POLICE OFFICER EXAM: POWER PRACTICE

Other Titles of Interest by LearningExpress

Becoming a Police Officer

Math for Law Enforcement Exams

Police Sergeant Exam

Reasoning for Law Enforcement Exams

State Trooper Exam

Police Officer Exam, 4e

POLICE OFFICER EXAM: POWER PRACTICE

2nd Edition

LEARNINGEXPRESS®

NEW YORK

Copyright © 2011 Learning Express, LLC.

All rights reserved under International and Pan American Copyright Conventions.
Published in the United States by LearningExpress, LLC, New York.

Library of Congress Cataloging-in-Publication Data: On File

Printed in the United States of America

9 8 7 6 5 4 3 2 1

Second Edition

978-1- 61103-012-9

For more information or to place an order, contact LearningExpress at:
  80 Broad Street
  4th Floor
  New York, NY 10034

Or visit us at:
  www.learnatest.com

CONTENTS

ABOUT THE CONTRIBUTORS

The following individuals contributed to the content of this book.

Lieutenant Raymond E. Foster, LAPD (ret.), MPA, is a 24-year veteran of policing. Currently, he is a university lecturer and the author of several books, including *Police Technology, Leadership: Texas Hold 'em Style*, and *From LAPD to NYPD: An Introduction to Policing*.

Kimberly Collica, PhD, has a doctorate in Criminal Justice and is a professor in the Justice Studies/Criminal Justice Department at Berkeley College. She has many years of experience working within the state prison and county jail systems. Her research focuses on HIV, correctional populations, rehabilitation, and reintegration.

Gennifer Furst, PhD, has a doctorate in Criminal Justice and is an assistant professor in the Sociology Department at William Paterson University. Her research focuses on issues related to incarceration, prison-based animal programs, and the use of animals by the criminal justice system.

ABOUT *POLICE OFFICER EXAM: POWER PRACTICE*

LearningExpress understands the importance of achieving a top score on your police officer exam, and we strive to publish the most authentic and comprehensive police officer test preparation materials available today. Practice does indeed make perfect, and that's why we've created this book composed of six full-length police officer practice exams (plus a seventh online) complete with detailed answer explanations—it offers you all the extra practice you need to get a great score. Whether used on its own or as a powerful companion to other police officer exam preparation titles, *Police Officer Exam: Power Practice* is the key to a top score and a brighter future!

POLICE OFFICER EXAM: POWER PRACTICE

1 ▶ THE LEARNINGEXPRESS TEST PREPARATION SYSTEM

CHAPTER SUMMARY

Taking the police officer written exam can be tough. It demands a lot of preparation if you want to achieve a top score. Your rank on the eligibility list may be determined largely by this score. The LearningExpress Test Preparation System, developed by leading test experts, gives you the discipline and attitude you

To be a winner.

This chapter can help you take control of the entire test preparation process. It clearly explains the steps you need to take to achieve a top score on the written exam. Do not underestimate the importance of doing well on the written exam: Your future career in law enforcement depends on it. This chapter will help you to

- become familiar with the format of the exam.
- overcome excessive test anxiety.
- prepare gradually for the exam instead of cramming.
- understand and use vital test-taking skills.
- know how to pace yourself through the exam.
- learn how to use the process of elimination.
- know when and how to guess.
- be in tip-top mental and physical shape on the day of the exam.

The purpose of this chapter is to ensure that you are in control of the test-prep process. You do not want the exam to control you.

The LearningExpress Test Preparation System puts you in control. In just nine easy-to-follow steps, you will learn everything you need to know to make sure that you are in charge of your preparation and your performance on the exam. Other test takers may let the test get the better of them; other test takers may be unprepared or out of shape, but not you. You will have taken all the steps you need to take to get a high score on the police exam.

Here's how the LearningExpress Test Preparation System works: Nine easy steps lead you through everything you need to know and do to get ready to master your exam. The time listed next to each of the steps includes both reading about the step and one or more activities. It's important that you do the activities along with the reading, or you won't be getting the full benefit of the system. Each step tells you approximately how much time that step will take you to complete.

We estimate that working through the entire system will take you approximately three hours, though it's perfectly okay if you work faster or slower than the time estimates assume. If you can take a whole afternoon or evening, you can work through the whole LearningExpress Test Preparation System in one sitting. Otherwise, you can break it up and do just one or two steps a day for the next several days. It's up to you—remember, you are in control.

Nine Steps to Success	Time
Step 1. Get Information	30 minutes
Step 2. Conquer Test Anxiety	20 minutes
Step 3. Make a Plan	50 minutes
Step 4. Learn to Manage Your Time	10 minutes
Step 5. Learn to Use the Process of Elimination	20 minutes
Step 6. Know When to Guess	20 minutes
Step 7. Reach Your Peak Performance Zone	10 minutes
Step 8. Get Your Act Together	10 minutes
Step 9. Do It!	10 minutes
Total	**3 hours**

Step 1: Get Information

Time to complete: 30 minutes
Activity: Research your specific police officer exam

Knowledge is power. The first step in the LearningExpress Test Preparation System is finding out everything you can about your police officer written exam. If you have access to the Internet, you can perform a search on any basic search engine to find out whether the police department you want to apply to has a website. Or you can check out a site that contains a long list of links to police departments around the country: www.police one.com/careers. If you find that your targeted police department has a website, review it carefully to see whether it contains any information about the written exam. If not, contact the police department you want to apply to and ask for the personnel office. In larger cities, you will be referred to a recruiting unit or to the human resources department. In smaller towns, you may speak to someone right there in the department. Request a position announcement, find out whether an exam bulletin is available, and ask when the next written exam is scheduled. If the department issues an exam bulletin, then you'll get a brief outline of what skills will be tested on the written exam.

What You Should Find Out

The more details you can find out about the written exam, either from the bulletin online or from speaking with a recruiter, the more efficiently you'll be able to study. Here's a list of some things you might want to find out about your exam:

- What skills are tested?
- How many sections are on the exam?
- How many questions does each section have?

- Are the questions ordered from easy to hard, or is the sequence random?
- How much time is allotted for each section?
- Are there breaks in between sections?
- What is the passing score, and how many questions do you have to answer correctly in order to get that score?
- Does a higher score give you any advantages, like a better rank on the eligibility list?
- How is the test scored: Is there a penalty for incorrect answers?
- Are you permitted to go back to a prior section or move on to the next section if you finish early?
- Can you write in the test booklet or will you be given scratch paper?
- What should you bring with you on exam day?

What's on Most Police Officer Exams

The skills that the police officer written exam tests vary from city to city. That's why it's important to contact the recruiting office of your police department to find out exactly what skills are covered. Below are the most commonly tested subjects:

- reading comprehension
- grammar
- vocabulary and spelling
- math
- judgment
- map reading
- memory and observation
- number and letter recall
- personal background

Let's move on to the next step to find out how you can get a handle on test anxiety.

Step 2: Conquer Test Anxiety

Time to complete: 20 minutes
Activity: Take the Test Stress Test

Having as much information as possible about the exam is the first step in getting control of the exam. Next, you have to overcome one of the biggest obstacles to test success: test anxiety. Test anxiety can not only impair your performance on the exam itself, but it can even keep you from preparing! In Step 2, you'll learn stress management techniques that will help you succeed on your exam. Learn these strategies now, and practice them as you work through the exams in this book, so they will be second nature to you by exam day.

Combating Test Anxiety

The first thing you need to know is that a little test anxiety is a good thing. Everyone gets nervous before a big exam—and if that nervousness motivates you to prepare thoroughly, so much the better. It's said that Sir Laurence Olivier, one of the foremost British actors of the twentieth century, was ill before every performance. His stage fright didn't impair his performance; in fact, it probably gave him a little extra edge—just the kind of edge you need to do well, whether on a stage or in an examination room.

Stress Management before the Test

Stress is the difference between your capabilities and the environment. The more prepared you are to handle the examination, the greater your capabilities and the less stress you feel. Preparation for the written exam, oral board, and physical agility test is the only surefire way to increase your score and reduce stress-related anxiety.

If you feel your level of anxiety rising in the weeks before your test, here is what you can do to bring the level down again:

- **Get prepared.** There's nothing like knowing what to expect and being prepared for it to put you in control of test anxiety. That's why you are using this book. Use it faithfully, and remind yourself that you are better prepared than most of the people who will be taking the test.
- **Practice self-confidence.** A positive attitude is a great way to combat test anxiety. This is no time to be humble or shy. Stand in front of the mirror and say to your reflection, "I'm prepared. I'm full of self-confidence. I'm going to ace this test. I know I can do it." If you hear it often enough, you will believe it.
- **Fight negative messages.** Every time someone starts telling you how hard the exam is or how it's almost impossible to get a high score, fight back by telling them your self-confidence messages. If the someone with the negative messages is you, telling yourself *you don't do well on exams, you just can't do this*, don't listen. Listen to your self-confidence messages instead.
- **Visualize.** Imagine yourself reporting for duty on your first day of police academy training. Think of yourself wearing your uniform with pride and learning the skills you will use for the rest of your life. Visualizing success can help make it happen—and it reminds you of why you are doing all this work in preparing for the exam.
- **Exercise.** Physical activity helps calm your body down and focus your mind. Being in good physical shape can actually help you do well on the exam, as well as prepare you for the physical agility test. So, go for a run, lift weights, go swimming—and do it regularly.

Stress Management on Test Day

There are several ways you can bring down your level of test anxiety on test day. They will work best if you practice them in the weeks before the test, so you know which ones work for you.

Test Stress Test

You need to worry about test anxiety only if it is extreme enough to impair your performance. The following questionnaire will provide a diagnosis of your level of test anxiety. In the blank before each statement, write the number that most accurately describes your experience.

0 = Never 1 = Once or twice 2 = Sometimes 3 = Often

____ I have gotten so nervous before an exam that I simply put down the books and didn't study for it.

____ I have experienced disabling physical symptoms such as vomiting and severe headaches because I was nervous about an exam.

____ I have simply not showed up for an exam because I was afraid to take it.

____ I have experienced dizziness and disorientation while taking an exam.

____ I have had trouble filling in the little circles because my hands were shaking too hard.

____ I have failed an exam because I was too nervous to complete it.

____ **Total: Add up the numbers you entered in the blanks.**

Your Test Stress Score

Here are the steps you should take, depending on your score. If you scored

- **below 3,** your level of test anxiety is nothing to worry about; it is probably just enough to give you that little extra edge.
- **between 3 and 6,** your test anxiety may be enough to impair your performance, and you should practice the stress management techniques listed in this section to try to bring your test anxiety down to manageable levels.
- **above 6,** your level of test anxiety is a serious concern. In addition to practicing the stress management techniques listed in this section, you may want to seek additional, personal help. Call your local high school or community college and ask for the academic counselor. Tell the counselor that you have a level of test anxiety that sometimes keeps you from being able to take an exam. The counselor may be willing to help you or may suggest someone else you should talk to.

- **Deep breathing.** Take a deep breath while you count to five. Hold it for a count of one, then let it out on a count of five. Repeat several times.
- **Move your body.** Try rolling your head in a circle. Rotate your shoulders. Shake your hands from the wrist. Many people find these movements very relaxing.

- **Visualize again.** Think of the place where you are most relaxed: lying on the beach in the sun, walking through the park, or wherever is most comforting to you. Now close your eyes and imagine you are actually there. If you practice in advance, you'll find that you need only a few seconds of this exercise to experience a significant increase in your sense of well-being.

When anxiety threatens to overwhelm you right there during the exam, there are still things you can do to manage the stress level:

- **Repeat your self-confidence messages.** You should have them memorized by now. Say them silently to yourself, and believe them!
- **Visualize one more time.** This time, visualize yourself moving smoothly and quickly through the test, answering every question right and finishing just before time is up. Like most visualization techniques, this one works best if you have practiced it ahead of time.
- **Find an easy question.** Skim over the test until you find an easy question, and answer it. Getting even one circle filled in can get you into the test-taking groove.
- **Take a mental break.** Everyone loses concentration once in a while during a long test. It's normal, so you shouldn't worry about it. Instead, accept what has happened. Say to yourself, "Hey, I lost it there for a minute. My brain is taking a break." Put down your pencil, close your eyes, and do some deep breathing for a few seconds. Then you'll be ready to go back to work.

Answer the questions on the Test Stress Test to learn more about your level of test anxiety.

Step 3: Make a Plan

Time to complete: 50 minutes
Activity: Construct a study plan

One of the most important things you can do to get control of yourself and your exam is to make a study plan. Too many people fail to prepare simply because they fail to plan. Spending hours the day before the exam poring over sample test questions not only raises your level of test anxiety, but it also is simply no substitute for careful preparation and practice over time.

Police Officer Exams	Skills Tested
Exam 1, Chapter 2 Exam 5, Chapter 6 *These exams test your basic reading and writing skills.*	Reading Text, Tables, Charts, and Graphs Grammar Vocabulary and Spelling
Exam 2, Chapter 3 Exam 4, Chapter 5 Exam 6, Chapter 7 *These exams test job-related skills, such as memory and observation.*	Reading Text, Tables, Charts, and Graphs Math Judgment Map Reading Memory and Observation
Exam 3, Chapter 4 Free Online Exam *These exams are similar to the Law Enforcement Candidate Record (LECR) exam.*	Vocabulary and Spelling Number and Letter Recall Personal Background

Don't fall into the cram trap. Take control of your preparation time by mapping out a study schedule. There are four sample schedules on the following pages, based on the amount of time you have before the exam. If you are the kind of person who needs deadlines and assignments to motivate you for a project, here they are. If you are the kind of person who doesn't like to follow other people's plans, you can use the suggested schedules here to construct your own.

An important aspect of a study plan is flexibility. Your plan should help you, not hinder you, so be prepared to alter your study schedule once you get started, if necessary. You will probably find that one or more steps will take longer to complete than you had anticipated, while others will go more quickly.

In constructing your study plan, you should take into account how much work you need to do. If your score on the first practice test wasn't what you had hoped, consider taking some of the steps from Schedule A and fitting them into Schedule D, even if you have only three weeks before the exam.

You can also customize your study plan according to the information you gathered in Step 1. If the exam you have to take doesn't include memory questions, for instance, you don't have to study that skill and can concentrate instead on some other area that *is* covered. The table on page 6 lists all the skills you need to study for each exam.

Even more important than making a plan is making a commitment. You can't improve your skills in reading, writing, and judgment overnight. You have to set aside some time every day for study and practice. Try for at least 20 minutes a day. Twenty minutes daily will do you much more good than two hours on Saturday.

If you have months before the exam, you are lucky. Don't put off your study until the week before the exam! Start now. Even 10 minutes a day, with half an hour or more on weekends, can make a big difference in your score—and in your chances of making the force!

Schedule A: The Leisure Plan

If no test has been announced yet in your city, you may have a year or more in which to get ready. This schedule gives you six months to sharpen your skills. If an exam is announced in the middle of your preparation, you can use one of the later schedules to help you compress your study program. Study only the skills that are relevant to the type of exam you will be taking.

Time	Preparation
6 months before the test	Take one of the exams, then study the explanations for the answers until you know you could answer all the questions right. Start going to the library once every two weeks to read books or magazines about law enforcement, or browse through police-related websites.
5 months before the test	Practice your reading, grammar, vocabulary, and spelling skills. If possible, find other people who are preparing for the test and form a study group.
4 months before the test	Sharpen your judgment and problem-solving skills with a book like LearningExpress's *Reasoning Skills for Law Enforcement Exams*. Start making flash cards of vocabulary and spelling words.
3 months before the test	Practice your math by making up problems from everyday events or with a test-prep book such as LearningExpress's *Math Skills for Law Enforcement Exams*. Exercise your memory by making note of people and places you see each day. Continue to read and work with your flash cards.
6 weeks before the test	Take another sample test in the book. Use your score to help you decide where to concentrate your efforts. Practice the relevant skills, or get the help of a friend or teacher.
1 week before the test	Review the sample tests you took. See how much you've learned in the past months. Concentrate on what you have done well and resolve not to let any areas where you still feel uncertain bother you.
1 day before the test	Relax. Do something unrelated to police exams. Eat a good meal and go to bed at your usual time.

Schedule B: The Just-Enough-Time Plan

If you have three to six months before your exam, that should be enough time to prepare for the written test, especially if you score above 70% on the first sample test you take. This schedule assumes four months; stretch it out or compress it if you have more or less time, and study only the skills that are relevant to the type of exam you will be taking.

Time	Preparation
4 months before the test	Take one of the exams, then study the explanations for the answers until you know you could answer all the questions right. Start going to the library once every two weeks to read books or magazines about law enforcement, or browse through police-related websites. Also, make flash cards of vocabulary and spelling words.
3 months before the test	Practice your reading, grammar, vocabulary, and spelling skills. If possible, find other people who are preparing for the test and form a study group. Continue to read and work with your flash cards.
2 months before the test	Sharpen your judgment and problem-solving skills with a book like LearningExpress's *Reasoning Skills for Law Enforcement Exams.* Practice your math by making up problems from everyday events or with a test-prep book such as LearningExpress's *Math Skills for Law Enforcement Exams.* Exercise your memory by making note of people and places you see each day. Continue to read and work with your flash cards.
1 month before the test	Take another practice test. Use your score to help you decide where to concentrate your efforts. Focus on the relevant skills, or get the help of a friend or teacher.
1 week before the test	Review both of the sample tests you took. See how much you have learned in the past months. Concentrate on what you have done well, and resolve not to let any areas where you still feel uncertain bother you.
1 day before the test	Relax. Do something unrelated to police exams. Eat a good meal and go to bed at your usual time.

Schedule C: More Study in Less Time

If you have one to three months before the exam, you still have enough time for some concentrated study that will help you improve your score. This schedule is built around a two-month time frame. If you have only one month, spend an extra couple of hours a week to get all these steps in. If you have three months, take some of the steps from Schedule B and fit them in. Study only the skills that are relevant to the type of exam you will be taking.

Time	Preparation
8 weeks before the test	Take one sample test to find your weakest subjects. Focus on studying those weak subjects in these two weeks.
6 weeks before the test	Practice your grammar, vocabulary, and spelling skills.
5 weeks before the test	Practice your reading comprehension and judgment skills.
4 weeks before the test	Work on your math and memory skills.
2 weeks before the test	Take one of the second sample tests. Then score it and read the answer explanations until you are sure you understand them. Review the areas where your score is lowest.
1 week before the test	Concentrate on studying the areas where a little work can help the most.
1 day before the test	Relax. Do something unrelated to police exams. Eat a good meal and go to bed at your usual time.

Schedule D: The Fast Track

If you have three weeks or less before the exam, you really have your work cut out for you. Carve half an hour out of your day, *every day*, for study. This schedule assumes you have the whole three weeks to prepare in; if you have less time, you'll have to compress the schedule accordingly. Study only the skills that are relevant to the type of exam you will be taking.

Time	Preparation
3 weeks before the test	Take one practice exam. Then focus on your weakest subject areas.
2 weeks before the test	Focus on other subjects. Take another one of the sample tests.
1 week before the test	Evaluate your performance on the second sample test. Review the skills where you had the most trouble. Get a friend or teacher to help you with the test section you found to be the most difficult.
2 days before the test	Review both of the sample tests you took. Make sure you understand all of the answer explanations.
1 day before the test	Relax. Do something unrelated to police exams. Eat a good meal and go to bed at your usual time.

Step 4: Learn to Manage Your Time

Time to complete: 10 minutes to read, many hours of practice!
Activities: Practice these strategies as you take the sample tests in this book

Steps 4, 5, and 6 of the LearningExpress Test Preparation System put you in charge of your exam by showing you test-taking strategies that work. Practice these strategies as you take the sample tests in this book, and then you will be ready to use them on test day.

First, you will take control of your time on the exam. The first step in achieving this control is to find out the format of the exam you're going to take. Some police exams have different sections that are each timed separately. If this is true of the exam you'll be taking, you'll want to practice using your time wisely on the practice exams and trying to avoid mistakes while working quickly. Other types of exams don't have separately timed sections. If this is the case, just practice pacing yourself on the practice exams, so you don't spend too much time on difficult questions.

- **Listen carefully to directions.** By the time you get to the exam, you should be familiar with how all the sections work, but listen to the person who is administering the exam just in case something has changed.
- **Pace yourself.** Glance at your watch every few minutes, and compare the time to how far you've gotten in the sections. When one-quarter of the time has elapsed, you should be a quarter of the way through the sections, and so on. If you're falling behind, pick up the pace a bit.
- **Keep moving.** Don't spend too much time on any one question. If you don't know the answer, skip the question and move on. Circle the num-

ber of the question in your test booklet in case you have time to come back to it later.
- **Keep track of your place on the answer sheet.** If you skip a question, make sure you skip that space on the answer sheet too. Check yourself every 5–10 questions to make sure the question number and the answer sheet number are still the same.
- **Don't rush.** Though you should keep moving steadily through the test, rushing won't help. Try to keep calm and work methodically and quickly.

Step 5: Learn to Use the Process of Elimination

Time to complete: 20 minutes
Activity: Complete worksheet on Using the Process of Elimination

After time management, your next most important tool for taking control of your exam is using the process of elimination wisely. It's standard test-taking wisdom that you should always read all the answer choices before choosing your answer. This practice helps you find the right answer by eliminating wrong answer choices. And, sure enough, that standard wisdom applies to your exam, too.

Let's say you're facing a vocabulary question that goes like this:

13. "Biology uses a <u>binomial</u> system of classification." In this sentence, the word *binomial* most nearly means
   a. understanding the law.
   b. having two names.
   c. scientifically sound.
   d. having a double meaning.

If you happen to know what *binomial* means, of course, you don't need to use the process of elimination, but let's assume that, like many people, you don't. So you look at the answer choices. "Understanding the law" sure doesn't sound very likely for something having to do with biology. So you eliminate choice **a**—and now you have only three answer choices to deal with. Mark an **X** next to choice **a** so you never have to read it again.

On to the other answer choices. If you know that the prefix *bi-* means *two*, as in *bicycle*, flag answer **b** as a possible answer. Place a check mark beside it, meaning "good answer, I might use this one."

Choice **c**, "scientifically sound," is a possibility. At least it's about science, not law. It could work here, although, when you think about it, having a "scientifically sound" classification system in a scientific field is kind of redundant. You remember the *bi* thing in *binomial*, and probably continue to like answer **b** better. But you are not sure, so you put a question mark next to **c**, meaning "well, maybe."

Now, choice **d**, "having a double meaning." You are still keeping in mind that *bi-* means *two*, so this one looks possible at first. But then you look again at the sentence the word belongs in, and you think, "Why would biology want a system of classification that has two meanings? That wouldn't work very well!" If you are really taken with the idea that *bi* means *two*, you might put a question mark here. But if you are feeling a little more confident, you'll put an **X**. You already have a better answer picked out.

Now your question looks like this:

13. "Biology uses a <u>binomial</u> system of classification." In this sentence, the word *binomial* most nearly means
  X **a.** understanding the law.
  ✔ **b.** having two names.
  ? **c.** scientifically sound.
  ? **d.** having a double meaning.

You have just one check mark, for a good answer. If you are pressed for time, you should simply mark choice **b** on your answer sheet. If you have the time to be extra careful, you could compare your check-mark answer to your question-mark answers to make sure that it's better. (It is: The *binomial* system in biology is the one that gives a two-part genus and species name like *homo sapiens*.)

It's good to have a system for marking good, bad, and maybe answers. We're recommending this one:

  X = bad
  ✔ = good
  ? = maybe

If you don't like these marks, devise your own system. Just make sure you do it long before test day—while you are working through the practice exams in this book—so you won't have to worry about it during the test.

Even when you think you're absolutely clueless about a question, you can often use the process of elimination to get rid of at least one answer choice. If so, you're better prepared to make an educated guess, as you will see in Step 6. More often, the process of elimination allows you to get down to only two possibly right answers. Then you're in a strong position to guess. And sometimes, even though you don't know the right answer, you can find it simply by getting rid of the wrong ones, as you did in the last example.

Try using your powers of elimination on the questions in the worksheet entitled Using the Process of Elimination that begins on page 14. The answer explanations there show one possible way you might use the process to arrive at the right answer.

The process of elimination is your tool for the next step, which is knowing when to guess.

Use the process of elimination to answer the following questions.

1. Ilsa is as old as Meghan will be in five years. The difference between Ed's age and Meghan's age is twice the difference between Ilsa's age and Meghan's age. Ed is 29. How old is Ilsa?
   a. 4
   b. 10
   c. 19
   d. 24

2. "All drivers of commercial vehicles must carry a valid commercial driver's license whenever operating a commercial vehicle." According to this sentence, which of the following people need NOT carry a commercial driver's license?
   a. a truck driver idling his engine while waiting to be directed to a loading dock
   b. a bus operator backing her bus out of the way of another bus in the bus lot
   c. a taxi driver driving his personal car to the grocery store
   d. a limousine driver taking the limousine to her home after dropping off her last passenger of the evening

3. Smoking tobacco has been linked to
   a. increased risk of stroke and heart attack.
   b. all forms of respiratory disease.
   c. increasing mortality rates over the past ten years.
   d. juvenile delinquency.

4. Which of the following words is spelled correctly?
   a. incorrigible
   b. outragous
   c. domestickated
   d. understandible

Answers

Here are the answers, as well as some suggestions as to how you might have used the process of elimination to find them.

1. d. You should have eliminated choice a off the bat. Ilsa can't be four years old if Meghan is going to be Ilsa's age in five years. The best way to eliminate the other answer choices is to try plugging them into the information given in the problem. For instance, for choice b, if Ilsa is 10, then Meghan must be 5. The difference in their ages is 5. The difference between Ed's age, 29, and Meghan's age, 5, is 24. Is 24 two times 5? No. Then choice b is wrong. You could eliminate choice c in the same way and be left with choice d.

2. c. Note the word *not* in the question, and go through the answers one by one. Is the truck driver in choice a "operating a commercial vehicle"? Yes, idling counts as "operating," so he needs to have a commercial driver's license. Likewise, the bus operator in choice b is operating a commercial vehicle; the question doesn't say the operator has to be on the street. The limo driver in d is operating a commercial vehicle, even if it doesn't have passengers in it. However, the cabbie in choice c is not operating a commercial vehicle, but his own private car.

3. a. You could eliminate choice **b** simply because of the presence of the word *all*. Such absolutes hardly ever appear in correct answer choices. Choice **c** looks attractive until you think a little about what you know—aren't *fewer* people smoking these days, rather than more? So how could smoking be responsible for a higher mortality rate? (If you didn't know that *mortality rate* means the rate at which people die, you might keep this choice as a possibility, but you'd still be able to eliminate two answers and have only two to choose from.) And choice **d** seems seems unlikely, so you could eliminate that one, too. And you're left with the correct choice, **a**.

4. a. How you used the process of elimination here depends on which words you recognized as being spelled incorrectly. If you knew that the correct spellings were *outrageous*, *domesticated*, and *understandable*, then you were home free.

Step 6: Know When to Guess

Time to complete: 20 minutes
Activity: Complete worksheet on Your Guessing Ability

Armed with the process of elimination, you're ready to take control of one of the big questions in test taking: Should I guess? Unless the exam has a guessing penalty, you have nothing to lose and everything to gain from guessing. The more complicated answer depends both on the exam and on you—your personality and your guessing intuition.

Most police officer written exams don't use a guessing penalty. The number of questions you answer correctly yields your score, and there's no penalty for wrong answers. So most of the time, you don't have to worry—simply go ahead and guess. But if you find that your exam does have a guessing penalty, you should read this section to find out what that means to you.

How the Guessing Penalty Works

A guessing penalty really works only against *random* guessing—filling in the little circles to make a nice pattern on your answer sheet. If you can eliminate one or more answer choices, as outlined previously, you're better off taking a guess than leaving the answer blank, even on the sections that have a penalty.

Here's how a guessing penalty works: Depending on the number of answer choices in a given exam, some proportion of the number of questions you get incorrect is subtracted from the total number of questions you got correct. For instance, if there are four answer choices, typically the guessing penalty is one-third of your wrong answers. Suppose you took a test of 100 questions. You answered 88 of them correctly and 12 incorrectly.

If there's no guessing penalty, your score is simply 88. But if there's a one-third-point guessing penalty, the scorers take your 12 incorrect answers and divide by 3 to come up with 4. Then they subtract that 4 from your correct-answer score of 88 to leave you with a score of 84. Thus, you would have been better off if you had simply not answered those 12 questions that you weren't sure of. Then your total score would still be 88, because there wouldn't be anything to subtract.

What You Should Do about the Guessing Penalty

That's how a guessing penalty works. The first thing this means for you is that marking your answer sheet at random doesn't pay. If you're running out of time

The following are ten really hard questions. You're not supposed to know the answers. Rather, this is an assessment of your ability to guess when you don't have a clue. Read each question carefully, just as if you did expect to answer it. If you have any knowledge at all of the subject of the question, use that knowledge to help you eliminate wrong answer choices. Use this answer grid to fill in your answers to the questions.

1.	(a)	(b)	(c)	(d)
2.	(a)	(b)	(c)	(d)
3.	(a)	(b)	(c)	(d)
4.	(a)	(b)	(c)	(d)

5.	(a)	(b)	(c)	(d)
6.	(a)	(b)	(c)	(d)
7.	(a)	(b)	(c)	(d)
8.	(a)	(b)	(c)	(d)

9.	(a)	(b)	(c)	(d)
10.	(a)	(b)	(c)	(d)

1. September 7 is Independence Day in
   a. India.
   b. Costa Rica.
   c. Brazil.
   d. Australia.

2. Which of the following is the formula for determining the momentum of an object?
   a. $p = mv$
   b. $F = ma$
   c. $P = IV$
   d. $E = mc^2$

3. Because of the expansion of the universe, the stars and other celestial bodies are all moving away from each other. This phenomenon is known as
   a. Newton's first law.
   b. the big bang.
   c. gravitational collapse.
   d. Hubble flow.

4. American author Gertrude Stein was born in
   a. 1713.
   b. 1830.
   c. 1874.
   d. 1901.

5. Which of the following is NOT one of the Five Classics attributed to Confucius?
   a. *I Ching*
   b. *Book of Holiness*
   c. *Spring and Autumn Annals*
   d. *Book of History*

6. The religious and philosophical doctrine that holds that the universe is constantly in a struggle between good and evil is known as
   a. Pelagianism.
   b. Manichaeanism.
   c. neo-Hegelianism.
   d. Epicureanism.

7. The third chief justice of the Supreme Court was
   a. John Blair.
   b. William Cushing.
   c. James Wilson.
   d. John Jay.

8. Which of the following is the poisonous portion of a daffodil?
   a. the bulb
   b. the leaves
   c. the stem
   d. the flowers

9. The winner of the Masters golf tournament in 1953 was

    a. Sam Snead.

    b. Cary Middlecoff.

    c. Arnold Palmer.

    d. Ben Hogan.

10. The state with the highest per capita personal income in 1980 was

    a. Alaska.

    b. Connecticut.

    c. New York.

    d. Texas.

Answers

Check your answers against the correct answers below.

  1. c.

  2. a.

  3. d.

  4. c.

  5. b.

  6. b.

  7. b.

  8. a.

  9. d.

 10. a.

How Did You Do?

You may have simply gotten lucky and actually known the answers to one or two questions. In addition, your guessing was more successful if you were able to use the process of elimination on any of the questions. Maybe you didn't know who the third Chief Justice was (question 7), but you knew that John Jay was the first. In that case, you would have eliminated choice **d** and, therefore, improved your odds of guessing correctly from one in four to one in three.

According to probability, you should get $2\frac{1}{2}$ answers correct by guessing, so getting either two or three correct would be average. If you got four or more correct, you may be a really terrific guesser. If you got one or none correct, you may not be a very strong guesser.

Keep in mind, though, that this is only a small sample. You should continue to keep track of your guessing ability as you work through the practice questions in this book. Circle the numbers of questions you guess on as you make your guess, or, if you don't have time while you take the practice exams, go back afterward and try to remember which questions you guessed at. Remember, on a test with four answer choices for each question, your chances of getting a right answer is one in four. So keep a separate "guessing" score for each exam. How many questions did you guess on? How many did you get correct? If the number you got correct is at least one-fourth of the number of questions you guessed on, you are at least an average guesser, maybe better—and you should go ahead and guess on the real exam. If the number you got correct is significantly lower than one-fourth of the number you guessed on, you should not guess on exams where there is a guessing penalty, unless you can eliminate a wrong answer. If there's no guessing penalty, however, you would be safe in guessing anyway.

on an exam that has a guessing penalty, you should not use your remaining seconds to mark a pretty pattern on your answer sheet. Take those few seconds to try to answer one more question right.

But as soon as you get out of the realm of random guessing, the guessing penalty no longer works against you. If you can use the process of elimination to get rid of even one incorrect answer choice, the odds stop being against you and start working in your favor.

Sticking with our example of an exam that has four answer choices, eliminating just one incorrect answer makes your odds of choosing the correct answer one in three. That's the same as the one-out-of-three guessing penalty—even odds. If you eliminate two answer choices, your odds are one in two—better than the guessing penalty. In either case, you should go ahead and choose one of the remaining answer choices.

But what if you're not much of a risk taker, *and* you think of yourself as the world's worst guesser? Complete the Your Guessing Ability worksheet to get an idea of how good your intuition is.

Step 7: Reach Your Peak Performance Zone

Time to complete: 10 minutes to read; weeks to complete!
Activity: Complete the Physical Preparation Checklist

To get ready for a challenge like a big exam, you have to take control of your physical, as well as your mental, state. Exercise, proper diet, and rest will ensure that your body works with, rather than against, your mind on test day, as well as during your preparation.

Exercise

If you don't already have a regular exercise program, the time during which you're preparing for your writ-

ten exam is an excellent time to start one. You'll have to be in shape to pass the physical agility test and to make it through the first weeks of basic training anyway. And if you're already keeping fit—or trying to get that way—don't let the pressure of preparing for the written exam be an excuse for quitting now. Exercise helps reduce stress by pumping wonderful good-feeling hormones called endorphins into your system. It also increases the oxygen supply throughout your body, including your brain, so you'll be at peak performance on test day.

A half hour of vigorous activity—enough to raise a sweat—every day should be your aim. If you're really pressed for time, every other day is okay. Choose an activity you like and get out there and do it. Jogging with a friend always makes the time go faster, or take a radio.

But don't overdo it. You don't want to exhaust yourself so much that you can't study. Moderation is the key.

Diet

First of all, cut out the junk food. Go easy on caffeine, and try to eliminate alcohol and nicotine from your system at least two weeks before the exam. Promise yourself a celebration the night after the exam, if need be.

What your body needs for peak performance is simply a balanced diet. Eat plenty of fruits and vegetables, along with protein and complex carbohydrates. Foods that are high in lecithin (an amino acid), such as fish and beans, are especially good brain foods.

Rest

You probably know how much sleep you need every night to be at your best, even if you don't always get it. Make sure you do get that much sleep, though, for at least a week before the exam. Moderation is important here, as well. Too much extra sleep could just make you groggy.

If you're not a morning person and your exam will be given in the morning, you should reset your internal clock so that your body doesn't think you're taking an exam at 3 A.M. You have to start this process well before the exam. The way it works is to get up half an hour earlier each morning, and then go to bed half an hour earlier that night. Don't try it the other way around; you'll just toss and turn if you go to bed early without having gotten up early. The next morning, get up another half an hour earlier, and so on. How long you will have to do this depends on how late you're used to getting up.

Step 8: Get Your Act Together

**Time to complete: 10 minutes to read; time to
   complete will vary**
Activity: Complete Final Preparations worksheet

You're in control of your mind and body; you're in charge of test anxiety, your preparation, and your test-taking strategies. Now it's time to take charge of external factors, like the testing site and the materials you need to take the exam.

Find Out Where the Test Is and Make a Trial Run

The exam bulletin or notice the recruiting office sent you will tell you when and where your exam is being held. Do you know how to get to the testing site? Do you know how long it will take you to get there? If not, make a trial run, preferably on the same day of the week at the same time of day. Make note, on the Final Preparations worksheet, of the amount of time it will take you to get to the exam site. Plan on arriving 10 or 15 minutes early so you can get the lay of the land, use the bathroom, and calm down. Then figure out how early you will have to get up that morning, and make sure you get up that early every day for a week before the exam.

Gather Your Materials

The night before the exam, lay out the clothes you will wear and the materials you have to bring with you to the exam. Plan on dressing in layers; you won't have any control over the temperature of the examination room. Have a sweater or jacket you can take off if it's warm or put on if the air conditioning is on full blast. Use the checklist on the Final Preparations worksheet on page 22 to help you pull together what you will need.

Don't Skip Breakfast

Even if you don't usually eat breakfast, do so on exam morning. A cup of coffee doesn't count. Don't eat doughnuts or other sweet foods, either. A sugar high will leave you with a sugar low in the middle of the exam. A mix of protein and complex carbohydrates is best: Cereal with milk or eggs with toast will do your body a world of good.

Physical Preparation Checklist

During the week before the test, write down (1) what physical exercise you engaged in and for how long and (2) what you ate for each meal. Remember, you're trying for at least a half an hour of exercise every other day (preferably every day) and a balanced diet that's light on junk food.

7 Days before the Exam

Exercise: _____ for _____ minutes

Breakfast: _____

Lunch: _____

Dinner: _____

Snacks: _____

6 Days before the Exam

Exercise: _____ for _____ minutes

Breakfast: _____

Lunch: _____

Dinner: _____

Snacks: _____

5 Days before the Exam

Exercise: _____ for _____ minutes

Breakfast: _____

Lunch: _____

Dinner: _____

Snacks: _____

4 Days before the Exam

Exercise: _____ for _____ minutes

Breakfast: _____

Lunch: _____

Dinner: _____

Snacks: _____

3 Days before the Exam

Exercise: _____ for _____ minutes

Breakfast: _____

Lunch: _____

Dinner: _____

Snacks: _____

2 Days before the Exam

Exercise: _____ for _____ minutes

Breakfast: _____

Lunch: _____

Dinner: _____

Snacks: _____

1 Day before the Exam

Exercise: _____ for _____ minutes

Breakfast: _____

Lunch: _____

Dinner: _____

Snacks: _____

Step 9: Do It!

Time to complete: 10 minutes, plus test-taking time
Activity: Ace the Police Officer written exam!

Fast forward to exam day. You're ready. You made a study plan and followed through. You practiced your test-taking strategies while working through this book. You're in control of your physical, mental, and emotional state. You know when and where to show up and what to bring with you. In other words, you're better prepared than most of the other people taking the exam with you.

Just one more thing. When you're finished with the police officer written exam, you will have earned a reward. Plan a celebration. Call up your friends and plan a party, or have a nice dinner for two—whatever your heart desires. Give yourself something to look forward to.

And then do it. Go into the exam, full of confidence, armed with the test-taking strategies you've practiced till they're second nature. You're in control of yourself, your environment, and your performance on the exam. You're ready to succeed. So do it. Go in there and ace the exam. And look forward to your future career in law enforcement!

Getting to the Exam Site

Location of exam: _____

Date of exam: _____

Time of exam: _____

Do I know how to get to the exam site?   Yes ____   No ____ (If no, make a trial run.)

Time it will take to get to exam site: _____

Things to Lay Out the Night Before

Clothes I will wear   ____

Sweater/jacket   ____

Watch   ____

Photo ID   ____

Admission card   ____

4 No. 2 pencils   ____

_____   _____

_____   _____

2 ▶ POLICE OFFICER PRACTICE EXAM 1

CHAPTER SUMMARY

The first practice exam gives you an example of a police officer exam based primarily on your basic reading and writing skills. It is similar to tests used by many police departments around the nation. Remember that all test questions rely on reading comprehension and English skills, so mastering these skills is very important for all types of entry exams.

This first practice exam is an example of a basic reading and writing skills exam like those used by many agencies around the country. This exam contains 100 questions and is divided into two parts:

Part One: 60 clarity of expression (grammar), vocabulary, spelling, and reading comprehension questions.

Part Two: 40 questions that require you to fill in the missing words in two passages. This portion of the exam is different from fill-in exams you may be familiar with. Read the instructions carefully before filling in any blank spaces.

The directions for each type of question are included in the test. Since you are now experienced at taking the practice exams, decide before you begin whether you will take your time and analyze along the way how you are doing or whether you will create conditions similar to the actual test and time yourself closely. Since the amount of time you will be given for the actual test may be different for different departments, rather than setting a hard time limit, see how long it takes you to complete the test and then try to find out what the time limits are for the departments you plan to test for.

When you turn the page, you will find the answer sheet for Part One, followed by the answer sheet for Part Two, the test itself, the answers and explanations, and, finally, information about scoring the test.

Police Officer Practice Exam 1: Part One

1.	ⓐ	ⓑ	ⓒ	ⓓ	21.	ⓐ	ⓑ	ⓒ	ⓓ	41.	ⓐ	ⓑ	ⓒ	ⓓ
2.	ⓐ	ⓑ	ⓒ	ⓓ	22.	ⓐ	ⓑ	ⓒ	ⓓ	42.	ⓐ	ⓑ	ⓒ	ⓓ
3.	ⓐ	ⓑ	ⓒ	ⓓ	23.	ⓐ	ⓑ	ⓒ	ⓓ	43.	ⓐ	ⓑ	ⓒ	ⓓ
4.	ⓐ	ⓑ	ⓒ	ⓓ	24.	ⓐ	ⓑ	ⓒ	ⓓ	44.	ⓐ	ⓑ	ⓒ	ⓓ
5.	ⓐ	ⓑ	ⓒ	ⓓ	25.	ⓐ	ⓑ	ⓒ	ⓓ	45.	ⓐ	ⓑ	ⓒ	ⓓ
6.	ⓐ	ⓑ	ⓒ	ⓓ	26.	ⓐ	ⓑ	ⓒ	ⓓ	46.	ⓐ	ⓑ	ⓒ	ⓓ
7.	ⓐ	ⓑ	ⓒ	ⓓ	27.	ⓐ	ⓑ	ⓒ	ⓓ	47.	ⓐ	ⓑ	ⓒ	ⓓ
8.	ⓐ	ⓑ	ⓒ	ⓓ	28.	ⓐ	ⓑ	ⓒ	ⓓ	48.	ⓐ	ⓑ	ⓒ	ⓓ
9.	ⓐ	ⓑ	ⓒ	ⓓ	29.	ⓐ	ⓑ	ⓒ	ⓓ	49.	ⓐ	ⓑ	ⓒ	ⓓ
10.	ⓐ	ⓑ	ⓒ	ⓓ	30.	ⓐ	ⓑ	ⓒ	ⓓ	50.	ⓐ	ⓑ	ⓒ	ⓓ
11.	ⓐ	ⓑ	ⓒ	ⓓ	31.	ⓐ	ⓑ	ⓒ	ⓓ	51.	ⓐ	ⓑ	ⓒ	ⓓ
12.	ⓐ	ⓑ	ⓒ	ⓓ	32.	ⓐ	ⓑ	ⓒ	ⓓ	52.	ⓐ	ⓑ	ⓒ	ⓓ
13.	ⓐ	ⓑ	ⓒ	ⓓ	33.	ⓐ	ⓑ	ⓒ	ⓓ	53.	ⓐ	ⓑ	ⓒ	ⓓ
14.	ⓐ	ⓑ	ⓒ	ⓓ	34.	ⓐ	ⓑ	ⓒ	ⓓ	54.	ⓐ	ⓑ	ⓒ	ⓓ
15.	ⓐ	ⓑ	ⓒ	ⓓ	35.	ⓐ	ⓑ	ⓒ	ⓓ	55.	ⓐ	ⓑ	ⓒ	ⓓ
16.	ⓐ	ⓑ	ⓒ	ⓓ	36.	ⓐ	ⓑ	ⓒ	ⓓ	56.	ⓐ	ⓑ	ⓒ	ⓓ
17.	ⓐ	ⓑ	ⓒ	ⓓ	37.	ⓐ	ⓑ	ⓒ	ⓓ	57.	ⓐ	ⓑ	ⓒ	ⓓ
18.	ⓐ	ⓑ	ⓒ	ⓓ	38.	ⓐ	ⓑ	ⓒ	ⓓ	58.	ⓐ	ⓑ	ⓒ	ⓓ
19.	ⓐ	ⓑ	ⓒ	ⓓ	39.	ⓐ	ⓑ	ⓒ	ⓓ	59.	ⓐ	ⓑ	ⓒ	ⓓ
20.	ⓐ	ⓑ	ⓒ	ⓓ	40.	ⓐ	ⓑ	ⓒ	ⓓ	60.	ⓐ	ⓑ	ⓒ	ⓓ

Police Officer Practice Exam 1: Part Two

WRITE 1ST LETTER OF WORD HERE

CODE LETTERS HERE

1	2	3	4	5	6	7	8	9	10

A A A A A A A A A A
B B B B B B B B B B
C C C C C C C C C C
D D D D D D D D D D
E E E E E E E E E E
F F F F F F F F F F
G G G G G G G G G G
H H H H H H H H H H
I I I I I I I I I I
J J J J J J J J J J
K K K K K K K K K K
L L L L L L L L L L
M M M M M M M M M M
N N N N N N N N N N
O O O O O O O O O O
P P P P P P P P P P
Q Q Q Q Q Q Q Q Q Q
R R R R R R R R R R
S S S S S S S S S S
T T T T T T T T T T
U U U U U U U U U U
V V V V V V V V V V
W W W W W W W W W W
X X X X X X X X X X
Y Y Y Y Y Y Y Y Y Y
Z Z Z Z Z Z Z Z Z Z

11	12	13	14	15	16	17	18	19	20

A A A A A A A A A A
B B B B B B B B B B
C C C C C C C C C C
D D D D D D D D D D
E E E E E E E E E E
F F F F F F F F F F
G G G G G G G G G G
H H H H H H H H H H
I I I I I I I I I I
J J J J J J J J J J
K K K K K K K K K K
L L L L L L L L L L
M M M M M M M M M M
N N N N N N N N N N
O O O O O O O O O O
P P P P P P P P P P
Q Q Q Q Q Q Q Q Q Q
R R R R R R R R R R
S S S S S S S S S S
T T T T T T T T T T
U U U U U U U U U U
V V V V V V V V V V
W W W W W W W W W W
X X X X X X X X X X
Y Y Y Y Y Y Y Y Y Y
Z Z Z Z Z Z Z Z Z Z

21	22	23	24	25	26	27	28	29	30

A A A A A A A A A A
B B B B B B B B B B
C C C C C C C C C C
D D D D D D D D D D
E E E E E E E E E E
F F F F F F F F F F
G G G G G G G G G G
H H H H H H H H H H
I I I I I I I I I I
J J J J J J J J J J
K K K K K K K K K K
L L L L L L L L L L
M M M M M M M M M M
N N N N N N N N N N
O O O O O O O O O O
P P P P P P P P P P
Q Q Q Q Q Q Q Q Q Q
R R R R R R R R R R
S S S S S S S S S S
T T T T T T T T T T
U U U U U U U U U U
V V V V V V V V V V
W W W W W W W W W W
X X X X X X X X X X
Y Y Y Y Y Y Y Y Y Y
Z Z Z Z Z Z Z Z Z Z

31	32	33	34	35	36	37	38	39	40

A A A A A A A A A A
B B B B B B B B B B
C C C C C C C C C C
D D D D D D D D D D
E E E E E E E E E E
F F F F F F F F F F
G G G G G G G G G G
H H H H H H H H H H
I I I I I I I I I I
J J J J J J J J J J
K K K K K K K K K K
L L L L L L L L L L
M M M M M M M M M M
N N N N N N N N N N
O O O O O O O O O O
P P P P P P P P P P
Q Q Q Q Q Q Q Q Q Q
R R R R R R R R R R
S S S S S S S S S S
T T T T T T T T T T
U U U U U U U U U U
V V V V V V V V V V
W W W W W W W W W W
X X X X X X X X X X
Y Y Y Y Y Y Y Y Y Y
Z Z Z Z Z Z Z Z Z Z

Practice Exam 1: Part One

Section One: Clarity

In each of the following sets of sentences, select the one that is most clearly written.

1. a. The graduating class of new police officers stood at attention for its graduation picture last week.
   b. The graduating class of new police officers stands at attention for its graduation picture last week.
   c. The graduating class of new police officers stand at attention for their graduation picture last week.
   d. The graduating class of new police officers is standing at attention for their graduation picture last week.

2. a. There was fewer incidents of use of force this year compared to last year.
   b. There was less incidents of use of force this year compared to last year.
   c. There were less incidents of use of force this year compared to last year.
   d. There were fewer incidents of use of force this year compared to last year.

3. a. Whether the firehouse remained open is going to be decided by the mayor.
   b. Weather the firehouse remains open is going to be decided by the mayor.
   c. Whether the firehouse remains open is going to be decided by the mayor.
   d. Weather the firehouse remains open was decided by the mayor.

4. a. How to handle last week's hostage situation is handles by the president, with the help of advisors.
   b. The president, with the help of advisors, decided how to handle last week's hostage situation.
   c. How to handle last week's hostage situation decides the president, with the help of advisors.
   d. The president, with the help of advisors, deciding how to handle last week's hostage situation.

5. a. A police officer is at risk when on the job.
   b. A police officer are at risk when on the job.
   c. Police officers is at risk when on the job.
   d. Police officers was at risk on when on the job.

6. a. Detective Scalzo and me responded to the call for police assistance on Park Avenue.
   b. I and Detective Scalzo responded to the call for police assistance on Park Avenue.
   c. Me and Detective Scalzo responded to the call for police assistance on Park Avenue.
   d. Detective Scalzo and I responded to the call for police assistance on Park Avenue.

7. a. Its a hot day to be wearing a bullet-proof vest.
   b. It's a hot day to be wearing a bullet-proof vest.
   c. Its's a hot day to be wearing a bullet-proof vest.
   d. Its' a hot day to be wearing a bullet-proof vest.

8. **a.** Me and Officer Gurick were told by our sergeant to arrive on the scene and start questioning bystanders about what they witnessed.

  b. Arrive on the scene and start questioning bystanders about what they witnessed Officer Gurick and I were told by our sergeant.

  c. Officer Gurick and I were told by our sergeant to arrive on the scene and start questioning bystanders about what they witnessed.

  d. I and Officer Gurick were told by our sergeant to arrive on the scene and start questioning bystanders about what they witnessed.

9. **a.** Neither Eddie nor I were aware of the meeting called by the lieutenant.

  b. Neither Eddie nor I was aware of the meeting called by the lieutenant.

  c. Neither Eddie or I were aware of the meeting called by the lieutenant.

  d. Neither Eddie or I was aware of the meeting called by the lieutenant.

10. **a.** The success of a drug treatment program is measured by a client's time spent sober.

  b. The success of a drug treatment program are measured by clients' time spent sober.

  c. The successes of a drug treatment program is measured by client's time spent sober.

  d. The success's of a drug treatment program is measured by client's time spent sober.

11. **a.** The mayor's annual report indicated the 23rd precinct had fewer arrests then the 68th precinct.

  b. The mayor's annual report indicated the 23rd precinct's had fewer arrests then the 68th precinct.

  c. The mayor's annual report indicated the 23rd precinct's had fewer arrests than the 68th precinct.

  d. The mayor's annual report indicated the 23rd precinct had fewer arrests than the 68th precinct.

12. **a.** Last week Kyle performed good at the firing range.

  b. Last week Kyle performed well at the firing range.

  c. Last week Kyle performs good at the firing range.

  d. Last week Kyle performs well at the firing range.

13. **a.** Sir Robert Peele, of England, is often recognized as the founder of modern policing throughout the world.

  b. Of England, throughout the world, Sir Robert Peele is often recognized as the founder of modern policing.

  c. Often recognized as the founder of modern policing, Sir Robert Peele, of England, throughout the world.

  d. Sir Robert Peele, of England, then is often recognized as the founder of modern policing throughout the world.

14. **a.** When we caught the perpetrator she said she threw the gun over their.
   b. When we caught the perpetrator she said she threw the gun over there.
   c. When we caught the perpetrator she said she had through the gun over their.
   d. When we caught the perpetrator she said she through the gun over their.

15. **a.** Officer Cartman had to decide witch shift she wanted to work.
   b. Officer Cartman had to deciding which shift she wanted to work.
   c. Officer Cartman had to decide which shift she wanted to work.
   d. Officer Cartman had to deciding witch shift she wanted to work.

Section Two: Vocabulary

In each of the following sentences, select the word or phrase that most nearly means the same as the underlined word.

16. While working undercover, Officer Hudson became <u>intrigued</u> by the activities occurring in the supposedly vacant house.
   a. interested
   b. threatened
   c. examined
   d. angered

17. Detective Vedder asked the victim to <u>articulate</u> what he saw prior to being attacked outside the bar.
   a. perceive
   b. communicate
   c. imagine
   d. delay

18. As a result of Officer Lincoln's <u>perseverance</u>, the circuit of people manufacturing and distributing narcotics was uncovered and seven people were arrested.
   a. ability
   b. intelligence
   c. luckiness
   d. determination

19. The judge faced a <u>dilemma</u> when the jury members said they could not come to an agreement on a verdict.
   a. argument
   b. predicament
   c. fist fight
   d. contradiction

20. When presented with the evidence, the suspect had to <u>concede</u> that he was, in fact, at the scene of the crime.
   a. argue
   b. complain
   c. admit
   d. reiterate

21. Because the person on trial had a <u>resemblance</u> to the actual perpetrator of the crime, the jury wrongfully convicted an innocent person.
   a. closeness
   b. connection
   c. similarity
   d. suspicion

22. After years of questioning suspects, Detective Grover knew the story of the person he was interrogating was <u>contrived</u>.
   a. false
   b. believable
   c. argumentative
   d. easy

23. During the sentencing, the convicted murderer of five teenagers appeared <u>callous</u> as he rolled his eyes at the judge and showed no emotion when the victims' family members spoke.
   a. certain
   b. immoral
   c. uncaring
   d. overjoyed

24. Officers from the 47th precinct were involved in <u>philanthropic</u> work for the community's children, who needed a new playground.
   a. historical
   b. charitable
   c. athletic
   d. expensive

25. After nine years on the same patrol, Officer Gossard found the work <u>mundane</u> and decided to take the sergeant's exam.
   a. exciting
   b. challenging
   c. easy
   d. boring

26. For firefighters, hot summer temperatures are a <u>hindrance</u> to their already difficult work.
   a. supplement
   b. aid
   c. obstacle
   d. relief

27. After nearly being caught inside a house, the burglar learned not to choose a target <u>haphazardly</u>.
   a. arbitrarily
   b. carefully
   c. pointedly
   d. smartly

28. Captain Hamm <u>espoused</u> a high level of esprit de corps.
   a. criticized
   b. ridiculed
   c. undermined
   d. supported

29. After having six drinks and then getting behind the wheel of a car, it was almost <u>inevitable</u> that Jeremy was going to get into an accident.
   a. unavoidable
   b. doubtful
   c. routine
   d. unlikely

30. When Kyle and Stan got together for lunch they <u>reminisced</u> about their younger days in the academy.
   a. excused
   b. allowed
   c. recalled
   d. supported

Section Three: Spelling

In each of the following sentences, select the correct spelling of the missing word.

31. It was _____ that the person the officers caught was guilty.
   a. aparent
   b. apparent
   c. apparrent
   d. aparrant

32. An interpreter was brought in to _____ the witness who did not speak English.
   a. accamindate
   b. acomodate
   c. accommodate
   d. acomindate

33. There would be an _____ of false tips called in to the hotline.
   a. abundance
   b. abundence
   c. abuntence
   d. abundanse

34. Every person's fingerprints are _____, so no two people have the same fingerprint pattern.
   a. uneque
   b. unique
   c. uneeck
   d. uneke

35. The smell of marijuana in the air was _____, but Officer Nelson could smell it when she pulled over the car.
   a. suttile
   b. suttel
   c. suttle
   d. subtle

36. Even though no one came forward, it was _____ that someone in the store had stolen money from the cash register.
   a. evidant
   b. evadent
   c. evedant
   d. evident

37. While writing a paper for his criminology class, Sergeant Phil kept his books nearby for _____.
   a. refrence
   b. reference
   c. refrince
   d. refrance

38. The house where the crime _____ was on the corner of 68th Street.
   a. ocurred
   b. occured
   c. acurd
   d. occurred

39. The field where the evidence was found was covered in _____ dirt.
   a. sparce
   b. sperce
   c. sparse
   d. spaerse

40. Lieutenant Pearl told her officers to _____ with the plans as discussed at the meeting.
   a. proceed
   b. procede
   c. preceed
   d. precede

41. At a parade, crowd control is always _____.
   a. nesasary
   b. nessasary
   c. necessary
   d. neccasary

42. After the promotion exam, Elizabeth was being a _____ and was sure she did not pass.
   a. pesamist
   b. pessimist
   c. pessamist
   d. pesimist

43. It is not unusual for a serial killer to be charming and leave a positive _____ on the people around him.
   a. empression
   b. impresion
   c. immpresion
   d. impression

44. The cost of the damage was _____ to be five or six million dollars.
   a. estimated
   b. estamated
   c. estamatted
   d. esstimated

45. The meeting at headquarters was _____ for all.
   a. manditory
   b. mandatory
   c. mandetory
   d. mendatory

Section Four:
Reading Comprehension

For each of the reading passages, answer the questions based on what is stated or implied in the passage.

Read the following passage, then answer questions 46 through 52.

Educators have suggested several ways in which race and ethnicity can be incorporated into criminology/criminal justice course curriculum. The first way is through cultural literacy, or the traditional study of the field of criminal justice/criminology. Students would be required to read classic, mainstream scholars with little to no mention of works addressing race/ethnicity or inclusion of scholars of color. The second way is through a black criminology similar to the existing feminist criminology. Black criminology would encourage theoretical development regarding race and crime by scholars of color. However, work by African American criminologists has traditionally been ignored. A third approach incorporating race/ethnicity into the curriculum, often referred to as historical multiculturalism, is meant to foster critical thinking skills among students. Research has found that students lack critical analytic skills, allowing them to adhere to myths and generalizations about crime. By providing a historical background, students are better prepared to discuss the impact of current policies and implications of the criminal justice system.

The importance of not omitting race and ethnicity from training in criminal justice should not be underestimated. Academics warn that the exclusion of multicultural perspectives has consequences beyond the criminal justice system and impacts society as a whole. The uniquely practical nature of this field makes the training and knowledge future practitioners receive particularly significant and therefore must be part of all students' training.

46. The passage makes which suggestion?
   a. Students should study criminology/criminal justice from the black criminology perspective.
   b. Students should study a multicultural perspective of crime.
   c. Students should not have to study criminology/criminal justice while considering the history of race in our country.
   d. Students generally do not read their textbooks.

47. According to the passage, a multicultural perspective is important because
   a. many professors have refused to teach how race and ethnicity affects the criminal justice system.
   b. professors do not teach the history of race correctly.
   c. other fields are taught from a multicultural perspective.
   d. criminal justice policy directly affects people's lives.

48. This passage includes a discussion of each of the following methods of incorporating race and ethnicity EXCEPT
  a. black criminology.
  b. cultural literacy.
  c. practical understanding.
  d. historical multiculturalism.

49. According to the passage, many students
  a. have called for a ban on the study of crime from a multicultural perspective.
  b. believe myths and generalizations about crime.
  c. already know about how race and ethnicity impact people in the criminal justice system.
  d. report they do not understand the link between race and crime.

50. Reading the historically significant classic texts about crime/criminology is advocated by which perspective?
  a. black criminology
  b. cultural literacy
  c. practical understanding
  d. historical multiculturalism

51. Which method discussed in the passage is meant to combat crime myths students may believe?
  a. black criminology
  b. cultural literacy
  c. practical understanding
  d. historical multiculturalism

52. The passage supports which of the following?
  a. incorporating race and ethnicity into teaching criminology/criminal justice
  b. not incorporating race and ethnicity into teaching criminology/criminal justice
  c. Cultural literacy is the best perspective from which to teach criminology/criminal justice.
  d. The general public has called for students to be taught about the role of race and ethnicity in the criminal justice system.

Read the following passage, then answer questions 53 through 56.

Animal-assisted activities have been incorporated into a growing range of social programs, including different types of prison programming. These prison-based animal programs have primarily been implemented in order to provide a service to the external community, such as having inmates train or care for animals for adoption or service use in the community. The programs are viewed as successful from a service perspective and are appealing on an intuitive level. However, they have been regarded as successful according to anecdotal information, not empirical research. Additional research is needed regarding the long-term effects of these programs.

53. According to the passage, animal programs in prisons
  a. are growing in number.
  b. have been around since prisons were invented.
  c. have been shown to be ineffectual.
  d. are popular with the prison inmates.

54. The author of the passage argues
   a. against putting animals in prison.
   b. that prison inmates like cats and dogs.
   c. that there is a growing demand for service animals.
   d. in support of more scientific research.

55. Which of the following statements is the author of this passage most likely to agree with?
   a. Prison inmates should have few privileges.
   b. Prison inmates provide a valuable service in training service animals for disabled people.
   c. Prison inmates generally do not care about people in the community outside prison.
   d. Prison officials do not care about people in the community outside prison.

56. According to the article, which of the following statements is true?
   a. Americans generally do not like animals.
   b. Prison administrators generally do not like animals inside their prisons.
   c. An example of an animal-assisted activity is when inmates train or groom animals.
   d. Animals are increasingly being permitted in more places such as shops and restaurants.

Read the following passage, then answer questions 57 through 60.

A relationship is formed when law enforcement officers are partnered with canines. The use of police service dogs in a variety of capacities—from explosives and drug detection to cadaver and missing person searches—has gained much visibility since the attacks on 9/11. The limited research that has been conducted on officer-service dog relationships has found ambivalence about officer attitudes. Sometimes they give their dogs a human-like identity, even while generally considering the dog as less than human. However, a canine partner brings to the working relationship abilities such as smell and speed that surpass those of a human. The dog enables the partners to perform at a level that is otherwise unattainable for traditional police teams comprised of two humans. A second dimension of the officer-dog relationship stems from the officer being partnered with someone considered different. Based largely on gender differences, there is a body of research examining status differences among law enforcement. Since traditionally masculine traits (e.g., aggressiveness, competitiveness) are valued in policing, females are generally thought to be less able than males to achieve success in law enforcement. But this line of thinking cannot be applied to officer-canine partners because of the contradictory status of the dog—both less than human, but also in possession of skills that are valued in policing. When a canine partner is portrayed as a brave and loyal hero, how does the human partner feel?

57. According to the passage,
   a. there is a bias against law enforcement officers who are partnered with canines.
   b. there is limited research on the relationship formed when law enforcement officers are partnered with canines.
   c. the general public supports law enforcement officers being partnered with canines.
   d. more research needs to be done because no one is sure why law enforcement officers are being partnered with canines.

58. The relationship between a law enforcement officer and a canine partner
  a. has been thoroughly studied.
  b. need not be studied.
  c. is just like the relationship between two human law enforcement officers.
  d. is complex or multi-dimensional.

59. Which of the following statements would the author of this passage be most likely to agree with?
  a. Canines should be used in law enforcement because they have a better sense of smell and can run faster than humans.
  b. Canines cannot be trusted to work in law enforcement due to a lack of research.
  c. Human law enforcement officers partnered with canines are at a disadvantage when at a crime scene.
  d. Being partnered with a canine is just like when a male law enforcement officer is partnered with a female law enforcement officer.

60. The author of this passage is curious about
  a. how fellow law enforcement officers regard a fellow human officer who is partnered with a canine.
  b. the complexities of the relationship formed when a human law enforcement officer is partnered with a canine.
  c. how the human who is partnered with a canine feels when her dog saves the day or solves a crime.
  d. all of the above.

Practice Exam 1: Part Two

This is a test of your reading ability. In the following passages, words have been omitted. Each numbered set of dashed blank lines indicates where a word is left out; each dash represents one letter of the missing word. The correct word should not only make sense in the sentence but also have the number of letters indicated by the dashes.

Read through the whole passage, and then begin filling in the missing words. Fill in as many missing words as possible. If you aren't sure of the answer, take a guess.

Then mark your answers on the answer sheet on page 27 as follows: Write the first letter of the word you have chosen in the square under the number of the word. Then blacken the circle of that letter of the alphabet under the square.

In part as a rejection of theories that do
1 _ _ _ account for changes that occur
in people naturally over the life course,
researchers developed life course theory, which
considers how turning points or significant
life events can alter the criminal pathways of
career **2** _ _ _ _ _ _ _ _ _. Based in part on
3 _ _ _ _ _ _ bonds and the resulting social
capital, or positive benefits from those
relations, the **4** _ _ _ _ _ _ considers how
these factors contribute to desistance from
and persistence in crime. Some people stop
committing **5** _ _ _ _ _ _ when they get married,
6 _ _ _ _ a child, or **7** _ _ _ _ the military. An
example of such research is work **8** _ _ _ _
considers the roles of social **9** _ _ _ _ _,
personal attributes, **10** _ _ _ _-control, drug
11 _ _ _, and peer association in boot
12 _ _ _ _ success. Being connected, or bonded,
to others has been shown to help some people
13 _ _ _ _ committing crimes. A person who is
bonded to others generally will **14** _ _ _ risk

losing the relationship in order to commit
15 _ _ _ _ _ _. Exploring gender differences in
the application of **16** _ _ _ _ course theory,
researchers have also examined the criminality
of women. Researchers have considered
how relationships and turning **17** _ _ _ _ _ _
may affect the criminality of **18** _ _ _ and
women differently. Women, who are usually the
primary caregiver to **19** _ _ _ _ _ _ _ _, have
different roles than men. Women become
responsible for another life as soon as they are
pregnant. Maybe this is why some people argue
women mature faster than men. But then how
do we explain the increasing number of women
going to **20** _ _ _ _ _ _?

Social process theorists examine the influence
of social interactions that take place among
all segments of society. The approach has
21 _ _ _ _ main branches—social learning,
labeling, social bond, and **22** _ _ _ _-control.
According to **23** _ _ _ _ _ _ learning theories,
people acquire the techniques and thinking
associated with crime from relations with
others **24** _ _ _ are engaged in the behaviors.
When criminality is rewarded more than
punished, or its benefits outweigh its risks, it is
reinforced and **25** _ _ _ _ likely to reoccur.
One of the main underlying principles of
social learning theory is that it takes place in
26 _ _ _ of us; even **27** _ _ _ enforcement
officers may learn to engage in criminal
behaviors. According to some researchers
learning occurs when there is an association
with those engaged in the behavior and
available **28** _ _ _ _ models. Society's reaction
to crime, through negative labeling and
stigmatizing, plays a role in a person's
criminality. Although some people may be

more likely to engage in crime due to the
influence of a **29** _ _ _ _ _ _ _ _ label, there
are also people who are **30** _ _ _ _ likely to
engage in crime in order to avoid that
31 _ _ _ _ _. Some research points out the
limits of labeling theory in **32** _ _ _-Western
cultures and outlines how Chinese society uses
stigma and labeling to achieve desistance from
33 _ _ _ _ _. According to social control theory,
criminality occurs when a **34** _ _ _ _ _ _ is only
weakly connected to conventional others.
Research has examined how social bonds with
others influence the probation experiences of
people convicted of **35** _ _ _ _ _ molestation.
Using what is arguably the most stigmatized
and estranged group of offenders to be released
from **36** _ _ _ _ _ _, research has tested the
hypothesis that bonds with others will affect
adjustment to probation. In contrast,
Gottfredson and Hirschi's general theory of
37 _ _ _ _ _ argues that criminal propensity is
fixed within an individual early in **38** _ _ _ _.
Previous research using their theory has
examined levels of self-control, **39** _ _ _ _-
reported engagement in criminal activity, and
attitudes of youth in several cities at multiple
points in **40** _ _ _ _.

Answers: Part One

Section One: Clarity

1. a. Choice **a** is the only one with subject-verb agreement. In choices **b**, **c**, and **d** the verbs *stands*, *stand*, and *is standing* are not past tense; the photo was taken *last* week, which calls for past tense.

2. d. Subject-verb agreement is only correct in **d**. When writing about a number of something, use *fewer*, not *less*, which is used with things that cannot be counted (e.g., less fun, less danger).

3. c. *Whether* not *weather* is the correct form of the word. Choice **a** starts in the past tense with *remained* but then uses the future tense with *is going*.

4. b. Choice **b** is the only one with subject-verb agreement, correctly using the past tense throughout the sentence.

5. a. Choice **a** is the only one with subject-verb agreement.

6. d. *I* is the correct pronoun, not *me*. And the other person is placed in the sentence first, before the writer, *I*.

7. b. While contractions should be avoided in formal writing, choice **b** is the only correct form of the contraction *it is*.

8. c. Choice **a** uses *me* instead of *I* and puts the writer first. Choice **b** is awkward. Choice **d** also puts the writer, not the other person, first.

9. b. When using *neither . . . nor*, use a singular verb. Choices **a** and **c** use plural verbs. In choices **c** and **d**, *or* rather than *nor* was used.

10. a. Only choice **a** has subject-verb agreement, and *successes* is not used.

11. d. *Then* is used to describe when one event occurs after another while *than* is used to make comparisons. Only choices **c** and **d** had the correct usage. Choice **c** uses the possessive *precinct's* incorrectly.

12. b. *Well* is used to describe performance or a state of being while *good* is used to describe the quality of something—for example, you feel well but have a good view. Only choices **b** and **d** use *well* correctly. Choice **d** has inconsistent verb tenses; the present tense of the verb is used to describe something that happened in the past.

13. a. Choices **b**, **c**, and **d** do not make sense. Choice **a** is the only choice without subordination errors.

14. b. *There* is used to indicate a place, and *threw* is used as a verb. Only choice **b** uses both words correctly.

15. c. *Which* is the correct word choice. Only choice **c** uses the past tense of verbs throughout the sentence.

Section Two: Vocabulary

16. a. *Intrigued* means to become fascinated or interested in something.

17. b. *Articulate* is a verb meaning to tell or describe, making **b** the best answer.

18. d. To *persevere* means to be persistent or to keep working for some goal, so determination, choice **d**, is the best answer.

19. b. To face a *dilemma* is to have a problem or to struggle over a decision, making choice **b** the best answer.

20. c. To *concede* means to acknowledge or accept something, making choice **c** the best answer.

21. c. *Resemblance* means to be similar to or look like something else, making choice **c** the best answer.

22. a. *Contrived* describes something as artificial or forced, making choice **a** the best answer.

23. c. To be *callous* is to be unfeeling or insensitive, making choice **c** the best answer.

24. b. To be *philanthropic* means to be generous, such as volunteering or doing charity work.

25. d. When something is *mundane,* it is dull or routine, making choice **d** the best answer.

26. c. When something is a *hindrance,* it interferes or makes something more difficult to accomplish, making choice **c** the best answer.

27. a. When something is done *haphazardly,* it is done in a random or indiscriminate manner, making choice **a** the best answer.

28. d. *Espoused* means supported or adopted a position or cause.

29. a. When something is *inevitable,* it is certain or expected to happen, making choice **a** the best answer.

30. c. When someone *reminisces,* they remember or bring to mind something that occurred in the past, making choice **c** the best answer.

Section Three: Spelling

31. b. This is the proper spelling of *apparent.*

32. c. This is the proper spelling of *accommodate.*

33. a. This is the proper spelling of *abundance.*

34. b. This is the proper spelling of *unique.*

35. d. This is the proper spelling of *subtle.*

36. d. This is the proper spelling of *evident.*

37. b. This is the proper spelling of *reference.*

38. d. This is the proper spelling of *occurred.*

39. c. This is the proper spelling of *sparse.*

40. a. This is the proper spelling of *proceed.*

41. c. This is the proper spelling of *necessary.*

42. b. This is the proper spelling of *pessimist.*

43. d. This is the proper spelling of *impression.*

44. a. This is the proper spelling of *estimated.*

45. b. This is the proper spelling of *mandatory.*

Section Four: Reading Comprehension

46. b. The first sentence of the last paragraph states that it is important not to omit studying race and ethnicity when studying criminal justice.

47. d. In the last paragraph, the second sentence states that a multicultural perspective of criminal justice impacts society as a whole. Also, the last sentence describes the field as practical.

48. c. Practical understanding is not one of the three methods mentioned.

49. b. The passage includes a sentence stating that research has found students lack critical analytic skills, which allows them to adhere to myths and generalizations about crime.

50. b. The passage states that cultural literacy supports the traditional study of the field and would require students to read classic, mainstream scholars.

51. d. The passage states that historical multiculturalism teaches critical thinking skills, and without them students adhere to myths and generalizations about crime.

52. a. The passage describes ways to incorporate race and ethnicity into teaching criminology/ criminal justice.

53. a. The passage states that animals are increasingly being incorporated into different types of prison programming.

54. d. The final sentence of the passage states that additional research is needed regarding the long-term effects of these programs.

55. b. The passage states that the programs are successful from a service perspective.

56. c. According to the passage, when inmates train or care for animals for adoption or service use in the community, they are engaged in animal-assisted activity.

57. b. The third sentence of the passage states that limited research has been conducted.

58. d. The passage discusses several aspects of the relationship between a law enforcement officer and a canine partner.

59. a. The passage states that a canine partner has abilities such as smell and speed that surpass those of a human.

60. d. The passage mentions statements **a**, **b**, and **c**.

Answers: Part Two

1. not
2. criminals
3. social
4. theory
5. crimes
6. have
7. join
8. that
9. bonds
10. self
11. use
12. camp
13. stop
14. not
15. crimes
16. life
17. points
18. men
19. children
20. prison
21. four
22. self
23. social
24. who
25. more
26. all
27. law
28. role
29. negative
30. less
31. label
32. non
33. crime
34. person
35. child
36. prison
37. crime
38. life
39. self
40. time

Scoring

Most U.S. cities require a score of at least 70% to pass a police officer exam. Because this exam has 100 questions, the number you answered correctly is your percentage: If you got 70 questions correct, your score is 70%. What you should do next depends not only on how you score, but also on whether the city you're applying to uses your written score to help determine your rank on the eligibility list. Some cities use other factors, such as your performance in an oral board or interview, to decide whether to hire you. In that case, all you need to do is to pass the written exam in order to make it to the next step in the process, and a score of at least 70% is good enough. In other cities, however, your written score, either by itself or in combination with other factors, is used to place you on the eligibility list. The higher your score, the more likely you are to be hired.

Use this practice exam as a way to analyze your performance. Pay attention to the areas in which you missed the most questions. If most of your mistakes are in the reading comprehension questions, then you know you need to practice your reading skills. Or perhaps you had difficulty with the spelling section. Once you see where you need help, then your mission will be to hone the relevant skills to develop your test-taking strategies.

To help you see where your trouble spots are, break down your scores according to the four sections.

Part One

Section One: Clarity ___ questions correct

Section Two: Vocabulary ___ questions correct

Section Three: Spelling ___ questions correct

Section Four: Reading Comprehension ___ questions correct

Part Two

Reading ___ questions correct

Write down the number of correct answers for each section, and then add up all five numbers for your overall score. Each question is worth one point, and the total you arrive at after adding all the numbers is also the percentage of questions that you answered correctly on the test.

And now forget about your total score; what's more important right now is your score on the individual sections of the exam. Your best bet is to study and review all the tested skills carefully, but you'll want to spend the most time on the skills that correspond to the kind of questions that gave you the most trouble.

Remember, reading and writing skills are important not only for the exam, but also for your job as a police officer. So the time you spend improving those skills will pay off—not only in higher exam scores, but also in career success.

After you've reviewed and practiced the relevant skills, take the second exam of this type, in Chapter 6, to see how much you've improved.

3 ▶ POLICE OFFICER PRACTICE EXAM 2

CHAPTER SUMMARY

The practice exam in this chapter is an example of the kind of job-related exam used by many police departments around the country. It tests skills police officers actually use on the job—not only basic skills like math and reading, but also map reading, memory, and good judgment and common sense.

The first practice exam in this book showed you an example of a police exam that simply tests your reading and writing skills. This second practice exam shows you a somewhat different kind of test. It still includes reading comprehension—most police exams do, because reading is such a vital job-related skill—but it also tests your ability to memorize pictures and written material, your map-reading skills, and your ability to use judgment to solve the kinds of problems police officers typically encounter, including simple math problems. There are 100 questions on this test, broken down into three sections:

- Section One: Memorization and Visualization consists of a set of pictures and text that you have to study and then a set of questions that you must answer based on the visuals and the text. You will not be allowed to look back at the material as you respond to these questions.
- Section Two: Reading covers map reading and reading comprehension.
- Section Three: Judgment and Problem Solving consists of questions that test deductive and inductive reasoning, your ability to apply good judgment and common sense in specific situations, and your ability to solve problems involving numbers (math word problems).

For best results, approach this exam as if it were the real thing. Find a quiet place where you can take the exam, and arm yourself with a few sharp No. 2 pencils. Give yourself 15 minutes to study the memory material at the beginning of the exam. Then start the practice test, which begins with questions about what you memorized. Give yourself two and a half hours to complete the test, in addition to the 15 minutes you spent memorizing.

The exam is followed by an answer key complete with explanations of why the correct answer is the best choice. An explanation of how to interpret your test score follows the answer key.

Police Officer Practice Exam 2

1.	ⓐ	ⓑ	ⓒ	ⓓ
2.	ⓐ	ⓑ	ⓒ	ⓓ
3.	ⓐ	ⓑ	ⓒ	ⓓ
4.	ⓐ	ⓑ	ⓒ	ⓓ
5.	ⓐ	ⓑ	ⓒ	ⓓ
6.	ⓐ	ⓑ	ⓒ	ⓓ
7.	ⓐ	ⓑ	ⓒ	ⓓ
8.	ⓐ	ⓑ	ⓒ	ⓓ
9.	ⓐ	ⓑ	ⓒ	ⓓ
10.	ⓐ	ⓑ	ⓒ	ⓓ
11.	ⓐ	ⓑ	ⓒ	ⓓ
12.	ⓐ	ⓑ	ⓒ	ⓓ
13.	ⓐ	ⓑ	ⓒ	ⓓ
14.	ⓐ	ⓑ	ⓒ	ⓓ
15.	ⓐ	ⓑ	ⓒ	ⓓ
16.	ⓐ	ⓑ	ⓒ	ⓓ
17.	ⓐ	ⓑ	ⓒ	ⓓ
18.	ⓐ	ⓑ	ⓒ	ⓓ
19.	ⓐ	ⓑ	ⓒ	ⓓ
20.	ⓐ	ⓑ	ⓒ	ⓓ
21.	ⓐ	ⓑ	ⓒ	ⓓ
22.	ⓐ	ⓑ	ⓒ	ⓓ
23.	ⓐ	ⓑ	ⓒ	ⓓ
24.	ⓐ	ⓑ	ⓒ	ⓓ
25.	ⓐ	ⓑ	ⓒ	ⓓ
26.	ⓐ	ⓑ	ⓒ	ⓓ
27.	ⓐ	ⓑ	ⓒ	ⓓ
28.	ⓐ	ⓑ	ⓒ	ⓓ
29.	ⓐ	ⓑ	ⓒ	ⓓ
30.	ⓐ	ⓑ	ⓒ	ⓓ
31.	ⓐ	ⓑ	ⓒ	ⓓ
32.	ⓐ	ⓑ	ⓒ	ⓓ
33.	ⓐ	ⓑ	ⓒ	ⓓ
34.	ⓐ	ⓑ	ⓒ	ⓓ
35.	ⓐ	ⓑ	ⓒ	ⓓ

36.	ⓐ	ⓑ	ⓒ	ⓓ
37.	ⓐ	ⓑ	ⓒ	ⓓ
38.	ⓐ	ⓑ	ⓒ	ⓓ
39.	ⓐ	ⓑ	ⓒ	ⓓ
40.	ⓐ	ⓑ	ⓒ	ⓓ
41.	ⓐ	ⓑ	ⓒ	ⓓ
42.	ⓐ	ⓑ	ⓒ	ⓓ
43.	ⓐ	ⓑ	ⓒ	ⓓ
44.	ⓐ	ⓑ	ⓒ	ⓓ
45.	ⓐ	ⓑ	ⓒ	ⓓ
46.	ⓐ	ⓑ	ⓒ	ⓓ
47.	ⓐ	ⓑ	ⓒ	ⓓ
48.	ⓐ	ⓑ	ⓒ	ⓓ
49.	ⓐ	ⓑ	ⓒ	ⓓ
50.	ⓐ	ⓑ	ⓒ	ⓓ
51.	ⓐ	ⓑ	ⓒ	ⓓ
52.	ⓐ	ⓑ	ⓒ	ⓓ
53.	ⓐ	ⓑ	ⓒ	ⓓ
54.	ⓐ	ⓑ	ⓒ	ⓓ
55.	ⓐ	ⓑ	ⓒ	ⓓ
56.	ⓐ	ⓑ	ⓒ	ⓓ
57.	ⓐ	ⓑ	ⓒ	ⓓ
58.	ⓐ	ⓑ	ⓒ	ⓓ
59.	ⓐ	ⓑ	ⓒ	ⓓ
60.	ⓐ	ⓑ	ⓒ	ⓓ
61.	ⓐ	ⓑ	ⓒ	ⓓ
62.	ⓐ	ⓑ	ⓒ	ⓓ
63.	ⓐ	ⓑ	ⓒ	ⓓ
64.	ⓐ	ⓑ	ⓒ	ⓓ
65.	ⓐ	ⓑ	ⓒ	ⓓ
66.	ⓐ	ⓑ	ⓒ	ⓓ
67.	ⓐ	ⓑ	ⓒ	ⓓ
68.	ⓐ	ⓑ	ⓒ	ⓓ
69.	ⓐ	ⓑ	ⓒ	ⓓ
70.	ⓐ	ⓑ	ⓒ	ⓓ

71.	ⓐ	ⓑ	ⓒ	ⓓ
72.	ⓐ	ⓑ	ⓒ	ⓓ
73.	ⓐ	ⓑ	ⓒ	ⓓ
74.	ⓐ	ⓑ	ⓒ	ⓓ
75.	ⓐ	ⓑ	ⓒ	ⓓ
76.	ⓐ	ⓑ	ⓒ	ⓓ
77.	ⓐ	ⓑ	ⓒ	ⓓ
78.	ⓐ	ⓑ	ⓒ	ⓓ
79.	ⓐ	ⓑ	ⓒ	ⓓ
80.	ⓐ	ⓑ	ⓒ	ⓓ
81.	ⓐ	ⓑ	ⓒ	ⓓ
82.	ⓐ	ⓑ	ⓒ	ⓓ
83.	ⓐ	ⓑ	ⓒ	ⓓ
84.	ⓐ	ⓑ	ⓒ	ⓓ
85.	ⓐ	ⓑ	ⓒ	ⓓ
86.	ⓐ	ⓑ	ⓒ	ⓓ
87.	ⓐ	ⓑ	ⓒ	ⓓ
88.	ⓐ	ⓑ	ⓒ	ⓓ
89.	ⓐ	ⓑ	ⓒ	ⓓ
90.	ⓐ	ⓑ	ⓒ	ⓓ
91.	ⓐ	ⓑ	ⓒ	ⓓ
92.	ⓐ	ⓑ	ⓒ	ⓓ
93.	ⓐ	ⓑ	ⓒ	ⓓ
94.	ⓐ	ⓑ	ⓒ	ⓓ
95.	ⓐ	ⓑ	ⓒ	ⓓ
96.	ⓐ	ⓑ	ⓒ	ⓓ
97.	ⓐ	ⓑ	ⓒ	ⓓ
98.	ⓐ	ⓑ	ⓒ	ⓓ
99.	ⓐ	ⓑ	ⓒ	ⓓ
100.	ⓐ	ⓑ	ⓒ	ⓓ

Practice Exam 2

Section One: Memorization and Visualization

You have 15 minutes to study the following posters and to read the article on police procedure. After 15 minutes are up, turn the page and go on to answer the test questions, beginning with questions about the study material. Do not refer back to the posters and the article to answer the questions. When you have finished with Part One: Memorization and Visualization, you may continue with the rest of the exam.

MISSING

Leonard Prescott Smith

DESCRIPTION:

Age: 78
Race: White
Height: 6′0″
Weight: 185 lbs.
Hair: Bald
Eyes: Green

REMARKS: Alzheimer's patient last seen in lobby of Hillside Nursing Home on Christmas Day. Has been found wandering in Red Rock Park on other occasions.

IF LOCATED: Call Barnstable Police Department, Barnstable, Massachusetts, at 508-555-8000.

WANTED

Denise Gibbons

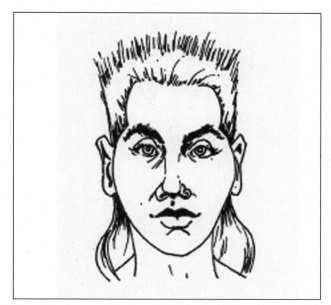

ALIASES: Dipsey Gibbons; Dee Gibbs
WANTED BY: Hays County Parole Board
CHARGES: Violation of Parole
DESCRIPTION:

Age: 26
Race: White
Height: 5′5″
Weight: 125 lbs.
Hair: Blond
Eyes: Hazel

IDENTIFYING SCARS OR MARKS: Six-inch surgical scar on front left knee; needle marks on inner right arm.
REMARKS: Known prostitute. Frequents Shady Grove area. Is thought to be active heroin addict. Last seen with short, purple-tinted hair. Wears small hoop nose ring. May head for sister's home in Bangor, Maine.
CAUTION: Has been known to carry knives and will fight police. Handle with caution.

WANTED

Jamil Jones

ALIASES: Jay Jones
WANTED BY: FBI
CHARGES: Kidnapping

DESCRIPTION:
Age: 22
Race: Black
Height: 5′10″
Weight: 165 lbs.
Hair: Black
Eyes: Brown

IDENTIFYING SCARS OR MARKS: Thin scar along left cheek.
REMARKS: Last known employer, Lucky Limo Service in Quincy, Massachusetts. Frequently seen with full black beard and mustache.
CAUTION: Jones is known to carry a .45 mm Browning.

WANTED

Louis James Serna

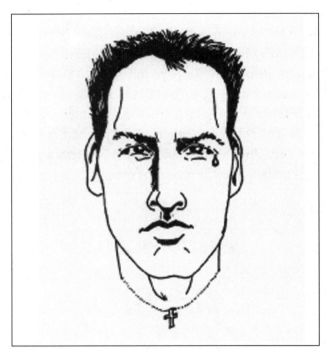

ALIASES: L.J. Serna
WANTED BY: Boston Police Department
CHARGES: Assault

DESCRIPTION:
Age: 17
Race: Hispanic
Height: 5′6″
Weight: 120 lbs.
Hair: Brown
Eyes: Brown

IDENTIFYING SCARS OR MARKS: Tattoos of a teardrop at base of left eye, "Angie" on right upper shoulder, and snake curling around left wrist.
REMARKS: Latino Riders gang member. Limps heavily on right leg.

WANTED

Alice Faye Bunn

ALIASES: Allie Jones
WANTED BY: Coal County Sheriff's Department
CHARGES: Abuse of the Elderly

DESCRIPTION:
Age: 40
Race: White
Height: 5′7″
Weight: 170 lbs.
Hair: Brown
Eyes: Blue

IDENTIFYING SCARS OR MARKS: Burn scars along top of right hand.
REMARKS: Frequently works as a nurse's aide. Last seen in Tempe, Arizona, but is believed to be en route to New Haven, Connecticut.

Roadblock Guidelines

The Advisory Committee of the State Police has issued the following guidelines for establishing a roadblock in order to identify and apprehend drunk drivers:

1. **Selecting the location.** The roadblock must be established in a location that affords motorists a clear view of the stop. It cannot be established, for example, just over a hill or around a curve. Motorists must be able to see that a roadblock is ahead and that cars are being stopped.

2. **Staffing the location.** A roadblock must display visible signs of police authority. Therefore, uniformed officers in marked patrol cars should primarily staff the roadblock. Plainclothes officers may supplement the staff at a roadblock, but the initial stop and questioning of motorists should be conducted by uniformed officers. In addition to the officers conducting the motorist stops, officers should be present to conduct field sobriety tests on suspect drivers. A command observation officer must also be present to coordinate the roadblock.

3. **Operation of the roadblock.** All cars passing through the roadblock must be stopped. It should not appear to an approaching motorist that cars are being singled out for some reason while others are not stopped, as this will generate unnecessary fear on the part of the motorist. The observation vehicle that is present at the roadblock will be able to pursue any motorists who refuse to stop.

4. **Questioning the drivers.** Each motorist stopped by the roadblock should be questioned only briefly. In most cases, an officer should ask directly if the driver has been drinking. In suspicious cases, an officer may engage in some further questioning to allow him or her to evaluate the driver's sobriety. A driver who appears

to have been drinking should be directed to the side of the road, out of the line of traffic, where other officers may conduct a field sobriety test. Each non-suspicious driver should be stopped only briefly, for approximately a minute or less.

5. **Duration of operation.** No drunk-driving roadblock should be in operation for more than two hours. Roadblocks in place for longer periods lose their effectiveness as word spreads as to the location of the roadblock, and motorists who have been drinking will avoid the area. In addition, on average, only about 1% of all the drivers who pass through a roadblock will be arrested for drunk driving, and after a short period of time, officers can be used more efficiently elsewhere.

6. **Charges other than drunk driving.** A roadblock may only be established for a single purpose—in this case, detecting drunk drivers—and should not be seen as an opportunity to check for a variety of motorist offenses. However, officers are not required to ignore what is plainly obvious. For example, motorists and passengers who are not wearing seat belts should be verbally warned that failure to do so is against the law. Detaining and ticketing such drivers is not the purpose of the roadblock and would unduly slow down the stops of other cars. An officer who spots a situation that presents a clear and present danger should follow through by directing the motorist to the side of the road where the officers are conducting field sobriety tests. These officers can then follow through on investigating the driver for crimes other than drunk driving.

Section One: Memorization and Visualization

Answer the following 30 questions based on the posters and police procedure article you have just studied. **Do not refer back to the study material to answer these questions.**

1. Denise Gibbons is wanted for
   a. armed robbery.
   b. fraud.
   c. sexual assault.
   d. violation of parole.

2. Leonard Prescott Smith is
   a. Middle Eastern.
   b. white.
   c. Hispanic.
   d. African American.

3. Leonard Prescott Smith has
   a. a mostly bald head.
   b. a tattoo near his eye.
   c. missing front teeth.
   d. a scar on his cheek.

4. Louis James Serna also goes by the name
   a. A.J. Serna.
   b. L.J. Serna
   c. Allie Jones.
   d. Louie Serna.

5. Jamil Jones's last known employer was
   a. L.J.'s Limo Service.
   b. Lucky Limo Service.
   c. Smith's Limo Service.
   d. Hillside Limo Service.

6. Alice Faye Bunn is wanted for
   a. kidnapping.
   b. violation of parole.
   c. abuse of the elderly.
   d. assault.

7. Denise Gibbons's hair is
   a. spiked on top.
   b. curly.
   c. dyed blond.
   d. wavy.

8. Louis James Serna's snake tattoo is located on his
   a. right shoulder.
   b. chest.
   c. forehead.
   d. left wrist.

9. Alice Faye Bunn is believed to be en route to
   a. Quincy, Massachusetts.
   b. Tempe, Arizona.
   c. Barnstable, Massachusetts.
   d. New Haven, Connecticut.

10. Jamil Jones's scar runs
   a. vertically down his chin.
   b. vertically down his right cheek.
   c. horizontally along his left cheek.
   d. horizontally along his forehead.

11. Which of the following is true of Leonard Prescott Smith?
   a. He is wanted for violation of parole.
   b. He is an Alzheimer's patient.
   c. He is armed and dangerous.
   d. He is a former nursing home employee.

12. Louis James Serna has been seen wearing
   a. a scarf around his head.
   b. a T-shirt.
   c. a heavy jacket.
   d. a cross around his neck.

13. Which two suspects are known to carry weapons?
   a. Jones and Bunn
   b. Gibbons and Serna
   c. Serna and Bunn
   d. Gibbons and Hassid

14. Which suspect walks with a limp?
   a. Smith
   b. Jones
   c. Serna
   d. Bunn

15. Which two suspects are in their twenties?
   a. Smith and Jones
   b. Gibbons and Jones
   c. Bunn and Jones
   d. Gibbons and Bunn

16. Which two suspects have black hair?
   a. Gibbons and Bunn
   b. Jones and Bunn
   c. Serna and Gibbons
   d. Jones and Serna

17. Of the people listed below, which is tallest?
   a. Smith
   b. Jones
   c. Bunn
   d. Serna

18. Which suspect is known to carry a gun?
   a. Serna
   b. Gibbons
   c. Jones
   d. Bunn

19. Based on the information in the posters, which of the following is true?
   a. Bunn is the only suspect with blue eyes.
   b. Serna is the only suspect with brown eyes.
   c. Bunn and Gibbons both have blue eyes.
   d. Smith and Gibbons both have hazel eyes.

20. Based on the information in the Wanted posters, which of the following is false?
   a. Gibbons wears a nose ring.
   b. Serna has a tattoo of the name "Angie."
   c. Serna and Jones both have beards.
   d. Bunn wears glasses.

21. According to the Roadblock Guidelines, officers must make sure they set up a drunk-driving roadblock that
   a. can be seen by motorists from a distance.
   b. provides a well-hidden place for officers to park their cars.
   c. is near a bar or tavern.
   d. is near a busy street or highway.

22. While questioning motorists at a drunk-driving roadblock, Officer Firth notices that, although the driver of a particular car appears to be sober, the passenger in that car seems extremely nervous and has bruises on his face. She asks the passenger if he is all right, and after glancing at the driver, the passenger nods yes. According to the guidelines, Officer Firth should
   a. let the car pass through because the driver is not drunk.
   b. question the passenger and driver further about the passenger's condition.
   c. arrest the driver on suspicion of assault.
   d. direct the driver to pull to the side of the road where other officers can investigate further.

23. Officers have been conducting a drunk-driving roadblock since 7:00 P.M. and have made 35 drunk-driving arrests, which is one-quarter of all cars stopped. It is now 9:00 P.M. According to the guidelines, the officers should
   a. continue the roadblock because they are making a high percentage of arrests.
   b. reestablish the roadblock one-quarter mile down the road.
   c. ask the Advisory Committee for permission to operate the roadblock longer.
   d. dismantle the roadblock because it has been in operation for two hours.

24. Officers have been directed to operate a drunk-driving roadblock from 6:00 P.M. to 8:00 P.M. at the corner of Greene and First. At 6:45, the unusually heavy traffic begins to back up. According to the guidelines, officers should NOT
   a. dismantle the roadblock early.
   b. begin stopping only every third car.
   c. move the roadblock to a quieter intersection.
   d. ask for extra officers to help staff the roadblock.

25. According to the guidelines, the officers stopping and questioning motorists at a drunk-driving roadblock should be in uniform so that motorists
   a. will take the roadblock more seriously.
   b. will answer their questions more truthfully.
   c. can identify which agency they are from.
   d. can tell from a distance that this is an official activity.

26. Officer Robb is stopping and questioning eastbound cars at the drunk-driving roadblock on Highway 7. He asks one driver if she has been drinking. The driver says, "No, Officer, I haven't," but she slurs her words. According to the guidelines, Officer Robb should
   a. ask the driver a few more questions.
   b. arrest the driver for drunk driving.
   c. ask the driver to take a breathalyzer test.
   d. pass the driver through with a warning.

27. A car approaching a drunk-driving roadblock slows down, then at the last minute speeds up and passes through the roadblock without stopping. According to the guidelines,
   a. the officers should note the car's license number and radio headquarters.
   b. the officers should request backup to pursue the car.
   c. the officers conducting field sobriety tests should pursue the vehicle.
   d. the officer in the command observation vehicle should pursue the motorist.

28. Based on the guidelines, which of the following statements is true?
   a. Guidelines for drunk-driving roadblocks are determined by the state police.
   b. Guidelines for drunk-driving roadblocks are determined by local police departments.
   c. Guidelines for drunk-driving roadblocks are determined by the state legislature.
   d. Guidelines for drunk-driving roadblocks are determined by the county sheriff.

29. According to the guidelines, officers operating a drunk-driving roadblock can expect
   a. cooperation from most drivers.
   b. to arrest only about 1% of the drivers stopped.
   c. to issue several tickets for failure to wear a seat belt.
   d. that many cars will refuse to stop.

30. According to the guidelines, the main role of the command observation officer at a drunk-driving roadblock is to
   a. conduct field sobriety tests.
   b. establish the official police presence.
   c. determine when to dismantle the roadblock.
   d. coordinate the roadblock.

Section Two: Reading

Read the following passage, then answer questions 31 through 35.

In order for our society to make decisions about the kinds of punishments we will impose on convicted criminals, we must understand why we punish criminals. Some people argue that retribution is the purpose of punishment and that, therefore, the punishment must in some direct way fit the crime. This view is based on the belief that a person who commits a crime deserves to be punished. Because the punishment must fit the specific crime, the *theory of retribution* allows a sentencing judge to consider the circumstances of each crime, criminal, and victim in imposing a sentence.

Another view, the *deterrence theory*, promotes punishment in order to discourage commission of future crimes. In this view, punishment need not relate directly to the crime committed, because the point is to deter both a specific criminal and the general public from committing crimes in the future. However, punishment must necessarily be uniformly and consistently applied, in order for the members of the public to understand how they would be punished if they committed a crime. Laws setting sentencing guidelines are based on the deterrence theory and do not allow a judge to consider the specifics of a particular crime in sentencing a convicted criminal.

31. According to the passage, punishment
  a. is rarely an effective deterrent to future crimes.
  b. must fit the crime in question.
  c. is imposed solely at the discretion of a judge.
  d. may be imposed for differing reasons.

32. The retribution theory of punishment
  a. is no longer considered valid.
  b. holds that punishment must fit the crime committed.
  c. applies only to violent crimes.
  d. allows a jury to recommend the sentence that should be imposed.

33. The passage suggests that a person who believes that the death penalty results in fewer murders most likely also believes in
  a. the deterrence theory.
  b. the retribution theory.
  c. giving judges considerable discretion in imposing sentences.
  d. the integrity of the criminal justice system.

34. Which of the following would be a good title for this passage?
  a. "Sentencing Reform: A Modest Proposal"
  b. "More Criminals Are Doing Time"
  c. "Punishment: Deterrent or Retribution?"
  d. "Why I Favor Uniform Sentencing Guidelines"

35. A person who believes in the deterrence theory would probably also support
  a. non-unanimous jury verdicts.
  b. early release of prisoners because of prison overcrowding.
  c. a broad definition of the insanity defense.
  d. allowing television broadcasts of court proceedings.

Read the following passage, then answer questions 36 through 40.

At 12:15 A.M., while riding the uptown-bound 12 train, transit officers Cobb and Wilson received a report of a disturbance in the fourth car of a downtown-bound 12 train. That train was held at the Fourth Street station until the arrival of the officers, who found complainant Alan Sterns tending his injured eye. Mr. Sterns told Officer Wilson that he had been attacked by Caroline Simpson when he attempted to move her bags, after politely asking her to do so, in order to make room to sit down. He said Ms. Simpson poked him in the eye and then threatened him with a switchblade. Ms. Simpson told Officer Cobb that she had been harassed by Mr. Sterns and struck him in self-defense. The officers asked Mr. Sterns, Ms. Simpson, and witnesses Lisa Walker and Lois Casey to step off the train, and proceeded to question them on the platform. Ms. Walker, whose view of the incident had been partially obstructed by a metal pole, stated that Mr.

Sterns had only raised his arm after being struck, but she was not sure whether the gesture was threatening or defensive. Ms. Casey, who sat on the other side of Ms. Simpson, maintained that Mr. Sterns was only protecting himself and had behaved in a polite manner. Ms. Simpson was placed under arrest for carrying a concealed weapon.

36. Where did the assault occur?
   a. on a subway platform
   b. on the fourth car of the uptown-bound 12 train
   c. at the Fourth Street station
   d. on the fourth car of the downtown-bound 12 train

37. Which of the following actions caused the arrest?
   a. injuring the complainant's eye
   b. threatening the complainant
   c. carrying a switchblade
   d. disturbing the peace

38. The complainant's last name is
   a. Sterns.
   b. Simpson.
   c. Walker.
   d. Cobb.

39. Where was Ms. Casey sitting?
   a. beside the complainant
   b. across the car, behind a metal pole
   c. between the complainant and the accused
   d. beside the accused

40. According to the complainant, he was struck because
   a. he handled the woman's property.
   b. he asked the woman to move her bags.
   c. he politely asked the woman to move over.
   d. he appeared to raise his arm in a threatening manner.

Study the following map, then answer questions 41 through 45.

A police officer is often required to assist civilians who seek travel directions or referral to city agencies and facilities. This is a map of a section of the city where some public buildings are located. Each of the squares represents one city block. Street names are as shown. If there is an arrow next to the street name, it means the street is one way only in the direction of the arrow. If there is no arrow next to the street name, two-way traffic is allowed.

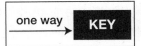

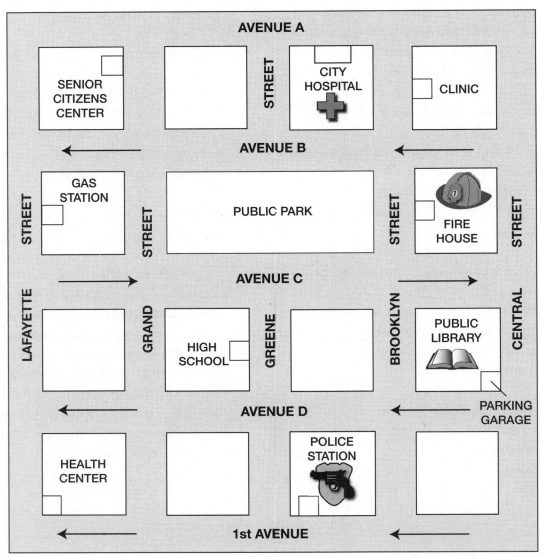

41. While you are on foot patrol, an elderly man stops you in front of the firehouse and asks you to help him find the senior citizens center. You should tell him to
   a. walk across the street to the senior citizens center.
   b. walk south to Avenue C, make a right, and walk west on Avenue C, make a right on Grand Street and walk up to the senior citizens center.
   c. walk north to Avenue B and then west on Avenue B to the end of the park, make a right and go one block.
   d. walk north to Avenue B and then west on Avenue B to Lafayette Street, make a right, and go one block.

42. The head librarian needs gasoline for his automobile. He is leaving the Avenue D garage exit from the library. His quickest legal route is to go
   a. north on Central Street to Avenue C and west on Avenue C to the gas station.
   b. west on Brooklyn Street to Avenue B and north on Avenue B to the gas station.
   c. west on Avenue D to Grand Street and north on Grand Street to the gas station.
   d. west on Avenue D to Lafayette Street and north on Lafayette Street to the gas station.

43. You are dispatched from the police station to an altercation occurring at the northwest corner of the public park. Which is the most direct legal way to drive there?
   a. east to Central Street, north on Central Street to Avenue B, and west on Avenue B to Grand Street
   b. west to Grand Street and north on Grand Street to Avenue B
   c. east to Brooklyn Street, north on Brooklyn Street to Avenue B, and west on Avenue B to Grand Street
   d. west to Greene Street, north on Greene Street to Avenue C, and east on Avenue C to Brooklyn Street

44. Your spouse is a nurse at the city hospital and goes to the public library every Monday as a volunteer. What would be the shortest legal route from the hospital to the library?
   a. west on Avenue A, south on Lafayette Street, east on Avenue C, and south on Central Street to the library entrance
   b. east on Avenue B and south on Central Street to the library entrance
   c. west on Avenue A, south on Lafayette Street, and east on Avenue D to the library entrance
   d. east on Avenue A and south on Central Street to the library entrance

45. After responding to a call at the firehouse, you are ready to drive back to the police station for the end of your shift. What is the quickest legal route?
   a. south on Brooklyn Street and west on 1st Avenue to the police station
   b. north on Brooklyn Street, west on Avenue A, south on Lafayette Street, and east on 1st Avenue to the police station
   c. north on Brooklyn Street and east on 1st Avenue to the police station
   d. south on Brooklyn Street, west on Avenue C, south on Grand Street, and east on 1st Avenue to the police station

Read the following passage, then answer questions 46 through 48.

Law enforcement officers often do not like taking time from their regular duties to testify in court, but testimony is an important part of an officer's job. To be good witnesses, officers should keep complete notes detailing any potentially criminal or actionable incidents. When on the witness stand, officers may refer to those notes to refresh their memories about particular events. It is also very important for officers to listen carefully to the questions asked by the lawyers and to provide only the information requested. Officers should never volunteer opinions or any extra information that is beyond the scope of a question.

46. According to the passage, an officer who is testifying in court
   a. will be questioned by the judge.
   b. may refer to his or her notes while on the witness stand.
   c. must do so without pay.
   d. appreciates taking a break from routine assignments.

47. This passage is probably taken from a(n)
  a. memo entitled "Proper Arrest Procedure."
  b. newspaper article.
  c. best-selling novel.
  d. officers' training manual.

48. According to the passage, testifying in court is
  a. an important part of a police officer's job.
  b. difficult, because lawyers try to trick witnesses.
  c. less stressful for police officers than for other witnesses.
  d. a waste of time, because judges usually let criminals off.

Read the following passage, then answer questions 49 and 50.

Detectives who routinely investigate violent crimes can't help but become somewhat jaded. Paradoxically, the victims and witnesses with whom they work closely are often in a highly vulnerable and emotional state. The emotional fallout from a sexual assault, for example, can be complex and long lasting. Detectives must be trained to handle people in emotional distress and must be sensitive to the fact that for the victim, the crime is not routine. At the same time, detectives must recognize the limits of their role and resist the temptation to act as therapists or social workers, instead referring victims to the proper agencies.

49. What is the main idea of the passage?
  a. Detectives who investigate violent crimes must not become emotionally hardened by the experience.
  b. Victims of violent crime should be referred to therapists and social workers.
  c. Detectives should be sensitive to the emotional state of victims of violent crime.
  d. Detectives should be particularly careful in dealing with victims of sexual assault.

50. According to the passage, what is "paradoxical" about the detective's relationship to the victim?
  a. Detectives know less about the experience of violent crime than do victims.
  b. What is routine for the detective is a unique and profound experience for the victim.
  c. Detectives must be sensitive to victims' needs but can't be social workers or psychologists.
  d. Not only must detectives solve crimes, but they must also handle the victims with care.

Read the following passage, then answer questions 51 through 53.

At 12:45 A.M. on October 15, while parked at 1910 Fairlane, police officers Flores and Steinbrenner were asked to respond to a disturbance at 1809 Clarkson. When they arrived at the one-story dwelling, the complainant, Alan Weber, who resides next door at 1807 Clarkson, told them that he had been kept awake for two hours by the sound of yelling and breaking glass. He said the occupant of 1809 Clarkson, Mr. Everett Hayes, lived alone. When the officers knocked on the door, Mr. Hayes answered promptly and said, "It's about time you got here." Inside, broken furniture was strewn about. Mr. Hayes stated that he had been protecting himself from persons who lived inside the woodwork of his home. He went willingly with the officers to Fairfield County Hospital at 1010 Market, where he was admitted to the psychiatric unit for observation. No arrests were made.

51. The call to the police was most likely made from which of the following addresses?
  a. 1910 Fairlane
  b. 1809 Clarkson
  c. 1807 Clarkson
  d. 1010 Market

52. Based on the passage, what was the most likely reason the police were called?
- **a.** A neighbor was bothered by the noise coming from Mr. Hayes's home.
- **b.** A neighbor was worried for Mr. Hayes's safety.
- **c.** A neighbor was worried for the safety of Mr. Hayes's family.
- **d.** A neighbor was curious about Mr. Hayes's personal life.

53. What was Mr. Hayes's demeanor when the police arrived at his door?
- **a.** He seemed surprised.
- **b.** He seemed to have been expecting them.
- **c.** He seemed frightened and distrustful.
- **d.** He seemed angered by their presence.

Read the following passage, then answer questions 54 and 55.

Police officers must read suspects their Miranda rights when taking them into custody. When a suspect who is merely being questioned incriminates himself, he might later claim to have been in custody and seek to have the case dismissed on the grounds of having been unapprised of his Miranda rights. In such cases, a judge must make a determination as to whether a reasonable person would have believed himself to have been in custody, based on certain criteria. The judge must determine whether the suspect was questioned in a threatening manner (for example, if the suspect was seated while both officers remained standing) and whether the suspect was aware that he was free to leave at any time. Officers must be aware of these criteria and take care not to give suspects grounds for later claiming they believed themselves to be in custody.

54. What is the main idea of the passage?
- **a.** Officers must remember to read suspects their Miranda rights.
- **b.** Judges, not police officers, make the final determination as to whether a suspect was in custody.
- **c.** Officers who are merely questioning a suspect must not give the suspect the impression that he or she is in custody.
- **d.** Miranda rights need not be read to all suspects before questioning.

55. When is a suspect not in custody?
- **a.** when free to refuse to answer questions
- **b.** when free to leave the police station
- **c.** when apprised of his or her Miranda rights
- **d.** when not apprised of his or her Miranda rights

Study the following map, then answer questions 56 through 60.

A police officer is often required to assist civilians who seek travel directions or referral to city agencies and facilities. This is a map of a section of the city where some public buildings are located. Each of the squares represents one city block. Street names are as shown. If there is an arrow next to the street name, it means the street is one way only in the direction of the arrow. If there is no arrow next to the street name, two-way traffic is allowed.

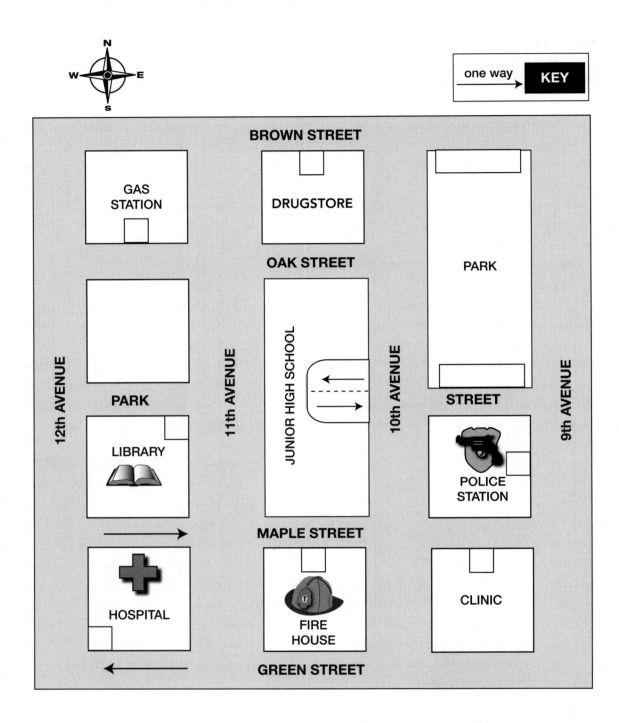

56. You arrive at the scene of a vehicular accident at the corner of Brown Street and 9th Avenue to find gasoline leaking from one of the cars. What is the most direct, legal way for the fire engine to travel to the scene of the accident?

a. east on Maple Street and north on 9th Avenue to the accident

b. west on Maple Street, north on 12th Avenue, and east on Brown Street to the accident

c. east on Maple Street and north on 11th Avenue to the accident

d. west on Maple Street, north on 11th Avenue, and east on Brown Street to the accident

57. What streets run north and south of the park?
   a. Brown Street and Oak Street
   b. Maple Street and Park Street
   c. Brown Street and Park Street
   d. Green Street and Oak Street

58. A civilian leaving the clinic needs to drive to the drugstore. If you were giving her directions from the clinic, what would be the most direct, legal route?
   a. east on Maple Street, north on 9th Avenue, and west on Brown Street to the store entrance
   b. west on Maple Street, north on 10th Avenue, and west on Brown Street to the store entrance
   c. west on Green Street, north on 12th Avenue, and east on Brown Street to the store entrance
   d. east on Oak Street, north on 11th Avenue, and east on Brown Street to the store entrance

59. Someone at the junior high school has been injured and needs to go to the hospital. What directions from the junior high school would you give to the ambulance driver?
   a. north on 10th Avenue, west on Brown Street, and south on 12th Avenue to the hospital entrance
   b. south on 10th Avenue and west on Green Street to the hospital entrance
   c. north on 10th Avenue and south on Brown Street to the hospital entrance
   d. south on 10th Avenue, west on Maple Street, and west on Green Street to the hospital entrance

60. You are leaving work at the police station and need to fill your gas tank before you go home. What is the quickest legal route to the gas station?
   a. south on 9th Avenue, west on Maple Street, north on 11th Avenue, and west on Oak Street to the entrance
   b. east on Maple Street, north on 10th Avenue, and west on Oak Street to the entrance
   c. north on 9th Avenue and west on Brown Street to the entrance
   d. north on 9th Avenue, west on Park Street, north on 10th Avenue, and west on Oak Street to the entrance

Section Three:
Judgment and Problem Solving

Use good judgment and common sense, as well as the information provided in each question, to answer the following questions.

61. While on foot patrol downtown, Officer Gutierrez is approached by Ms. Louise Herald, who says that a man snatched a shopping bag full of gifts from her arm and ran away. Ms. Herald remembers the contents of the shopping bag as follows:

- 1 cashmere sweater valued at $260
- 3 diamond bracelets, each valued at $365
- 1 computer game valued at $78
- 1 cameo brooch valued at $130

Later, Officer Gutierrez receives a call from Ms. Herald, who says she has found the receipts for the stolen merchandise. She says that what she told the officer was correct, except that there were only two diamond bracelets, not three, and that the value of the cashmere sweater was $245. What should Officer Gutierrez write as the total value of the stolen property?
a. $833
b. $1,183
c. $1,198
d. $1,563

62. Officer Kemp has worked more night shifts in a row than Officer Rogers, who has worked five. Officer Miller has worked 15 night shifts in a row, more than Officers Kemp and Rogers combined. Officer Calvin has worked eight night shifts in a row, less than Officer Kemp. How many night shifts in a row has Officer Kemp worked?
a. eight
b. nine
c. ten
d. eleven

63. For the past two months, stereo shops all over the city have been hit by burglars in the early morning hours. Sergeant Adams tells Officer Bryant that he should carefully watch the stores in his area that specialize in stereo equipment. Which one of the following situations should Officer Bryant investigate?
a. a truck with its motor running, backed up to the rear door of the House of Stereos at 1:00 A.M.
b. a lone man going through a Dumpster at the rear of the House of Stereos at 2:00 A.M.
c. a delivery van marked "House of Stereos" parked in the rear of the store at 2:00 A.M.
d. two teenage boys intently examining a stereo system in the window of House of Stereos just after midnight

64. Four eyewitnesses saw a vehicle being stolen and noted the license plate number. Each wrote down a different number. Which one of the following is probably right?
a. KLV 017
b. XIW 007
c. XIW 017
d. XIV 017

Read the following instructions, then answer questions 65 and 66.

An officer responding alone to the scene of a burglar alarm call should do the following:

1. Turn off siren and emergency lights as soon as possible to keep from alerting suspects.
2. Park the patrol car away from the building.
3. Notify the dispatcher of his or her arrival and location.
4. Begin checking the outside of the building for signs of entry.
5. Notify the dispatcher if signs of entry are discovered.
6. Wait for backup if it is available before going inside a building where entry has been made.
7. Tell backup officers where to position themselves as they arrive.

65. Officer Kim is dispatched to a burglar alarm call at 100 South Main Street, where the Quik Stop convenience store is located. The store closed at 1:00 A.M. and it is now 3:00 A.M. Officer Kim is parked in the parking lot of the pawnshop next door, writing a report, when the call comes out. Officer Kim's next step should be to

a. walk up to the building from the side so her approach is undetected.

b. wait for backup before approaching the building.

c. inform the dispatcher that she has arrived at 100 South Main Street.

d. check the outside of the building for signs of entry.

66. Officer Smith is sent to 1313 Milbury Way on a residential burglary alarm call at 1:00 P.M. Traffic is heavy on the way to the call, and he turns on his emergency lights to help clear the way. Officer Smith is notified that no backup is available in his sector. What is the next thing Officer Smith should do?

a. Park his patrol car a house or two away from 1313 Milbury Way.

b. Inform the dispatcher when he arrives.

c. Approach the front door, since any suspects are probably gone by now.

d. Turn off his emergency lights as soon as he can safely do so.

67. Police officers may find themselves in situations in which using a normal, conversational tone of voice is not enough to get an individual to do what the officer needs done. Which of the following situations calls for an officer to shout using a firm, authoritative tone of voice?

a. asking to see a driver's proof of automobile insurance after an accident

b. advising a new partner of a recently implemented departmental policy

c. chasing a burglar out of a house

d. asking a boy why he is not in school on a Monday morning

68. On Monday morning, officers Rosen and McNalty respond to a call reporting a burglary that apparently took place over the weekend at Datamation Computer Consultants. The owner of the business says that the following equipment is missing:

- 3 telephone sets, each valued at $125
- 2 computers, each valued at $1,300
- 2 computer monitors, each valued at $950
- 1 printer valued at $600
- 1 answering machine valued at $50

Officer McNalty is preparing a complaint report on the burglary. What should he write as the total value of the missing property?

a. $3,025

b. $5,400

c. $5,525

d. $6,525

69. In a four-day period—Monday through Thursday—each of the following officers worked only one day, each a different day. Officer Johnson was scheduled to work on Monday, but she traded with Officer Carter, who was originally scheduled to work on Wednesday. Officer Falk traded with Officer Kirk, who was originally scheduled to work on Thursday. After all the switching was done, who worked on Tuesday?

   a. Carter
   b. Falk
   c. Johnson
   d. Kirk

70. Mrs. Oneida has called the police to report that a man was looking into her bedroom window last night around 9:45 P.M. Officer Williams talks to residents in the area and finds out several people have seen a white male dressed in black walking up and down the street at about 10 P.M. for the past week. Officer Williams decides to patrol the area closely and is in the area by 9:30 P.M. Which situation should she investigate?

   a. two teenagers in jeans and dark T-shirts sitting on the curb, smoking cigarettes
   b. a man wearing black jogging shorts and dark shoes stretching his legs in the driveway of a house
   c. a man dressed in dark jeans and a navy blue turtleneck walking rapidly away from some shrubbery at the side of a house
   d. a man in dark clothing attaching a water hose to the faucet on the side of a house

71. Four people witnessed a mugging. Each gave a different description of the mugger. Which description is probably right?

   a. He was average height, thin, and middle-aged.
   b. He was tall, thin, and middle-aged.
   c. He was tall, thin, and young.
   d. He was tall, of average weight, and middle-aged.

Read the following instructions, then answer question 72.

All police officers are expected to know how to properly package evidence after the decision has been made to collect it. The following steps should be carried out in the order listed:

   1. Place each item in a separate container.
   2. Seal each container in such a way that it cannot be opened without breaking the seal.
   3. The officer collecting the evidence should write his or her name or employee number on the seal.
   4. Place a tag on the container that identifies the case number, the date and time collected, where the item was found, what the item is, who collected it, and what condition the item is in.
   5. Turn the evidence in personally to the Property Room without breaking the chain of custody by allowing someone else to do it.

72. Officer Jones is the first officer to arrive at the scene of a burglary at Wiggin's Liquor Store. After making sure the scene is secure, he begins to collect evidence. The first item he finds is a screwdriver lying on the sidewalk in front of the glass doors leading into the store. The second item he sees is a small flashlight on the floor inside the building. Officer Jones places the screwdriver in a small plastic bag. What is the next thing he should do?
   a. Lock the screwdriver in the trunk of his car.
   b. Seal the bag with evidence tape so that the bag cannot be opened.
   c. Write the case number and other information about the evidence on the outside of the bag.
   d. Put the flashlight in the bag with the screwdriver.

73. Officers Roberts and Reed are on bicycle patrol in the downtown area. Sergeant McElvey told them that a white male has been committing robberies along the nearby bike path by stepping out of the bushes and threatening bicyclists with an iron pipe until they give him their bicycles. There have been three separate incidents, and the suspect descriptions are from three different victims.

Robbery #1: Suspect is a white male, 20–25 years old, 5'9", 145 pounds, with a shaved head, wearing a skull earring in the left ear, floppy white T-shirt, worn light blue jeans, and black combat boots.

Robbery #2: Suspect is a white male, 25–30 years old, dark brown hair in a military-style crew cut, 6'2", 200 pounds, wearing a white T-shirt with the words "Just Do It" on the back, blue surgical scrub pants, and black combat boots.

Robbery #3: Suspect is a white male, 23 years old, 5'10", skinny build, no hair, wearing a Grateful Dead T-shirt, blue baggy pants, dark shoes, and one earring.

Three days after Sergeant McElvey told the officers about the robberies, Officer Reed arrested a suspect for attempting to take a woman's mountain bike from her on the bicycle path. The description of the suspect is as follows:

Robbery #4: Suspect is a white male, 22 years old, 140 pounds, 5'10", with a shaved head and one pierced ear, wearing a plain white T-shirt two sizes too large for him, faded baggy blue jeans, and scuffed black combat boots.

After comparing the suspect description with those in the first three robberies, Officer Reed should consider the arrested man as a suspect in which of the other robberies?
   a. Robbery #1, Robbery #2, and Robbery #3
   b. Robbery #1, but not Robbery #2 or Robbery #3
   c. Robbery #1 and Robbery #3, but not Robbery #2
   d. Robbery #1 and Robbery #2, but not Robbery #3

74. Officers are required to immediately report to their supervisor any damage to a patrol car. In which situation below should an officer call the supervisor to report a damaged patrol car?
   a. A disgruntled citizen kicks a tire on the patrol car as she walks past it.
   b. The driver's door is dented in by an irate man under arrest for public intoxication.
   c. The officer bumps a pole while backing out of an alley but finds no dents or scratches on the vehicle.
   d. The officer finds a dozen eggs smashed on the windshield.

Read the following instructions, then answer question 75.

The first officer to respond to the scene of a sexual assault has many responsibilities. The officer should take the following steps in the order listed:

1. Aid the victim if necessary by calling for an ambulance or administering first aid.
2. Try to calm and comfort the victim as much as possible.
3. If the attack is recent, get a suspect description from the victim and radio the dispatcher to put out a be-on-the-lookout broadcast.
4. Find out from the victim where the crime occurred.
5. Determine whether there is any physical evidence on the victim that may need to be preserved, such as pieces of the suspect's skin or blood under the victim's fingernails.
6. If possible, have the victim change clothing, and then take the clothing he or she was wearing as evidence.
7. Convince the victim to undergo a medical exam for his or her health and safety and so that evidence may be gathered.

75. Officer Augustine is at 2101 Reynolds Street talking to Betty Smith, the victim of a sexual assault. Ms. Smith is uninjured and is very calm. She gives Officer Augustine a detailed description of her attacker and says she thinks he may be headed for a nearby tavern. At this point, Officer Augustine should
a. get into his patrol car and drive to the tavern.
b. give the dispatcher the description of the suspect.
c. take the victim straight to the hospital for a medical exam.
d. have the victim change clothing.

76. Officer Bettis has arrived at the scene of a family disturbance. Two other officers are in the front yard of the residence, fighting with family members. Officer Bettis pulls out his departmentally approved nightstick and runs up to help one of the officers. A woman steps up and swings a broken beer bottle at Officer Bettis's head. What should he do next?
a. Try to snatch the beer bottle out of her hand and hope he doesn't get cut.
b. Strike her in a departmentally approved target area so she will drop the bottle.
c. Immediately call for more backup.
d. Dodge her blows and continue on to help the officer being attacked.

77. The new governor has decreed that one-quarter of all inmates in the state prison system must be released, due to overcrowding. She has directed police officials to release the inmates who have been held the longest. Weston has been in prison longer than Papak, but not as long as Gomez. Rashad has been in prison less time than Weston, but more time than Papak. Which prisoner should be released?
a. Gomez
b. Weston
c. Papak
d. Rashad

Read the following instructions, then answer questions 78 and 79.

Officers who use pepper spray to disperse a crowd should do the following:

1. Warn other officers that pepper spray is about to be deployed.
2. Order the crowd to disperse.
3. Take a position upwind of the crowd.

4. Direct the spray into the crowd while continuing to order them to disperse.
5. Provide first aid to anyone who is overcome by the spray.

78. Officers Brady, Dion, and Rodriguez are called to the scene of a large fight in front of Omar's Grill. When they arrive, they see around 15 adult males bunched up in the parking lot punching each other. Officer Dion pulls out his canister of pepper spray. What should he do next?
   a. order the crowd to stop fighting
   b. warn the other two officers that he's about to spray the crowd
   c. warn the crowd that he has pepper spray
   d. stand downwind of the crowd before spraying

79. Officers Perez and Navarro arrive at City Hall to find a mob rocking Mayor Dickson's car back and forth in the street. Officer Navarro shouts to Officer Perez that he is going to use his pepper spray. What should he do next?
   a. stand downwind of the crowd
   b. shout to the crowd to disperse
   c. warn the crowd that pepper spray is about to be deployed
   d. stand upwind of the crowd before using the spray

80. Officer Yang has noticed an increase in gang graffiti in his area. Store owners are complaining about the damage and have asked him to keep a closer eye on this problem. Which situation should Officer Yang investigate?
   a. Two teenagers are leaning against a park wall completely covered with gang-related graffiti.
   b. Four teenagers are leaning against the clean white wall of a neighborhood grocery store. One teenager has a can of spray paint hanging out of the rear pocket of his pants.
   c. Three teenagers are riding bicycles in a grocery store parking lot late at night.
   d. Six teenagers are walking along the sidewalk bouncing a basketball and yelling at passing cars while making gang signs with their hands.

81. Four people saw Ramirez snatch a woman's purse. Which description of Ramirez is probably right?
   a. He wore blue pants and an orange sweatshirt.
   b. He wore blue pants and a red sweatshirt.
   c. He wore black pants and an orange sweatshirt.
   d. He wore blue pants and an orange jacket.

82. Taylor, Hudson, Xavier, and Muller are on the security detail for the governor's visit. Taylor is in front of the stage, Hudson is behind the stage, Xavier is near the exit door, and Muller is at the back of the auditorium. If Hudson switches places with Xavier and Xavier then switches places with Muller, where is Muller?
   a. near the exit
   b. in front of the stage
   c. at the back of the auditorium
   d. behind the stage

83. Officer Rannick is meeting his girlfriend at the mall to see a movie. As he enters the mall, he sees a man about ten yards away grab a woman's purse, push her down, and take off running through the mall. What should Officer Rannick do?

a. Walk away because he is not on duty.

b. Have a store manager call mall security and then hurry on his way.

c. Chase the suspect.

d. Find mall security himself.

84. Officer Hesalroad has responded to the scene of a robbery. On the officer's arrival, the victim, Ms. Margaret Olsen, tells the officer that the following items were taken from her by a man who threatened her with a knife:

- 1 gold watch valued at $240
- 2 rings, each valued at $150
- 1 ring valued at $70
- Cash, $95

Officer Hesalroad is preparing her report on the robbery. Which of the following is the total value of the cash and property Ms. Olsen reported stolen?

a. $545

b. $555

c. $705

d. $785

85. The owner of the Sun Times Chevrolet dealership tells Officer Chervenack that someone is stealing running boards and other parts from the vans he has parked in the south lot sometime after 10:30 P.M. Officer Chervenack decides to patrol the area carefully. Which of the following situations should she investigate?

a. After midnight, an Hispanic male in his early twenties is walking up and down rows of new pickups parked near the edge of the dealership.

b. After midnight, a panel truck pulls out of the vacant lot next to the dealership near where the vans are lined up.

c. After midnight, two youths in baggy pants and T-shirts are Rollerblading around the new cars on the Sun Times lot.

d. After midnight, a station wagon drives into the lot and stops near the door to the main showroom. A man gets out and unloads a mop, a bucket, and a broom.

86. Officer Mattox is listening to Claude, an angry citizen. Claude is furious with Officer Mattox because he feels that he doesn't deserve a ticket for running a stop sign. At what point should the officer consider physically arresting Claude?

a. Claude is seated in his automobile shouting, "Why aren't you out catching real crooks?" while the officer opens his ticket book.

b. Claude is standing beside his car on the sidewalk holding his arms out, with palms up, shouting at passing cars while the officer writes the ticket.

c. Claude points his pen at Officer Mattox and says, "I want your name and badge number because I'm calling your supervisor."

d. Claude pokes his forefinger in Officer Mattox's chest and tells him he doesn't know what he's talking about.

87. Officer Littmar is driving by a mall when he is flagged down by four men at a bus stop. They tell him that they just watched a man jump out of a yellow taxicab and force a woman at gunpoint to get inside the cab with him. They drove away northbound on Exeter Street. All four witnesses say they saw the number painted on the side of the cab and give Officer Littmar the numbers. Which of the following numbers is most likely to be the true numbers painted on the side of the taxi?

 a. 9266
 b. 9336
 c. 9268
 d. 8266

88. Officer Manley is called to the scene of an auto parts theft at Lucky Lube Auto Parts. The store manager, Alfonso, tells the officer that while he was waiting on another customer, a woman came inside the store, picked up a pen-shaped tire gauge, and ran out of the store without paying. He shouted at her to stop, but she kept running. Alfonso says he thinks this is the same woman who has been shoplifting up and down the strip mall for the past two weeks. Alfonso describes the woman as white, 5′2″, 105 pounds, with light brown hair touching the tops of her shoulders, dark navy-blue wire-rimmed glasses, and wearing a pale blue dress. Officer Manley looks at four other reports to see if the same woman fits as a suspect in the other four thefts.

Suspect in Theft #1: Female, white, 5′2″, 105 lbs., shoulder-length brownish hair, glasses, white sandals, stained pale-colored dress.

Suspect in Theft #2: Female, white, 5′3″, 110 lbs., with shoulder-length brown hair and wire-rimmed glasses, wearing a green dress.

Suspect in Theft #3: Female, white, 5′5″, 125 lbs., dyed light blond hair, blue dress, bare feet.

Suspect in Theft #4: Female, white, 5′2″, 112 lbs., light hair worn slightly below the shoulder, thin-framed metal glasses, light-colored sandals, black dress.

In which of the above thefts is Alfonso's suspect the most likely culprit?

 a. 2, 3, 4
 b. 1, 2, 4
 c. 1, 2, 3
 d. 1, 3, 4

89. Officers aren't always required to make a custody arrest at the exact moment the law has been broken. A warrant can always be issued at a later date for the suspect if the person can be identified. Which of the following situations best illustrates this point?

 a. Jeremy is well-known in his community for his appearance at political demonstrations. Police are called to the scene of a massive riot where Jeremy has incited over 100 college students to throw rocks and attack the outnumbered police force.
 b. Melody is walking along the street when a man jumps out from the shadows, grabs her purse, and takes off running. Officer Bentley catches him one block later.
 c. Antonio tells Officer DiAngelo that his cousin has been threatening to burn his house down. While Antonio is telling this story, a gasoline can comes crashing through the living room window.
 d. Rachel walks up to Officer Xavier dragging a teenager by the jacket. She tells the officer that she caught the young man putting his hand into her coat pocket when she was waiting at the bus stop.

90. Officer Kim reports to the scene of a burglary at 125 Eastside Avenue, Apartment 3D. The resident, Anthony Blake, who is a musician, says that he returned from his girlfriend's house this morning to find his lock picked and his instruments missing:

- 1 violin valued at $3,500
- 2 violin bows, each valued at $850
- 2 music stands, each valued at $85
- 1 cello valued at $2,300

In addition, Mr. Blake says that his watch, valued at $250, and $85 in cash are missing. When Officer Kim writes his report on the burglary, what should he write as the total value of the stolen property and cash?
- **a.** $6,735
- **b.** $7,070
- **c.** $7,670
- **d.** $8,005

91. Officers Charles and Washington have been dispatched to 2104 Maple Avenue. Neighbors called 911 and said that they could hear Jeff threatening his wife Sara and that they were afraid he was about to beat her. Officer Charles notifies the dispatcher that they have arrived. He parks the car in front of 2102 Maple, and he and Officer Washington begin walking up the sidewalk to 2104 Maple Ave. What should the two officers do next?
- **a.** Knock on the front door and request entry.
- **b.** Listen at the door to see if they can tell what is going on inside.
- **c.** Talk to the neighbors who called before taking any action.
- **d.** Administer first aid to those who are injured.

92. Four police officers are chasing a suspect on foot. Officer Calvin is directly behind the suspect. Partners Jenkins and Burton are side by side behind Calvin. Officer Zeller is behind Jenkins and Burton. Burton trips and falls, and Calvin turns back to help him. An officer tackles the suspect. Which officer caught the suspect?
- **a.** Burton
- **b.** Zeller
- **c.** Jenkins
- **d.** Calvin

93. Officer Troy arrives at the scene of a hit and run traffic accident. Ms. Chen tells him she was waiting for the light to change when a car struck her from behind. The driver backed up and left the scene. She saw his license plate as he left, as did three teenaged witnesses waiting for the school bus. The choices below list what each one reported. Which license plate number below is most likely the license plate of the hit and run vehicle?
- **a.** JXK 12L
- **b.** JYK 12L
- **c.** JXK 12I
- **d.** JXX I2L

94. Four eyewitnesses give descriptions of the getaway car used in a bank robbery. Which description is probably right?
  a. dark blue with a white roof
  b. dark green with a gray roof
  c. black with a gray roof
  d. dark green with a tan roof

95. Officer Singh has been receiving neighborhood complaints about increased park vandalism in her area. Which situation should Officer Singh monitor more closely?
  a. a jogger with a dog
  b. a small group leaving the park's main entrance with blankets and coolers
  c. two people wearing backpacks running quickly away from a secluded area
  d. a lone cyclist

96. Shoplifting is a theft of goods from a store, shop, or place of business during business hours where the suspect takes the good(s) past the last point of opportunity to pay for the merchandise without attempting to offer payment. Which of the following is an example of shoplifting?
  a. Terry walks into the Bag and Save grocery store and gets a piece of candy. He takes it to the counter and discovers he has no money. The clerk tells him to go ahead and keep the candy this time. Terry leaves the store eating the candy.
  b. Gloria walks into an electronics store to get a pack of AAA batteries. She sticks the small package in her coat pocket while she looks at the computer display. After a few minutes, she turns to walk out. Before she reaches the door, she remembers the batteries and turns back to the counter to pay for them.
  c. Gail enters Philo's Pharmacy on 12th Street to pick up a prescription. After paying for the medicine, she walks over to the perfume counter, where she finds a small bottle of cologne she likes. She puts the cologne in her purse and walks out the front door of the pharmacy.
  d. Pete and his mother, Abby, are grocery shopping. Pete picks up a candy bar, peels off the wrapper, and hands Abby the wrapper. When they reach the checkout counter, Pete walks out of the store while Abby puts the groceries, along with the candy wrapper, on the stand for checkout. The clerk rings up the price of the candy along with the groceries.

Read the following information, then answer questions 97 and 98.

The use of warnings may sometimes provide a satisfactory solution to a problem and may enhance the public perception of the department. Normally, the use of a warning occurs in traffic offenses, but warnings may occasionally be applied to misdemeanor criminal offenses.

In determining whether a warning should be issued, the officer should consider:

1. the seriousness of the offense
2. the likelihood that the violator will heed the warning
3. the reputation of the violator (i.e., known repeat offender, has received previous warnings, etc.)

97. Which of the following is the best example of a situation in which a police officer might issue a warning?
   a. a city councilperson who has been stopped for drunk driving
   b. a known heroin addict who is trespassing in an abandoned building
   c. a group of 14-year-old boys who are throwing rocks at each other
   d. a 35-year-old woman on probation for shoplifting who has been detained for stealing $2 from a local store

98. Which of the following is a situation in which a police officer could NOT issue a warning?
   a. a minor traffic violation
   b. a ten-year-old who shoplifted a candy bar
   c. a felony assault
   d. a city councilperson accused of trespassing

Read the following information, then answer questions 99 and 100.

After arresting a suspect, officers should conduct a search for weapons and contraband by doing the following:

1. Make sure the prisoner's hands are handcuffed securely behind his or her back.
2. Check the waistband and area within reach of the prisoner's handcuffed hands.
3. Check the prisoner's cap or hat.
4. Check the neck area and both arms.
5. Check the prisoner's front pockets.
6. Check the inseam of the pants and crotch area.
7. Check the legs and ankles.
8. Check the prisoner's shoes.

99. Officer Linder arrests a man wearing a baseball cap, a T-shirt, blue jeans, and lace-up work boots. She checks to make sure the handcuffs are secure. She notices a bulge in his cap. What should Officer Linder do next?
   a. Check his front pockets.
   b. Check the cap for weapons.
   c. Check the prisoner's waistband.
   d. Check the area near his neck.

100. Officer Petrochowsky arrests a man for public intoxication. The man is wearing a cowboy hat, a long-sleeved shirt, dress slacks, and cowboy boots. The officer checks the prisoner's handcuffs and checks to make sure the waistband and back pocket area are clear of weapons. Suddenly, the prisoner sits down on the curb and refuses to stand up. Two other officers help get the prisoner to his feet. What should Officer Petrochowsky do next?
   a. Check the prisoner's cowboy hat.
   b. Check the prisoner's boots.
   c. Check the prisoner's waistband and back pocket area.
   d. Take the prisoner straight to jail before he tries to sit back down.

Answers

Section One:
Memorization and Visualization

1. d. Refer to the Charges section on Gibbons.

2. b. Refer to the Description section on Smith.

3. a. Refer to the drawing of Smith.

4. b. Refer to the Aliases section on Serna.

5. b. Refer to the Remarks section on Jones.

6. c. Refer to the Charges section on Bunn.

7. a. Refer to the drawing of Gibbons.

8. d. Refer to the Identifying Scars or Marks section on Serna.

9. d. Refer to the Remarks section on Bunn.

10. c. Refer to the drawing of Jones, as well as to the Identifying Scars or Marks section.

11. b. Refer to the Remarks section on Smith.

12. d. Refer to the drawing of Serna.

13. d. Refer to the Caution section on both Gibbons and Jones.

14. c. Refer to the Remarks section on Serna.

15. b. Refer to the Description section on both Gibbons and Jones.

16. d. Refer to the Description section on both Jones and Serna.

17. a. The Description section on Smith notes that he is six feet tall; thus, he is taller than any of the other persons depicted on the posters.

18. c. Refer to the Caution section on Jones.

19. a. Refer to the Description sections for all persons depicted on the posters.

20. c. Both Serna and Jones are clean-shaven. Don't forget that this question asks which statement is false.

21. a. See guideline 1, the last sentence.

22. d. See the second half of guideline 6.

23. d. See the second sentence of guideline 5.

24. b. See guideline 3.

25. d. See the second sentence of guideline 2.

26. a. See guideline 4, the fourth sentence.

27. d. See guideline 3, the fourth sentence.

28. a. See the first paragraph of the passage.

29. b. See the fourth sentence of guideline 5.

30. d. See guideline 2, the last sentence.

Section Two: Reading

31. d. The passage presents two reasons for punishment. The second sentence notes a view that "some people" hold. The first line of the second paragraph indicates "another view."

32. b. This is the main idea of the first paragraph.

33. a. This is an application of the main idea of the second paragraph to a specific crime.

34. c. The first sentence indicates that the passage is about punishment. The first paragraph is about retribution; the second is about deterrence.

35. d. The second paragraph notes that one reason behind the deterrence theory is the effect of deterring not only criminals, but also the public.

36. d. See the first sentence of the passage. The officers were initially in the uptown-bound train. The subway platform is where the questioning occurred.

37. c. Although Ms. Simpson allegedly assaulted the complainant and created a disturbance, she was arrested for the concealed weapon.

38. a. Alan Sterns is identified as the complainant in the second sentence of the passage.

39. d. See the next-to-last sentence in the passage.

40. a. According to Mr. Sterns, Ms. Simpson struck him when he attempted to move her bags.

41. c. Choice **a** takes the man to the park, not to the senior citizens center. Choice **b** takes the man too far south. Choice **d** takes him to Lafayette Street, while the entrance to the senior citizens center is on Grand Street.

42. d. Choice **a** takes the librarian the wrong way on Avenue C. Choice **b** shows the wrong directions for the streets—Brooklyn Street runs north-south, and Avenue B runs east-west. Choice **c** leaves the librarian one block east of the gas station.

43. b. Choices **a** and **c** take you the wrong way on 1st Avenue. Choice **d** will get you to the southeast, not the northwest, corner of the park.

44. d. Choice **a** is less direct. Choice **b** does not start from the hospital, and involves going the wrong way on Avenue B. Choice **c** is indirect and involves going the wrong way on Avenue D.

45. a. Choice **b** is less direct and involves going the wrong way on 1st Avenue. Choice **c** will lead you away from 1st Avenue, not toward it. Choice **d** takes you the wrong way on Avenue C and 1st Avenue.

46. b. The third sentence of the passage states that officers may refer to their notes.

47. d. The passage provides information for law enforcement officers; therefore, it is probably not from either a newspaper article (choice **b**) or a novel (choice **c**). Choice **a** refers to a memo directed to police officers, but the subject matter does not relate to this title.

48. a. The first sentence states the importance of officer testimony.

49. c. Choice **a** is incorrect because the first sentence suggests that becoming hardened is unavoidable. Choices **b** and **d** are mentioned in the passage but do not reflect the main idea.

50. b. See the first two sentences of the passage.

51. c. The complainant, Alan Weber, lives at 1807 Clarkson.

52. a. The neighbor, Mr. Weber, said the noise kept him awake for two hours. There is no mention in the passage of Mr. Weber being worried (choices **b** and **c**) or curious (choice **d**). If he had been worried, he probably wouldn't have waited two hours to call the police.

53. b. Mr. Hayes's first words to the police were, "It's about time you got here." There is no indication that Mr. Hayes was surprised— his statement shows the opposite—nor that he was frightened, distrustful, or angry at the police. He went with them willingly.

54. c. While choices **a** and **d** are also true, they are not the main idea, which is supported by the whole passage and spelled out in the last sentence.

55. b. This is implied in the next-to-last sentence.

56. a. The other routes are impossible or illegal.

57. c. Brown Street and Park Street are the two streets that run north and south of the park.

58. a. The other routes are impossible or illegal.

59. b. The other routes are impossible (choices **c** and **d**) or circuitous (choice **a**).

60. d. Choice **a** takes you the wrong way on Maple Street. Choice **b** starts from the firehouse, not the police station. Choice **c** will not get you to the entrance of the gas station.

Section Three: Judgment and Problem Solving

61. b. Add the corrected value of the sweater ($245) to the value of the two, not three, bracelets ($730), plus the other two items ($78 and $130).

62. b. Officer Kemp has worked more shifts in a row than Officer Calvin; therefore, Kemp has worked more than eight shifts. The number of Kemp's shifts plus the number of Rogers's shifts (five) cannot equal 15 or more, the number of Miller's shifts. Therefore, Kemp has worked nine shifts in a row (5 + 9 = 14).

63. a. A truck with the motor running, backed up to the rear door of a closed business at 1:00 A.M., is suspicious. Delivery vans owned by businesses are commonly parked on store property after hours (choice **c**). A lone man going through a Dumpster would have no way to carry stereo equipment (choice **b**), and it would not be unusual for teenage boys to be looking at a stereo system in the window, even at midnight (choice **d**).

64. c. The elements of the license plate number that most often repeat in the descriptions are XIW and 017. Therefore, the correct license number is most likely XIW 017.

65. c. The officer has already done steps 1 and 2 because she is already at the location. Her next step would be to let the dispatcher know that she is on the scene (step 3).

66. d. Officer Smith should turn off his emergency lights as the first step in answering a burglar alarm call.

67. c. It would not be appropriate to shout in the situations described in choices **a**, **b**, or **d**. An officer would shout at a burglar because the situation calls for identifying himself or herself as a police officer. A loud, authoritative shout in this situation is part of the voice control officers should exercise as the first step in the use of force.

68. c. The total value of all three telephone sets at $125 each is $375. The total value of both computers at $1,300 each is $2,600. The two computer monitors, each valued at $950, have a total value of $1,900. Add those three totals to the printer at $600 and the answering machine at $50 for a grand total of $5,525 for all the stolen property.

69. d. After all the switches were made, Officer Kirk worked on Tuesday. Officer Carter worked on Monday, Officer Johnson on Wednesday, and Officer Falk on Thursday.

70. c. The officer is looking for a suspect dressed in dark clothing who has been seen walking up and down a residential street during a specific time span—a window peeper. Choices **a**, **b**, and **d** suggest normal neighborhood activity because all the people involved are out in the open. The shrubbery the man in choice **c** is walking away from suggests a hiding place near a window.

71. b. Tall, thin, and middle-aged are the elements of the description repeated most often and are therefore the most likely to be accurate.

72. b. Sealing the bag is step 2 on the list of procedures.

73. c. The suspect described in Robbery #2 has a crew-cut hairstyle, is at least five inches taller than the other suspects, and is about 60 pounds heavier. The other three descriptions are much more likely to be of the same man because they all describe a similar build and mention one earring or a pierced ear.

74. b. No damage has been done to the patrol car in choices **a**, **c**, or **d**.

75. b. The officer has already taken care of steps 1 and 2: The victim doesn't need immediate medical help, and she is calm. Step 3 tells the officer to radio the suspect description to the dispatcher so a be-on-the-lookout bulletin can be issued.

76. b. Police officers are required to subdue combative suspects as quickly and safely as possible. If Officer Bettis is in a situation where the nightstick is an approved weapon and he or other officers are in physical danger, he should use his nightstick. The situation does not change because the attacker is female. No other option is safe or feasible.

77. a. Gomez has been in prison longer than Weston, who has been in longer than Rashad, who has been in longer than Papak.

78. b. According to step 1 in the procedure, the officer should warn the other officers before he takes further action. The officer does want the crowd to stop fighting and will order them to do so, but choice **a** is step 2. Choice **c** is not listed as a step, and choice **d** is not a good answer because the officer will always want to be upwind of pepper spray, not downwind.

79. b. The officer has already taken step 1, having warned his partner that he is about to use the spray. Step 2 is to order the crowd to disperse.

80. b. Seeing a teenager with a can of spray paint is the most suspicious of the incidents described, since Officer Yang is looking for graffiti artists. Spray paint is not an item most people carry around with them and is suspicious given the circumstances.

81. a. Blue pants, sweatshirt, and the color orange are the elements repeated most often by the eyewitnesses and are therefore most likely correct.

82. d. After all the switches are made, Muller is behind the stage, Hudson is near the exit, Xavier is at the back of the auditorium, and Taylor is still in front of the stage.

83. c. Officer Rannick is obligated to fulfill his duties as a police officer. He cannot allow a crime to occur in his presence.

84. c. The two rings, each valued at $150, have a total value of $300, but then it's important to note that there's another ring, worth $70. Add $370 for the three rings to $240 for the gold watch and $95 in cash for a total of $705 in stolen property and cash.

85. b. A panel truck pulling out of a vacant lot near a car dealership that has suffered a rash of theft of auto parts is suspicious. The truck would be able to hold plenty of auto parts. The two rollerbladers in choice **c** aren't likely to be able to carry off a new running board without attracting attention. The Hispanic male in his early twenties in choice **a** appears to be doing what a lot of people do late at night, which is look at new cars without having to worry about sales personnel. It is not unusual for cleanup crews to arrive late at night after everyone has gone, as in choice **d**.

86. d. Claude has just assaulted Officer Mattox by poking him in the chest. This is a safety issue for the officer, and he should not allow contact of this nature. Allowing an angry citizen to vent and release a certain amount of frustration, as in the other options, is appropriate in many situations.

87. a. Three of the witnesses agree that the first number is 9. Three agree that the second number is 2. Three witnesses agree that the third number is 6, and three others agree that the fourth number is also 6. Choice **a** is the best choice because it is made up of the numbers that most of the witnesses agree that they saw.

88. b. The suspect described in theft #3 does not match Alfonso's suspect description very closely. The women in 1, 2, and 4 all appear to be the same woman Alfonso saw because of the similarities in height, weight, hair, and eyewear.

89. a. Outnumbered officers attempting to control a hostile crowd may not be able to arrest the instigator safely; however, according to the situation, they will likely be able to find him later, since they are aware of his identity. In the other situations, custody arrests are appropriate and more easily accomplished. Although in choice **c**, it seems apparent that Antonio knows his cousin's identity, and therefore, a warrant could be issued at a later date, the violence of the situation makes immediate action necessary.

90. d. The two violin bows, each worth $850, have a total value of $1,700. The two music stands, each worth $85, have a total value of $170. Add those totals to $3,500 for the violin and $2,300 for the cello to get $7,670. Finally, don't forget to add the $250 watch and $85 in cash, for a grand total of $8,005.

91. b. The next thing the officers should do in this situation is to listen at the door to see if they can tell that is going on inside.

92. c. After all the switching was done, Officer Jenkins was directly behind the suspect. Officer Burton had fallen and Officer Calvin turned back to help him. Officer Zeller remained in the rear.

93. a. The witnesses seem to agree that the plate starts out with the letter J. Three witnesses agree that the plate ends with 12L. Three witnesses think that the second letter is X, and a different three think that the third letter is K. The plate description that has all these common elements is choice **a**.

94. b. Dark green and gray roof are the elements repeated most often by the eyewitnesses and are therefore most likely correct.

95. c. Seeing two people moving quickly away from a secluded area is the most suspicious of the incidents described since Officer Singh is looking for people who are trying not to get caught or who might have an opportunity to deface or steal public property.

96. c. Choice **c** is an example of shoplifting because Gail made no attempt to pay for the cologne before leaving the pharmacy. Choice **a** is not an example of shoplifting because the clerk told Terry he did not have to pay for the candy. Terry did not hide the candy or try to leave the store without an attempt to pay. The clerk had the option of having Terry put back the candy, but he instead chose to give it away. Choice **b** is not an example of shoplifting because Gloria did not pass the last point of opportunity to pay before leaving the store without making an attempt to pay for the batteries. In businesses where the checkout stands are located in the middle or toward the rear of the store, the benefit of the doubt goes to the shopper until he or she walks out the door. Choice **d** is not an example of shoplifting because Abby paid for her son's candy, even though he ate the candy in the store and eventually walked out of the store.

97. c. Choice **a** is not a strong choice because a person's reputation has more to do with criminal history, or lack thereof, than his or her standing in the community. Moreover, if the city councilperson were warned about drunk driving, there is nothing to indicate that he or she would not continue the behavior. Both the known heroin addict and the woman on probation have reputations, like a criminal history, that run counter to giving warnings.

98. c. Of all the situations, only the case of the felony crime clearly prohibits the issuance of a warning.

99. c. The officer has already performed step 1 by making sure the handcuffs are secure. Checking the suspect's waistband and back pocket area is step 2, which she should perform next. She should not be distracted by the bulge in the cap, so choice **b** is not correct.

100. a. The officer should check the arrestee's hat because that is the next step after checking the waistband and back pocket area. The officer should not be distracted from the proper procedures because the intoxicated man is difficult to control. The other officers are there to assist, and he should be able to safely conduct his search.

Scoring

A passing score for police exams in most cities is 70%. If the real exam consists of 100 questions, like the test you just took, each question would be worth one point. Thus, your score on this exam is the same as your percentage.

While a total score of at least 70 usually lands you on the eligibility list, in many cities you need to do much better than just pass the exam to have a chance at a job. Many cities rank applicants according to their test scores, so that the higher you score on the exam, the better your chance of being called to go through the next steps in the selection process. In addition, veterans and/or residents of the city may have points added to their test scores, so that the best possible score is actually more than 100. If your city conducts this kind of ranking, your goal isn't just to score 70 and pass—you need the highest score you can possibly reach.

Use this practice exam as a way to analyze your performance. Pay attention to the areas where you missed the most questions. If most of your mistakes are in the reading comprehension questions, then you know you need to practice your reading skills. Or perhaps you had difficulty memorizing the posters. Once you see where you need help, then you should hone the relevant skills to develop your test-taking strategies.

To help you see where you should concentrate, break down your scores according to the three sections below:

Part One: _____ questions correct

Part Two: _____ questions correct

Part Three: _____ questions correct

Write down the number of correct answers for each section and then add up all three numbers for your overall score. Each question is worth one point, and the total you arrive at after adding all the numbers is also the percentage of questions that you answered correctly on the test.

For now, forget about your total score; what's more important right now is your scores on the individual sections of the exam. Your best bet is to review all the skills tested on this exam carefully, but you will want to spend the most time on the skills that correspond to the kind of question that you found most difficult.

▶ POLICE OFFICER PRACTICE EXAM 3

CHAPTER SUMMARY

This is the third practice exam in this book based on the entry-level civil service exam that police departments around the country administer to prospective police officers. If the police department you're applying to uses an exam called the LECR (Law Enforcement Candidate Record), this is the exam for you.

This practice police exam has two parts. The first part has two sections: verbal comprehension and number and letter recall. In the verbal section, you are given ten minutes to answer questions on synonyms and antonyms. The number and letter recall section lasts only nine minutes and consists of 100 questions.

You are asked to remember certain number-letter combinations from a given table. You will have the table in front of you as you complete these questions.

The second part of the exam consists of 185 questions about your personal background. This exam includes 20 sample personal background questions to help familiarize you with the format.

Incorrect answers count against you in the first part of the exam. It's better to leave questions blank than to close your eyes and point at an answer. A good rule of thumb is to guess only if you can definitely eliminate at least two of the four given answers.

When you finish the exam, check the answer key at the end of the test and see how well you scored. Because there are no correct or incorrect answers on the personal background questions, no answer key is included for this section.

Police Officer Practice Exam 3: Part One

Verbal Comprehension Section

1.	(a) (b) (c) (d)
2.	(a) (b) (c) (d)
3.	(a) (b) (c) (d)
4.	(a) (b) (c) (d)
5.	(a) (b) (c) (d)
6.	(a) (b) (c) (d)
7.	(a) (b) (c) (d)
8.	(a) (b) (c) (d)
9.	(a) (b) (c) (d)
10.	(a) (b) (c) (d)
11.	(a) (b) (c) (d)
12.	(a) (b) (c) (d)
13.	(a) (b) (c) (d)
14.	(a) (b) (c) (d)
15.	(a) (b) (c) (d)
16.	(a) (b) (c) (d)
17.	(a) (b) (c) (d)
18.	(a) (b) (c) (d)
19.	(a) (b) (c) (d)
20.	(a) (b) (c) (d)
21.	(a) (b) (c) (d)
22.	(a) (b) (c) (d)
23.	(a) (b) (c) (d)
24.	(a) (b) (c) (d)
25.	(a) (b) (c) (d)
26.	(a) (b) (c) (d)
27.	(a) (b) (c) (d)
28.	(a) (b) (c) (d)
29.	(a) (b) (c) (d)
30.	(a) (b) (c) (d)
31.	(a) (b) (c) (d)
32.	(a) (b) (c) (d)
33.	(a) (b) (c) (d)
34.	(a) (b) (c) (d)
35.	(a) (b) (c) (d)
36.	(a) (b) (c) (d)
37.	(a) (b) (c) (d)
38.	(a) (b) (c) (d)
39.	(a) (b) (c) (d)
40.	(a) (b) (c) (d)
41.	(a) (b) (c) (d)
42.	(a) (b) (c) (d)
43.	(a) (b) (c) (d)
44.	(a) (b) (c) (d)
45.	(a) (b) (c) (d)
46.	(a) (b) (c) (d)
47.	(a) (b) (c) (d)
48.	(a) (b) (c) (d)
49.	(a) (b) (c) (d)
50.	(a) (b) (c) (d)

Number and Letter Recall Section

1.	(a) (b) (c) (d) (e)
2.	(a) (b) (c) (d) (e)
3.	(a) (b) (c) (d) (e)
4.	(a) (b) (c) (d) (e)
5.	(a) (b) (c) (d) (e)
6.	(a) (b) (c) (d) (e)
7.	(a) (b) (c) (d) (e)
8.	(a) (b) (c) (d) (e)
9.	(a) (b) (c) (d) (e)
10.	(a) (b) (c) (d) (e)
11.	(a) (b) (c) (d) (e)
12.	(a) (b) (c) (d) (e)
13.	(a) (b) (c) (d) (e)
14.	(a) (b) (c) (d) (e)
15.	(a) (b) (c) (d) (e)
16.	(a) (b) (c) (d) (e)
17.	(a) (b) (c) (d) (e)
18.	(a) (b) (c) (d) (e)
19.	(a) (b) (c) (d) (e)
20.	(a) (b) (c) (d) (e)
21.	(a) (b) (c) (d) (e)
22.	(a) (b) (c) (d) (e)
23.	(a) (b) (c) (d) (e)
24.	(a) (b) (c) (d) (e)
25.	(a) (b) (c) (d) (e)
26.	(a) (b) (c) (d) (e)
27.	(a) (b) (c) (d) (e)
28.	(a) (b) (c) (d) (e)
29.	(a) (b) (c) (d) (e)
30.	(a) (b) (c) (d) (e)
31.	(a) (b) (c) (d) (e)
32.	(a) (b) (c) (d) (e)
33.	(a) (b) (c) (d) (e)
34.	(a) (b) (c) (d) (e)
35.	(a) (b) (c) (d) (e)
36.	(a) (b) (c) (d) (e)
37.	(a) (b) (c) (d) (e)
38.	(a) (b) (c) (d) (e)
39.	(a) (b) (c) (d) (e)
40.	(a) (b) (c) (d) (e)
41.	(a) (b) (c) (d) (e)
42.	(a) (b) (c) (d) (e)
43.	(a) (b) (c) (d) (e)
44.	(a) (b) (c) (d) (e)
45.	(a) (b) (c) (d) (e)
46.	(a) (b) (c) (d) (e)
47.	(a) (b) (c) (d) (e)
48.	(a) (b) (c) (d) (e)
49.	(a) (b) (c) (d) (e)
50.	(a) (b) (c) (d) (e)
51.	(a) (b) (c) (d) (e)
52.	(a) (b) (c) (d) (e)
53.	(a) (b) (c) (d) (e)
54.	(a) (b) (c) (d) (e)
55.	(a) (b) (c) (d) (e)
56.	(a) (b) (c) (d) (e)
57.	(a) (b) (c) (d) (e)
58.	(a) (b) (c) (d) (e)
59.	(a) (b) (c) (d) (e)
60.	(a) (b) (c) (d) (e)
61.	(a) (b) (c) (d) (e)
62.	(a) (b) (c) (d) (e)
63.	(a) (b) (c) (d) (e)
64.	(a) (b) (c) (d) (e)
65.	(a) (b) (c) (d) (e)
66.	(a) (b) (c) (d) (e)
67.	(a) (b) (c) (d) (e)
68.	(a) (b) (c) (d) (e)
69.	(a) (b) (c) (d) (e)
70.	(a) (b) (c) (d) (e)
71.	(a) (b) (c) (d) (e)
72.	(a) (b) (c) (d) (e)
73.	(a) (b) (c) (d) (e)
74.	(a) (b) (c) (d) (e)
75.	(a) (b) (c) (d) (e)

Number and Letter Recall Section (continued)

76.	ⓐ ⓑ ⓒ ⓓ ⓔ	85.	ⓐ ⓑ ⓒ ⓓ ⓔ	94.	ⓐ ⓑ ⓒ ⓓ ⓔ
77.	ⓐ ⓑ ⓒ ⓓ ⓔ	86.	ⓐ ⓑ ⓒ ⓓ ⓔ	95.	ⓐ ⓑ ⓒ ⓓ ⓔ
78.	ⓐ ⓑ ⓒ ⓓ ⓔ	87.	ⓐ ⓑ ⓒ ⓓ ⓔ	96.	ⓐ ⓑ ⓒ ⓓ ⓔ
79.	ⓐ ⓑ ⓒ ⓓ ⓔ	88.	ⓐ ⓑ ⓒ ⓓ ⓔ	97.	ⓐ ⓑ ⓒ ⓓ ⓔ
80.	ⓐ ⓑ ⓒ ⓓ ⓔ	89.	ⓐ ⓑ ⓒ ⓓ ⓔ	98.	ⓐ ⓑ ⓒ ⓓ ⓔ
81.	ⓐ ⓑ ⓒ ⓓ ⓔ	90.	ⓐ ⓑ ⓒ ⓓ ⓔ	99.	ⓐ ⓑ ⓒ ⓓ ⓔ
82.	ⓐ ⓑ ⓒ ⓓ ⓔ	91.	ⓐ ⓑ ⓒ ⓓ ⓔ	100.	ⓐ ⓑ ⓒ ⓓ ⓔ
83.	ⓐ ⓑ ⓒ ⓓ ⓔ	92.	ⓐ ⓑ ⓒ ⓓ ⓔ		
84.	ⓐ ⓑ ⓒ ⓓ ⓔ	93.	ⓐ ⓑ ⓒ ⓓ ⓔ		

Personal Background Section

1.	ⓐ ⓑ ⓒ ⓓ	8.	ⓐ ⓑ ⓒ ⓓ ⓔ	15.	ⓐ ⓑ ⓒ ⓓ ⓔ
2.	ⓐ ⓑ ⓒ ⓓ ⓔ ⓕ	9.	ⓐ ⓑ ⓒ ⓓ ⓔ	16.	ⓐ ⓑ ⓒ ⓓ
3.	ⓐ ⓑ ⓒ ⓓ ⓔ ⓕ	10.	ⓐ ⓑ ⓒ ⓓ	17.	ⓐ ⓑ ⓒ ⓓ
4.	ⓐ ⓑ ⓒ ⓓ	11.	ⓐ ⓑ ⓒ ⓓ	18.	ⓐ ⓑ ⓒ ⓓ ⓔ ⓕ
5.	ⓐ ⓑ ⓒ ⓓ ⓔ ⓕ ⓖ ⓗ	12.	ⓐ ⓑ ⓒ ⓓ ⓔ	19.	ⓐ ⓑ ⓒ ⓓ
6.	ⓐ ⓑ ⓒ ⓓ ⓔ ⓕ	13.	ⓐ ⓑ ⓒ ⓓ ⓔ	20.	ⓐ ⓑ ⓒ ⓓ ⓔ ⓕ
7.	ⓐ ⓑ ⓒ ⓓ	14.	ⓐ ⓑ ⓒ ⓓ ⓔ ⓕ		

Practice Exam 3: Part One

Section One:
Verbal Comprehension Section

You have ten minutes for this section. Choose the correct answer for each question.

1. Which word means the same as *imagine*?
  a. envision
  b. critique
  c. evaluate
  d. inflame

2. Which word means the opposite of *obvious*?
  a. limit
  b. unclear
  c. judge
  d. promise

3. Which word means the same as *applicant*?
  a. student
  b. guard
  c. candidate
  d. needed

4. Which word means the opposite of *stagnant*?
  a. exhaustion
  b. moving
  c. calculation
  d. decreasing

5. Which word means the opposite of *conspire*?
  a. contrive
  b. launch
  c. unite
  d. disagree

6. Which word means the opposite of *empower*?
  a. laud
  b. jostle
  c. withhold
  d. accept

7. Which word means the opposite of *simplistic*?
  a. effective
  b. connection
  c. intricate
  d. opposition

8. Which word means the opposite of *effective*?
  a. incompetent
  b. useful
  c. forgiving
  d. successful

9. Which word means the same as *extinguish*?
  a. fuel
  b. terminate
  c. excessive
  d. congratulate

10. Which word means the same as *connection*?
  a. association
  b. exhaustion
  c. estranged
  d. clarify

11. Which word means the same as *empathy*?
  a. indifference
  b. understanding
  c. disagreeable
  d. justify

12. Which word means the same as *devote*?
  a. disloyal
  b. animate
  c. allocate
  d. return

13. Which word means the opposite of *sincere*?
  a. truthful
  b. relaxed
  c. earnest
  d. hypocritical

14. Which word means the opposite of
premeditated?
   a. intentional
   b. consortium
   c. impulsive
   d. careful

15. Which word means the same as *comfort*?
   a. difficulty
   b. reassurance
   c. insecure
   d. sloppy

16. Which word means the same as *oblivion*?
   a. extinction
   b. comprehend
   c. various
   d. similar

17. Which word means the same as *frivolous*?
   a. secure
   b. playful
   c. serious
   d. confuse

18. Which word means the opposite of *immune*?
   a. resistant
   b. cavity
   c. quasi
   d. vulnerable

19. Which word means the same as *destined*?
   a. intended
   b. accidental
   c. clean
   d. colored

20. Which word means the opposite of *descend*?
   a. slope
   b. derive
   c. rise
   d. related

21. Which word means the same as *intuitive*?
   a. thoughtless
   b. instinctual
   c. effective
   d. argue

22. Which word means the same as *alleviate*?
   a. aggravate
   b. intensify
   c. completely
   d. relieve

23. Which word means the same as *integrate*?
   a. individual
   b. separate
   c. combine
   d. prescribe

24. Which word means the opposite of *imposter*?
   a. fraud
   b. genuine
   c. explode
   d. spring

25. Which word means the opposite of *variety*?
   a. diversity
   b. collection
   c. similar
   d. tragedy

26. Which word means the same as *insidious*?
   a. deceptive
   b. honest
   c. extravert
   d. obvious

27. Which word means the opposite of *brilliance*?
   a. ability
   b. talent
   c. dullness
   d. smooth

28. Which word means the opposite of *precise*?
   a. correct
   b. unite
   c. deviant
   d. vague

29. Which word means the opposite of *bigot*?
   a. extremist
   b. racist
   c. impartial
   d. slanted

30. Which word means the same as *facet*?
   a. circular
   b. vision
   c. footing
   d. aspect

31. Which word means the opposite of *sanction*?
   a. support
   b. illegal
   c. prohibit
   d. consent

32. Which word means the same as *function*?
   a. gathering
   b. malfunction
   c. nearby
   d. unnatural

33. Which word means the same as *decisive*?
   a. unified
   b. clear
   c. uncertain
   d. negative

34. Which word means the opposite of *inept*?
   a. useless
   b. unified
   c. competent
   d. outside

35. Which word means the same as *resilient*?
   a. rigid
   b. weak
   c. assured
   d. elastic

36. Which word means the same as *exhaust*?
   a. reveal
   b. review
   c. use
   d. excessive

37. Which word means the opposite of *insight*?
   a. institution
   b. perceptive
   c. misunderstanding
   d. argue

38. Which word means the opposite of *vacuum*?
   a. blank
   b. full
   c. thin
   d. valid

39. Which word means the same as *lurch*?
   a. smooth
   b. short
   c. stable
   d. stagger

40. Which word means the same as *determine*?
   a. uncontrolled
   b. establish
   c. another
   d. wordy

41. Which word means the opposite of *deviate*?
   a. conform
   b. diverge
   c. clear
   d. shine

42. Which word means the same as *labored*?
 a. defending
 b. smooth
 c. thoughtful
 d. struggling

43. Which word means the same as *quasi*?
 a. anticipate
 b. impatient
 c. pseudo
 d. genuine

44. Which word means the same as *poise*?
 a. composure
 b. empty
 c. group
 d. flower

45. Which word means the opposite of *inundate*?
 a. examine
 b. starve
 c. overwhelm
 d. excessive

46. Which word means the same as *pertain*?
 a. bother
 b. complain
 c. selling
 d. concern

47. Which word means the opposite of *initiative*?
 a. ambition
 b. begin
 c. apathy
 d. ignore

48. Which word means the same as *lacerate*?
 a. win
 b. cut
 c. off
 d. sly

49. Which word means the opposite of *persuade*?
 a. disagree
 b. ignore
 c. within
 d. discourage

50. Which word means the same as *insulate*?
 a. expose
 b. opinion
 c. protect
 d. jostle

Section Two: Number and Letter Recall Section

In this section, each set of 25 questions is preceded by a key that consists of letter sets and numbers. Each question consists of one of the letter sets followed by numbers. Use the key to pick the number that goes with each letter set, and then fill in the appropriate circle on the answer sheet. You have nine minutes for this section.

KEY 1								
DFG	ILP	HMB	PNG	ZVX	JYD	QTJ	KMC	OMC
89	59	72	41	97	23	64	33	12
BVJ	YGH	LVS	CFM	HNE	DMG	FMP	RNP	NTW
47	30	83	17	52	65	74	58	38
KGD	VCJ	AFH	UHC	XDB	SQN	UGD	HKF	NSY
51	95	43	36	19	27	56	71	87

		a	b	c	d	e			a	b	c	d	e
1.	RNP	51	29	92	73	58	**14.**	KMC	84	47	15	52	33
2.	HMB	87	72	56	91	37	**15.**	ILP	59	36	89	72	12
3.	DFG	17	43	12	89	56	**16.**	JYD	32	96	23	52	71
4.	BVJ	52	47	56	74	12	**17.**	UGD	43	56	51	30	98
5.	VCJ	28	52	95	49	15	**18.**	NSY	19	43	71	87	27
6.	DMG	65	38	27	30	89	**19.**	LVS	83	27	38	47	52
7.	OMC	41	59	65	12	83	**20.**	UGD	11	75	56	30	19
8.	YGH	33	52	9	22	30	**21.**	ZVX	43	51	87	19	97
9.	AFH	41	43	56	83	52	**22.**	QTJ	38	64	52	30	42
10.	SQN	59	30	27	58	36	**23.**	NTW	22	45	67	38	98
11.	PNG	41	51	74	38	65	**24.**	FMP	74	38	89	65	12
12.	HNE	97	83	27	52	36	**25.**	CFM	32	59	22	43	17
13.	YGH	38	30	87	95	71							

KEY 2								
NJH	DFS	UHN	PLV	WFR	CGH	RTY	VCJ	KGY
67	23	56	71	61	98	21	45	33
KUH	BKI	FTY	PIO	GVC	CGI	WDC	PLM	IJN
73	54	16	64	19	40	83	39	26
NHU	YGB	ESD	ZMP	NCS	RFI	OGT	VGU	OIJ
17	43	78	29	37	62	57	85	96

		a	b	c	d	e
26.	VGU	72	81	56	23	85
27.	NJH	87	67	19	47	54
28.	KGY	33	15	27	86	43
29.	OIJ	25	49	96	71	38
30.	NHU	17	83	65	98	35
31.	KUH	41	93	29	73	12
32.	DFS	76	51	16	64	23
33.	OGT	96	57	47	29	18
34.	PLM	39	78	96	40	56
35.	VCJ	67	21	45	32	11
36.	CGI	93	36	81	40	65
37.	BKI	37	21	16	96	54
38.	UHN	56	67	73	64	85

		a	b	c	d	e
39.	NCS	26	37	98	83	39
40.	PIO	38	45	64	71	24
41.	WFR	85	72	85	43	61
42.	ZMP	26	33	73	29	85
43.	WDC	83	29	47	85	16
44.	IJN	96	17	9	61	26
45.	FTY	38	16	49	81	63
46.	YGB	62	57	96	43	87
47.	CGH	45	21	98	72	36
48.	PLV	71	85	48	97	39
49.	GVC	58	34	16	19	23
50.	RTY	87	21	65	73	18

KEY 3								
ERT	BHF	POU	YGV	COI	GFR	VHJ	PKN	DGT
77	13	25	92	31	88	49	60	58
HLP	LOI	BKO	XDT	MBG	POK	AWR	QNK	CXZ
19	71	86	27	53	97	61	38	41
SDI	GNJ	PGB	CFH	MOF	CYK	EBK	VYL	RGI
94	16	79	81	67	21	52	47	35

		a	b	c	d	e			a	b	c	d	e
51.	RGI	72	47	67	31	35	**64.**	POU	25	91	83	47	59
52.	QNK	54	38	25	86	54	**65.**	CXZ	30	72	41	68	17
53.	HLP	19	27	81	35	79	**66.**	DGT	96	58	27	39	81
54.	BKO	65	39	86	42	87	**67.**	CYK	52	16	79	21	34
55.	ERT	59	25	54	77	64	**68.**	MOF	71	56	83	49	67
56.	YGV	44	92	62	35	13	**69.**	COI	13	94	31	28	44
57.	AWR	61	53	34	68	30	**70.**	PKN	39	60	78	45	51
58.	GNJ	72	40	32	22	16	**71.**	XDT	27	31	62	59	48
59.	PGB	35	81	79	96	58	**72.**	SDI	30	89	26	94	65
60.	BHF	13	56	37	88	29	**73.**	POK	98	72	97	33	58
61.	VYL	34	47	19	79	26	**74.**	VHJ	15	22	56	11	49
62.	CFH	22	35	72	94	81	**75.**	LOI	29	71	41	92	54
63.	EBK	67	82	45	52	98							

KEY 4							
BNK	VJF	OGV	FTJ	IUB	MIO	XTC	CHK	WBG
78	56	39	97	42	88	13	61	54
ERN	HUO	KTC	COI	VGU	RYK	XDE	OHF	BIP
27	19	83	50	71	34	68	49	92
PBU	OBT	BOI	GVF	EUI	FTK	CDS	KIH	GFY
94	20	45	17	89	58	32	64	77

		a	b	c	d	e			a	b	c	d	e
76.	PBU	59	47	72	86	94	90.	XDE	65	21	54	71	68
77.	BNK	54	78	29	62	45	91.	BOI	98	45	84	63	12
78.	GFY	77	26	18	53	89	92.	FTJ	34	91	11	97	49
79.	VGU	12	90	71	48	55	93.	EUI	89	65	30	72	53
80.	FTK	39	27	93	58	62	94.	BIP	57	49	92	61	86
81.	HUO	19	74	27	49	87	95.	OBT	32	81	76	53	20
82.	RYK	71	34	68	23	88	96.	IUB	45	16	93	42	53
83.	ERN	65	39	75	49	27	97.	CHK	61	23	38	15	71
84.	XTC	11	43	13	52	95	98.	KIH	48	64	56	28	37
85.	OHF	49	58	27	34	94	99.	VJF	73	28	91	56	18
86.	MIO	89	88	16	49	79	100.	GVF	27	60	17	66	11
87.	CDS	28	65	52	32	30							
88.	WBG	21	54	82	28	61							
89.	KTC	30	66	83	57	29							

Practice Exam 3: Part Two

Personal Background Section

Answer each question honestly. Mark only one answer unless the question directs you otherwise. There is no time limit for this section.

1. If I were to witness a coworker involved in employee theft, my initial reaction would be to
   a. report the person to my superiors.
   b. reprimand the person myself.
   c. ignore the person's actions.
   d. document the person's actions.

2. As a job applicant, my most important goal in an employment interview is to
   a. impress the interviewer.
   b. learn about the position.
   c. learn about salary and benefits.
   d. demonstrate my positive characteristics.
   e. demonstrate my commitment and professionalism.
   f. demonstrate my sense of humor.

3. My favorite type of movie is
   a. action/adventure.
   b. suspense.
   c. romance.
   d. comedy.
   e. drama.
   f. other

4. I feel the primary role of a parent is to
   a. educate.
   b. discipline.
   c. protect.
   d. provide.

5. On a typical weekend afternoon, I am likely to (mark all that apply)
   a. catch up on work.
   b. go to a movie.
   c. go to a cultural event.
   d. go to a sporting event.
   e. spend quiet time alone.
   f. spend time with family or friends.
   g. engage in physical activity.
   h. do chores around the house.

6. If a close family member were in a local nursing home, I would prefer to visit
   a. several times a week.
   b. once a week.
   c. once or twice a month.
   d. irregularly.
   e. on holidays and special occasions.
   f. not at all.

7. If I come across a difficult word while reading or working, I am most likely to
   a. try to determine its meaning based on context.
   b. look it up in the dictionary.
   c. jot it down and ask someone about its meaning.
   d. skip over it on the assumption that I can understand what I am reading without knowing the word.

8. I believe my most productive work period is during
   a. the morning.
   b. the afternoon.
   c. the evening.
   d. the late night.
   e. any time period.

9. The word that best describes my driving style is
   a. patient.
   b. impatient.
   c. observant.
   d. aggressive.
   e. cautious.

10. If I observe a vehicle broken down along a busy highway, I am most likely to
   a. stop and offer assistance.
   b. call the police to report what I saw.
   c. continue driving, assuming someone else will help out.
   d. respond if I am not in a hurry.

11. In school, I generally completed assignments
   a. ahead of time.
   b. just in time.
   c. on time sometimes and late sometimes.
   d. most often late.

12. Other than gaining an education, my main priority in school was
   a. making friends.
   b. participating in sports.
   c. determining a career path.
   d. participating in extracurricular activities.
   e. having a good time

13. If I disagreed with the methods of a teacher, I would
   a. approach him or her directly.
   b. write him or her an e-mail.
   c. approach his or her supervisor.
   d. not do anything about it.
   e. drop the class.

14. In school, I demonstrated the most enthusiasm for
   a. math classes.
   b. science classes.
   c. social science/social studies classes.
   d. liberal arts classes.
   e. physical education classes.
   f. industrial arts classes.

15. When I complete a major project at work, I am most likely to
   a. begin focusing immediately on another project.
   b. expect immediate feedback from colleagues.
   c. expect feedback from supervisors.
   d. appreciate the sense of accomplishment.
   e. desire some time off.

16. I feel that becoming romantically involved with a coworker is
   a. wrong.
   b. sometimes unwise but unavoidable.
   c. acceptable under most circumstances.
   d. acceptable if kept discreet.

17. When I am given a rush assignment at work, I am most likely to feel
   a. challenged.
   b. that I am being treated unfairly.
   c. flustered or overwhelmed.
   d. energized.

18. If a coworker asks for a loan, I will
   a. provide it without hesitation.
   b. say yes if it is a small amount.
   c. say no.
   d. provide it, but set up a specific repayment date.
   e. base my decision on my evaluation of the particular coworker's trustworthiness.
   f. base my decision on the closeness of my relationship with this coworker.

19. In a small-class setting at school, I would
   a. speak up often.
   b. prefer that the teacher did not call on me.
   c. respond only if asked to.
   d. feel self-conscious about expressing myself.

20. If someone I know tells me he or she is considering dropping out of high school, my first reaction would be to
   a. express my disappointment.
   b. describe how the person's life might be with and without an education.
   c. try hard to convince him or her to remain in school.
   d. list his or her options and let the person decide for himself or herself.
   e. refer him or her to someone else.
   f. tell him or her dropping out is not an option.

Answers

Verbal

1. a. *Envision* means the same as *imagine.*
2. b. *Unclear* means the opposite of *obvious.*
3. c. *Candidate* means the same as *applicant.*
4. b. *Moving* means the opposite of *stagnant.*
5. d. *Disagree* means the opposite of *conspire.*
6. c. *Withhold* means the opposite of *empower.*
7. c. *Intricate* means the opposite of *simplistic.*
8. a. *Incompetent* means the opposite of *effective.*
9. b. *Terminate* means the same as *extinguish.*
10. a. *Association* means the same as *connection.*
11. b. *Understanding* means the same as *empathy.*
12. c. *Allocate* means the same as *devote.*
13. d. *Hypocritical* means the opposite of *sincere.*
14. c. *Impulsive* means the opposite of *premeditated.*
15. b. *Reassurance* means the same as *comfort.*
16. a. *Extinction* means the same as *oblivion.*
17. b. *Playful* means the same as *frivolous.*
18. d. *Vulnerable* means the opposite of *immune.*
19. a. *Intended* means the same as *destined.*
20. c. *Rise* means the opposite of *descend.*
21. b. *Instinctual* means the same as *intuitive.*
22. d. *Relieve* means the same as *alleviate.*
23. c. *Combine* means the same as *integrate.*
24. b. *Genuine* means the opposite of *imposter.*
25. c. *Similar* means the opposite of *variety.*
26. a. *Deceptive* means the same as *insidious.*
27. c. *Dullness* means the opposite of *brilliance.*
28. d. *Vague* means the opposite of *precise.*
29. c. *Impartial* means the opposite of *bigot.*
30. d. *Aspect* means the same as *facet.*
31. c. *Prohibit* means the opposite of *sanction.*
32. a. *Gathering* means the same as *function.*
33. b. *Clear* means the same as *decisive.*
34. c. *Competent* means the opposite of *inept.*
35. d. *Elastic* means the same as *resilient.*
36. c. *Use* means the same as *exhaust.*
37. c. *Misunderstanding* means the opposite of *insight.*

38. b. *Full* means the opposite of *vacuum*.

39. d. *Stagger* means the same as *lurch*.

40. b. *Establish* means the same as *determine*.

41. a. *Conform* means the opposite of *deviate*.

42. d. *Struggling* means the same as *labored*.

43. c. *Pseudo* means the same as *quasi*.

44. a. *Composure* means the same as *poise*.

45. b. *Starve* means the opposite of *inundate*.

46. d. *Concern* means the same as *pertain*.

47. c. *Apathy* means the opposite of *initiative*.

48. b. *Cut* means the same as *lacerate*.

49. d. *Discourage* means the opposite of *persuade*.

50. c. *Protect* means the same as *insulate*.

Recall

1. e.
2. b.
3. d.
4. b.
5. c.
6. a.
7. d.
8. e.
9. b.
10. c.
11. a.
12. d.
13. b.
14. e.
15. a.
16. c.
17. b.
18. d.
19. a.
20. c.
21. e.
22. b.
23. d.
24. a.
25. e.
26. e.
27. b.

28. a.
29. c.
30. a.
31. d.
32. e.
33. b.
34. a.
35. c.
36. d.
37. e.
38. a.
39. b.
40. c.
41. e.
42. d.
43. a.
44. e.
45. b.
46. d.
47. c.
48. a.
49. d.
50. b.
51. e.
52. b.
53. a.
54. c.
55. d.
56. b.
57. a.
58. e.
59. c.
60. a.
61. b.
62. e.
63. d.
64. a.
65. c.
66. b.
67. d.
68. e.
69. c.

70. b.
71. a.
72. d.
73. c.
74. e.
75. b.
76. e.
77. b.
78. a.
79. c.
80. d.
81. a.
82. b.
83. e.
84. c.
85. a.
86. b.
87. d.
88. b.
89. c.
90. e.
91. b.
92. d.
93. a.
94. c.
95. e.
96. d.
97. a.
98. b.
99. d.
100. c.

Scoring

The passing score for the exam is computed using formulas that subtract for incorrect answers and take into consideration the personal background section. Scoring on the personal background section varies, so focus on the first section in determining your score.

Verbal Score

First, count the questions you answered correctly. Then, count the number of questions you answered incorrectly and divide by four. Subtract the results of the division from the number you got correct for your raw score. Questions you didn't answer have no effect on your score.

1. Number of correct questions: _____
2. Number of incorrect questions: _____
3. Divide number 2 by 4: _____
4. Subtract number 3 from number 1: _____

The result of number 4 is your raw score on the verbal section.

Recall Score

Count the recall questions you answered correctly. Then, count the number of questions you answered incorrectly and divide by five. Subtract the results of the division from the number you got correct, and that's your score. Questions you didn't answer don't count.

1. Number of correct questions: _____
2. Number of incorrect questions: _____
3. Divide number 2 by 5: _____
4. Subtract number 3 from number 1: _____

The result of number 4 is your raw score on the recall section.

What the Scores Mean

Generally, if you scored at least 70% on each section—that's 35 on verbal and 70 on recall—you can figure that you would probably pass the first part of the test if you took it today. But your goal isn't just to pass. Because your rank on the eligibility list may be based on your written exam score among other factors, you want to score as high as you can. Unless you scored nearly 100%, you will want to spend some time in study and practice.

Your score isn't the main point of taking this practice exam. Analyzing your performance is much more important. Use this analysis to focus your study and practice between now and exam day.

5 ▶ POLICE OFFICER PRACTICE EXAM 4

CHAPTER SUMMARY

Practice Exam 4 tests map reading, memory, judgment, common sense, reading, and math. It is similar in structure to Practice Exam 2. Compare your performance specifically with Practice Exam 2, but also with the other practice exams you have completed.

This practice exam is an example of a test that focuses on job-related skills. Even if the exam you take does not look exactly like this one, many police exams test for the same skills, so taking the exam will provide you with important practice and with an opportunity to analyze your test-taking abilities.

In addition to the pencils you will need to fill in the answer sheet, try to take this exam using an alarm clock or stopwatch. Set the timer for 15 minutes to study the memory materials that come directly after the answer sheet.

Then reset your timer for $2\frac{1}{2}$ hours, which is about the amount of time you can expect on an actual test to answer 100 questions. To do this properly, you should set aside at least $3\frac{1}{2}$ hours, including the 15-minute study time, the time for the test, and time after the test to review your answers and see where you need to continue studying.

As in the other practice tests, the study material, answer sheet, and test questions are followed by an explanation of the correct answers and information on how to score your exam.

Police Officer Practice Exam 4

1. ⓐ ⓑ ⓒ ⓓ
2. ⓐ ⓑ ⓒ ⓓ
3. ⓐ ⓑ ⓒ ⓓ
4. ⓐ ⓑ ⓒ ⓓ
5. ⓐ ⓑ ⓒ ⓓ
6. ⓐ ⓑ ⓒ ⓓ
7. ⓐ ⓑ ⓒ ⓓ
8. ⓐ ⓑ ⓒ ⓓ
9. ⓐ ⓑ ⓒ ⓓ
10. ⓐ ⓑ ⓒ ⓓ
11. ⓐ ⓑ ⓒ ⓓ
12. ⓐ ⓑ ⓒ ⓓ
13. ⓐ ⓑ ⓒ ⓓ
14. ⓐ ⓑ ⓒ ⓓ
15. ⓐ ⓑ ⓒ ⓓ
16. ⓐ ⓑ ⓒ ⓓ
17. ⓐ ⓑ ⓒ ⓓ
18. ⓐ ⓑ ⓒ ⓓ
19. ⓐ ⓑ ⓒ ⓓ
20. ⓐ ⓑ ⓒ ⓓ
21. ⓐ ⓑ ⓒ ⓓ
22. ⓐ ⓑ ⓒ ⓓ
23. ⓐ ⓑ ⓒ ⓓ
24. ⓐ ⓑ ⓒ ⓓ
25. ⓐ ⓑ ⓒ ⓓ
26. ⓐ ⓑ ⓒ ⓓ
27. ⓐ ⓑ ⓒ ⓓ
28. ⓐ ⓑ ⓒ ⓓ
29. ⓐ ⓑ ⓒ ⓓ
30. ⓐ ⓑ ⓒ ⓓ
31. ⓐ ⓑ ⓒ ⓓ
32. ⓐ ⓑ ⓒ ⓓ
33. ⓐ ⓑ ⓒ ⓓ
34. ⓐ ⓑ ⓒ ⓓ
35. ⓐ ⓑ ⓒ ⓓ
36. ⓐ ⓑ ⓒ ⓓ
37. ⓐ ⓑ ⓒ ⓓ
38. ⓐ ⓑ ⓒ ⓓ
39. ⓐ ⓑ ⓒ ⓓ
40. ⓐ ⓑ ⓒ ⓓ
41. ⓐ ⓑ ⓒ ⓓ
42. ⓐ ⓑ ⓒ ⓓ
43. ⓐ ⓑ ⓒ ⓓ
44. ⓐ ⓑ ⓒ ⓓ
45. ⓐ ⓑ ⓒ ⓓ
46. ⓐ ⓑ ⓒ ⓓ
47. ⓐ ⓑ ⓒ ⓓ
48. ⓐ ⓑ ⓒ ⓓ
49. ⓐ ⓑ ⓒ ⓓ
50. ⓐ ⓑ ⓒ ⓓ
51. ⓐ ⓑ ⓒ ⓓ
52. ⓐ ⓑ ⓒ ⓓ
53. ⓐ ⓑ ⓒ ⓓ
54. ⓐ ⓑ ⓒ ⓓ
55. ⓐ ⓑ ⓒ ⓓ
56. ⓐ ⓑ ⓒ ⓓ
57. ⓐ ⓑ ⓒ ⓓ
58. ⓐ ⓑ ⓒ ⓓ
59. ⓐ ⓑ ⓒ ⓓ
60. ⓐ ⓑ ⓒ ⓓ
61. ⓐ ⓑ ⓒ ⓓ
62. ⓐ ⓑ ⓒ ⓓ
63. ⓐ ⓑ ⓒ ⓓ
64. ⓐ ⓑ ⓒ ⓓ
65. ⓐ ⓑ ⓒ ⓓ
66. ⓐ ⓑ ⓒ ⓓ
67. ⓐ ⓑ ⓒ ⓓ
68. ⓐ ⓑ ⓒ ⓓ
69. ⓐ ⓑ ⓒ ⓓ
70. ⓐ ⓑ ⓒ ⓓ
71. ⓐ ⓑ ⓒ ⓓ
72. ⓐ ⓑ ⓒ ⓓ
73. ⓐ ⓑ ⓒ ⓓ
74. ⓐ ⓑ ⓒ ⓓ
75. ⓐ ⓑ ⓒ ⓓ
76. ⓐ ⓑ ⓒ ⓓ
77. ⓐ ⓑ ⓒ ⓓ
78. ⓐ ⓑ ⓒ ⓓ
79. ⓐ ⓑ ⓒ ⓓ
80. ⓐ ⓑ ⓒ ⓓ
81. ⓐ ⓑ ⓒ ⓓ
82. ⓐ ⓑ ⓒ ⓓ
83. ⓐ ⓑ ⓒ ⓓ
84. ⓐ ⓑ ⓒ ⓓ
85. ⓐ ⓑ ⓒ ⓓ
86. ⓐ ⓑ ⓒ ⓓ
87. ⓐ ⓑ ⓒ ⓓ
88. ⓐ ⓑ ⓒ ⓓ
89. ⓐ ⓑ ⓒ ⓓ
90. ⓐ ⓑ ⓒ ⓓ
91. ⓐ ⓑ ⓒ ⓓ
92. ⓐ ⓑ ⓒ ⓓ
93. ⓐ ⓑ ⓒ ⓓ
94. ⓐ ⓑ ⓒ ⓓ
95. ⓐ ⓑ ⓒ ⓓ
96. ⓐ ⓑ ⓒ ⓓ
97. ⓐ ⓑ ⓒ ⓓ
98. ⓐ ⓑ ⓒ ⓓ
99. ⓐ ⓑ ⓒ ⓓ
100. ⓐ ⓑ ⓒ ⓓ

Practice Exam 4

Section One:
Memorization and Visualization

You have 15 minutes to study the memory material at the beginning of the exam before starting the practice test, which begins with questions about what you have memorized.

The memory questions are divided into two distinct forms of memorization. The first part contains wanted posters and the second part is an article on law enforcement concerns about the dangers of text messaging while driving. After reviewing the posters and reading the article for a total of 15 minutes for both sections, turn the page and answer the test questions about the material. To create the same conditions as the actual test, **do not refer back to the posters and the article to answer the questions**.

You have two options when you complete Section One. If you want to continue to create actual test conditions, go directly on to the rest of the test. If you are curious about how well you answered these questions, review the answers for this portion before continuing with the rest of the exam.

WANTED

Cynthia Josephine Dean

ALIASES: Sadie Dean
AGENCY ISSUE WARRANT: U.S. Marshal's Service
CHARGE(S): Unlawful Flight to Avoid Prosecution
DESCRIPTION:
Age: 22
Race: White
Height: 5′2″
Weight: 110 lbs.
Hair: Brown
Eyes: Brown

IDENTIFYING MARKS, SCARS, OR TATTOOS: The suspect has multiple ear piercings in the right ear, and a single nose piercing and single eyebrow piercing. She is also missing two lower front teeth.
REMARKS: The suspect is a known methamphetamine user and is known to support drug addiction through shoplifting. Suspect frequents shopping malls and large retail establishments.

WANTED

Henry Jacob Foster

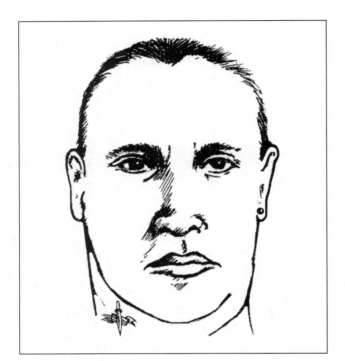

WANTED

Brian James Mesina

ALIASES: Jake the Snake
AGENCY ISSUE WARRANT: Chicago Police Department
CHARGE(S): Assault with a Deadly Weapon, Use of a Firearm
DESCRIPTION:
Age: 28
Race: White
Height: 6′3″
Weight: 270 lbs.
Hair: Black
Eyes: Blue

IDENTIFYING MARKS, SCARS, OR TATTOOS: Pierced left ear, tattoo of a sword and banner on right front side of neck.
REMARKS: Suspect should be considered armed and dangerous. He is a known associate of the White Only motorcycle gang, a white supremacy organization. He is known to frequent motorcycle clubs and strip clubs.

ALIASES: None Known
AGENCY ISSUE WARRANT: Chicago Police Department
CHARGE(S): Murder, Unlawful Flight to Avoid Prosecution
DESCRIPTION:
Age: 40
Race: White
Height: 5′10″
Weight: 200 lbs.
Hair: Black
Eyes: Brown

IDENTIFYING MARKS, SCARS, OR TATTOOS: Suspect was last seen wearing a Fu Manchu style mustache; suspect needs/wears corrective lenses.
REMARKS: Suspect should be considered armed and dangerous.

WANTED

Robert Percy Smith

WANTED

Raymond Eugene Miller

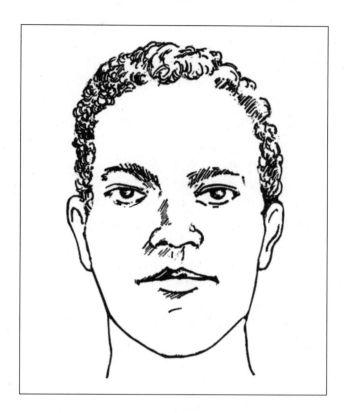

ALIASES: Bob Jones, Percy Smith, Michael Percy Smith, Michael Jones, David R. McIntyre
AGENCY ISSUE WARRANT: Los Angeles Police Department
CHARGE(S): Forgery
DESCRIPTION:
Age: 45
Race: White
Height: 6′0″
Weight: 195 lbs.
Hair: Bald
Eyes: Brown

IDENTIFYING MARKS, SCARS, OR TATTOOS: At the time of his last arrest, suspect was bald.
REMARKS: Suspect is known to disguise his appearance.

ALIASES: Ray Miller, Eugene R. Miller
AGENCY ISSUE WARRANT: Downey Police Department
CHARGE(S): Defrauding an Innkeeper
DESCRIPTION:
Age: Male
Race: Black
Height: 5′9″
Weight: 200 lbs.
Hair: Brown
Eyes: Brown

IDENTIFYING MARKS, SCARS, OR TATTOOS: Suspect has curly hair
REMARKS: None

Reading Passage

Good police management requires clear rules, regulations, procedures, and policies that not only guide a police officer's conduct but also help police managers determine whether a police officer acted correctly. Law enforcement is often conducted in a highly charged and fluid environment where a police officer rarely sees the exact situation twice. While most police officers act lawfully, they do occasionally make mistakes, and like all human beings in all occupations, there are those who commit acts of misconduct.

Part of the job of a police manager is to tailor an organizational response to a mistake or act of misconduct. An organizational response can run the spectrum from a verbal admonishment to termination of employment and perhaps even the filing of criminal charges. In order to craft the proper response, a police manager must consider the nature of police misconduct, the employee's history, the legal ramifications of the response, and the organizational values. At different times, these four factors can have different weight in the decision-making process. As an example, a new employee who makes a simple mistake will likely receive training, whereas a tenured employee making the same mistake should have known better and might receive a written admonishment. In that example, the nature of the misconduct (a simple mistake) has less weight in the decision-making process than the employee's time on the job. As another example, a new employee or a 15-year veteran of the job would likely have their employment terminated if they committed a felony. In this instance, the legal ramifications and the values of the organization strongly outweigh considerations about the employee.

Before a police manager can appropriately weigh these four factors, he or she must have a complete understanding of them. Understanding the law, the employee, and the organizational values are fairly straightforward. The law is written down. Indeed, organizational values are often also written down. A police manager can refer back to the appropriate criminal code or refer back to the department's value statement. Moreover, factors about the employee are often readily available in his or her personal work history, from statements by supervisors and peers, and by direct observation. What is generally misunderstood or cloudy in law enforcement is the nature of police misconduct.

Police misconduct can be analyzed in two broad categories: Job-related and non-job-related. Job-related misconduct relates to those acts that only a police officer could perform. They are directly related to the officer's employment. For instance, only a police officer can use emergency red lights and a siren to stop a motorist. Therefore, any acts of misconduct arising from a traffic stop are considered job-related. However, police officers, like all employees, can misuse sick time. Any employee of any organization who has sick time benefits is capable of misusing them. The abuse of sick time is not directly related to the job of a police officer, but can be applied to any employee. The important distinction is that job-related misconduct almost always involves a violation of the public trust whereas non-job-related misconduct does not.

Often, the primary concern of the police manager is the analysis of job-related misconduct. Here also, by categorizing the different types of police misconduct, under the general category of job-related misconduct, the manager may find insight into the appropriate organizational response. Under the category of job-related misconduct the three primary categories of police misconduct are: occupational deviance, noble cause misconduct, and brutality.

Occupational deviance is like job-related misconduct because it involves the use of the employee's position as a police officer to commit the misconduct. Some examples of this are gratuities, bribes, on-duty crimes, and other forms of internal corruption.

Noble cause misconduct is sometimes referred to as the Dirty Harry syndrome. This is when a police officer bends or breaks the law in order to facilitate the arrest and/or prosecution of a criminal. Typically, noble cause misconduct occurs when a police officer fabricates probable cause, plants evidence, commits perjury in court, and so forth. The key point of this type of misconduct is that the employee believes that the end justifies the means.

Police brutality comes in three forms: misuse of the law, speech, and force. Misuse of the law is significantly different than noble cause in that noble cause generally targets an offender because the police officer believes he or she is a criminal. Misuse of the law targets the offender because he or she belongs to a certain group. Typically, a police officer will have a personal zero-tolerance policy for minor violations of the law, which is directed at one particular group in society. For example, a police officer who issues a summons for littering in an African American neighborhood, but who would not issue the summons for the same violation in a white neighborhood, is misusing the law.

Section One: Memorization and Visualization

Answer questions 1 through 15 based on the wanted posters you have just studied. Do not refer back to the study material to answer these questions.

1. Which of the wanted persons are considered armed and dangerous?
   a. Raymond Eugene Miller and Cynthia Josephine Dean
   b. Henry Jacob Foster and Brian James Mesina
   c. Henry Jacob Foster and Raymond Eugene Miller
   d. Brian James Mesina and Raymond Eugene Miller

2. How many of the wanted persons are female?
   a. one
   b. two
   c. three
   d. four

3. Which of the wanted persons is both the tallest and has a tattoo of a sword on his neck?
   a. Brian James Mesina
   b. Raymond Eugene Miller
   c. Robert Percy Smith
   d. Henry Jacob Foster

4. Which two wanted persons have facial hair?
   a. Brian James Mesina and Raymond Eugene Miller
   b. Brian James Mesina and Robert Percy Smith
   c. Robert Percy Smith and Raymond Eugene Miller
   d. Robert Percy Smith and Henry Jacob Foster

5. Which suspects are wanted by the Chicago Police Department?
   a. Henry Jacob Foster and Brian James Mesina
   b. Henry Jacob Foster and Robert Percy Smith
   c. Raymond Eugene Miller and Robert Percy Smith
   d. Raymond Eugene Miller and Cynthia Josephine Dean

6. Which wanted person was wearing eyeglasses in the drawing?
   a. Cynthia Josephine Dean
   b. Raymond Eugene Miller
   c. Brian James Mesina
   d. Henry Jacob Foster

7. Which wanted person has the most visible piercings?
   a. Henry Jacob Foster
   b. Cynthia Josephine Dean
   c. Robert Percy Smith
   d. Raymond Eugene Miller

8. Which suspect has curly hair?
   a. Cynthia Josephine Dean
   b. Robert Percy Smith
   c. Brian James Mesina
   d. Raymond Eugene Miller

9. Which suspect is wanted only for Unlawful Flight to Avoid Prosecution?
   a. Cynthia Josephine Dean
   b. Robert Percy Smith
   c. Brian James Mesina
   d. Raymond Eugene Miller

10. According to the wanted poster, which suspect(s) frequents motorcycle clubs and strip bars?
   a. Henry Jacob Foster and Brian James Mesina
   b. Henry Jacob Foster and Robert Percy Smith
   c. Henry Jacob Foster
   d. Robert Percy Smith

11. Which of the suspects is most likely to be apprehended while shoplifting?
   a. Cynthia Josephine Dean
   b. Robert Percy Smith
   c. Brian James Mesina
   d. Raymond Eugene Miller

12. Which of the male suspects is the shortest?
   a. Henry Jacob Foster
   b. Robert Percy Smith
   c. Brian James Mesina
   d. Raymond Eugene Miller

13. Which of the suspects uses the alias David R. McIntyre?
   a. Cynthia Josephine Dean
   b. Robert Percy Smith
   c. Brian James Mesina
   d. Raymond Eugene Miller

14. Which suspect is missing his or her lower two front teeth?
   a. Cynthia Josephine Dean
   b. Robert Percy Smith
   c. Brian James Mesina
   d. Raymond Eugene Miller

15. Which wanted person's hair can best be described as a flattop?
   a. Cynthia Josephine Dean
   b. Robert Percy Smith
   c. Brian James Mesina
   d. Raymond Eugene Miller

Answer questions 16 through 30 based on the reading passage. Do not refer back to the study material to answer these questions.

16. According to the passage, which of the following is NOT required for good police management?
   a. rules
   b. regulations
   c. values
   d. policies

17. Which of the following is a factor that a police manager should consider when tailoring a response to a mistake or act of misconduct?
   a. Most police officers act lawfully.
   b. the nature of police misconduct
   c. Police work is conducted in a fluid environment.
   d. rules and regulations

18. Which of the four factors in evaluating police misconduct is likely written down?
   a. organizational values
   b. policies
   c. rules
   d. regulations

19. Which of the following is an example of job-related misconduct?
   a. misuse of sick time
   b. violations of rules
   c. deviance from policy
   d. occupational deviance

20. Noble cause misconduct is sometimes referred to as
   a. police brutality.
   b. the Dirty Harry syndrome.
   c. the white knight syndrome.
   d. internal corruption.

21. Which of the following CANNOT be described as noble cause misconduct?
   a. misuse of the law
   b. perjury in court
   c. fabricating probable cause
   d. planting evidence

22. Before police managers can appropriately weigh these four factors they must
   a. understand the law.
   b. weigh the alternative considerations.
   c. have a complete understanding of them.
   d. finish the decision-making process.

23. Which of the following almost always involves a violation of the public trust?
   a. job-related misconduct
   b. non-job-related misconduct
   c. crime
   d. police misconduct

24. Which of the following is NOT an example of occupational deviance?
   a. gratuities
   b. bribes
   c. brutality
   d. on-duty crimes

25. A police officer having a personal zero tolerance policy for minor violations of the law that is directed at one particular group in society best describes:
   a. the Dirty Harry syndrome
   b. misuse of the law
   c. occupational deviance
   d. a personal work history

26. Which of the following is NOT one of the stated ways a police manager can determine factors about a police officer's personal work history?
   a. statements from offenders
   b. statements from supervisors
   c. statements from peers
   d. direct observation

27. According to the passage, what is generally cloudy or misunderstood?
   a. how to craft a proper response to police misconduct
   b. the frequency of police misconduct
   c. the nature of police misconduct
   d. how to correct police misconduct

28. The "end justifies the means" best describes the attitude of police officers when they commit which type of misconduct?
   a. non-job-related
   b. excessive force misconduct
   c. misuse of the law
   d. noble cause misconduct

29. According to the passage, occupational deviance is like
   a. job-related misconduct
   b. non-job-related misconduct
   c. criminal law
   d. noble cause misconduct

30. According to the passage, which type of misconduct targets the offender because the police officer believes they committed a crime, not because they belong to a certain group?
   a. internal corruption
   b. on-duty crimes
   c. misuse of the law
   d. noble cause misconduct

Section Two: Reading Skills

Map 1

Answer questions 31 through 38 based on Map 1. Review the directional arrows and the map key. You are not permitted to go the wrong way on a one-way street.

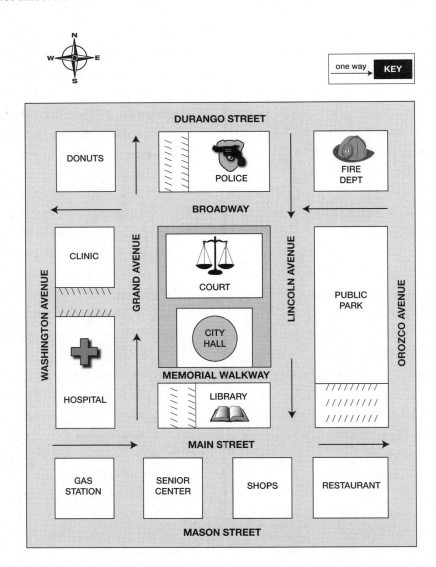

31. Which building is located in the northwest corner of the map?
  a. police station
  b. fire department
  c. donut shop
  d. senior center

32. Officer Jones is parked eastbound on the north side of the street in front of the library. He receives a call to go to the police station. What is the best route of travel?
  a. Make a U-turn on Main Street and head north on Grand Avenue.
  b. Proceed eastbound on Main Street, turn left on Orozco Avenue, and then left on Broadway.
  c. Proceed eastbound on Main Street, turn north on Lincoln Avenue, and then west on Broadway.
  d. Proceed westbound on Main Street, turn left on Orozco Avenue, and then west on Broadway.

33. How many streets are two-way streets?
  a. two
  b. three
  c. four
  d. five

34. Which avenue goes north only?
  a. Grand Avenue
  b. Lincoln Avenue
  c. Washington Avenue
  d. Orozco Avenue

35. Officer Jones is at the police station. He is in the parking lot, having just started his watch. The police station parking lot is indicated by diagonal lines. There are two exits to the parking lot, one on the north and one on the south. If he exits the south side of the parking lot, which street will he be on and which direction must he travel?
  a. Durango, east
  b. Durango, west
  c. Broadway, east
  d. Broadway, west

36. Officer Smith has just completed an injury investigation at the senior center. She is parked on the north side of Mason Street (legally parked at the curb) and must go to the hospital to interview the injured person. Since the hospital emergency room and emergency vehicle parking are on the north side of the hospital between the hospital and the clinic, what is her best route of travel?
  a. westbound Mason Street to southbound Grand Avenue
  b. westbound Mason Street to northbound Grand Avenue
  c. eastbound Mason Street to Orozco Avenue, westbound Broadway, southbound Grand Avenue
  d. eastbound Mason Street to Orozco Avenue, westbound Broadway, northbound Grand Avenue

37. The fire department is in what corner of the map?
  a. southeast
  b. southwest
  c. northeast
  d. northwest

38. Officer Smith sees a robbery suspect running from Grand Avenue, between the court and city hall, toward Lincoln. Officer Smith believes the suspect is going to make his escape through the park and wants to cut off the suspect's escape route on the east side of the park. Smith is parked on Main Street, on the south side of the hospital. What is her best route?

a. north on Grand Avenue, east on Broadway
b. left onto Grand Avenue, right onto Broadway
c. east on Main street, north on Orozco
d. east on main, north on Lincoln

Map 2

Answer questions 39 through 45 based on Map 2. Review the directional arrows and the map key. You are not permitted to go the wrong way on a one-way street.

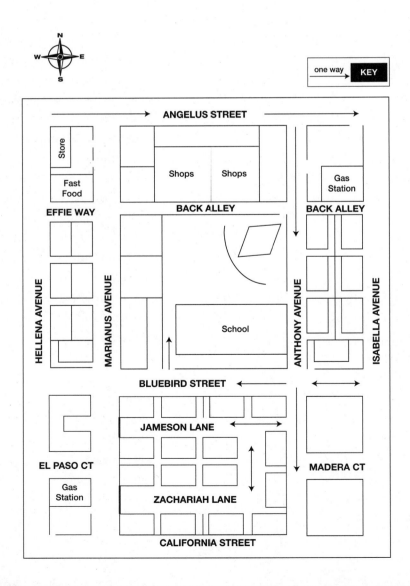

39. Gas stations are found on which two corners of the map?
  a. northeast and southwest
  b. northeast and northwest
  c. southwest and southeast
  d. northwest and southwest

40. Officer Smith receives a radio call reporting a fight at the school. He is parked on the north side of the street on El Paso Court. What is his best route of travel?
  a. north on Hellena Avenue, east on Bluebird
  b. north on Hellena Avenue, east on Angelus Street, south on Anthony Avenue, west on Bluebird
  c. south on Hellena Avenue, east on Bluebird
  d. south on Hellena Avenue, east on Angelus Street, south on Anthony Avenue, west on Bluebird

41. Which street is west of the school?
  a. Angelus Street
  b. Anthony Avenue
  c. Bluebird Street
  d. Marianus Avenue

42. Officer Smith completed the radio call at the school. He is parked on Anthony Avenue, just north of Bluebird Street when he hears another officer requesting a backup unit in the parking lot of the store located on the corner of Angelus Street and Marianus Avenue. What is his best route?
  a. north on Anthony Avenue, left on Bluebird Street, right onto Marianus Avenue
  b. south on Anthony Avenue, left on Bluebird Street, right onto Marianus Avenue
  c. north on Anthony Avenue, right turn onto Bluebird Street, north on Marianus Avenue
  d. south on Anthony Avenue, right turn onto Bluebird Street, north on Marianus Avenue

43. Which street, lane, or avenue gives access to Zachariah Lane?
  a. Anthony Avenue
  b. Bluebird Street
  c. Jameson Lane
  d. Marianus Avenue

44. After assisting the officer at the store on the corner of Angelus Street and Marianus Avenue, Officer Smith receives a call to meet her sergeant in the alley behind the gas station, east of Anthony Avenue. What is her best route?
  a. north on Marianus, east on Angelus Street, south on Anthony Avenue, turn left into the alley
  b. north on Marianus, east on Angelus Street, south on Anthony Avenue, turn right into the alley
  c. south on Marianus, left turn into the alley, drive across Anthony Avenue
  d. south on Marianus, right turn into the alley, drive across Anthony Avenue

45. The school is located on which corner of Anthony Avenue and Bluebird Street?
  a. northwest
  b. southwest
  c. northeast
  d. southeast

Reading Passage 1

Read the following passage, then answer questions 46 through 50.

By the time of Caesar Augustus, around 6 AD, the Romans began to develop a number of concepts that moved them closer to having a police force that we could recognize. Paramilitary units like vigiles, praetorian guards, and urban cohorts came into existence.

Caesar Augustus taxed the sale of slaves in order to finance night watchmen for the city of Rome. *Vigiles urbani* (literally, watchmen of the city) were founded primarily as a fire-prevention force, but they also provided patrol to prevent burglaries and occasionally pursued runaway slaves. Furthermore, like modern police agencies, these vigiles were organized along the military lines of the time. Whereas today a local police agency is headed by a chief who is assisted by captains, lieutenants, and sergeants, the Roman vigiles were commanded by a *praefectus vigilum*, who was assisted by a subpraefectus, tribunes, and centurions.

Just as modern police officers in large cities work out of precincts or stations and patrol specific geographic areas, Roman vigiles were assigned to cohorts (a cohort consisted of 560 men commanded by a tribune) that patrolled one of the 14 administrative districts of the City of Rome.

46. Caesar Augustus taxed the sale of slaves in order to finance
   a. the Roman police force.
   b. the administrative districts of the city.
   c. night watchmen.
   d. the establishment of cohorts.

47. Based on the passage, which of the following is a true statement?
   a. Modern police officers are assigned to specific areas.
   b. Modern police officers are assigned to cohorts.
   c. Modern police officers are assigned as night watchmen.
   d. Modern police officers are assigned as tribunes.

48. A modern police agency is headed by a
   a. sergeant.
   b. lieutenant.
   c. captain.
   d. chief.

49. The original Roman night watchmen were a
   a. group of tax collectors.
   b. fire-prevention force.
   c. paramilitary group.
   d. cohort of slaves.

50. Roman cohorts patrolled
   a. one of 14 administrative districts.
   b. precincts.
   c. vigiles.
   d. specific tribunes.

Reading Passage 2

Read the following passage, then answer questions 51 through 55.

While the FBI is probably the best known law enforcement agency, it isn't the oldest. The Judiciary Act of 1789 created the office of attorney general and the first law enforcement agency, the U.S. Marshals Service (USMS).

Today, the USMS serves a myriad of federal law enforcement missions, including the transportation and guarding of federal prisoners and serving federal warrants. The U.S. Marshals are also responsible for investigating and bringing to justice federal fugitives and for the operation and management of the Federal Witness Security Program. The Witness Security Program was authorized by the Organized Crime Control Act of 1970 and amended by the Comprehensive Crime Control Act of 1984. Since its inception, more than 7,500 witnesses and over 9,500 family members have entered the program and have been protected, relocated, and given new identities by the Marshals Service. Finally, the USMS provides professional services in the area of U.S. court security, personal protection, and asset seizures.

51. Which law created the U.S. Marshals?
   a. Judiciary Act of 1789
   b. Organized Crime Control Act of 1970
   c. Comprehensive Crime Control Act of 1984
   d. Comprehensive Judiciary Act of 1975

52. Which of the following is NOT one of the U.S. Marshals professional services?
   a. asset seizures
   b. organized crime investigations
   c. personal protection
   d. witness security

53. According to the passage, which agency is the oldest federal law enforcement agency?
   a. the federal Indian police
   b. the federal judiciary
   c. the Federal Bureau of Investigation
   d. the U.S. Marshals Service

54. The U.S. Marshals Federal Witness Protection Program involves
   a. security, asset protection, and relocation.
   b. protection, relocation, and new identities.
   c. warrant service, relocation, and protection.
   d. asset seizure, relocation, and security.

55. The Federal Witness Security Program was authorized by
   a. the chief U.S. Marshal.
   b. the Organized Crime Control Act of 1970.
   c. the Judiciary Act of 1789.
   d. the Comprehensive Crime Control Act of 1984.

Reading Passage 3

Read the following passage, then answer questions 56 through 60.

Airborne Law Enforcement Operations are becoming very common nationwide. As of April 2006, the Airborne Law Enforcement Association's (ALEA) database of air unit operations was tracking the operations of over 185 Airborne Law Enforcement–related units. The largest of these Airborne Law Enforcement units is maintained by the LAPD. The LAPD's Air Support Division (ASD) averages 18,000 flight hours a year with an aircraft fleet of 17 helicopters and one fixed-wing aircraft. Many other state and local police agencies have airborne capabilities, and some police agencies share helicopter service. In some instances, a nearby small city will contract for flight time with a larger city that has an airborne unit. Moreover, there are some private companies that provide airborne law enforcement services for a fee.

Air support operations are designed to assist patrol officers in a number of ways. A helicopter can often respond to a call for service much more rapidly than a patrol car. A number of research studies have observed that rapid response to calls for service is not correlated with an increase in solving a crime or capturing an offender. Nonetheless, no clear research on the impact of rapid response by aircraft supports a conclusion either way. There is significant anecdotal information that rapidly responding helicopters and fixed-wing aircraft have been highly successful in arriving before patrol cars, seeing suspects flee, and directing officers to those suspects.

56. Which of the following is NOT a way in which a police department can obtain airborne law enforcement?
   a. develop its helicopter patrol
   b. share with an adjacent city
   c. contract from the military
   d. contract from a private company

57. According to the passage, which of the following sentences is NOT true?
   a. Helicopter response is directly correlated to an increase in solving crime.
   b. Helicopter response is often faster than a patrol car.
   c. Helicopters have directed officers to suspects.
   d. Helicopters have seen suspects fleeing the location of a call.

58. According to the passage, which of the following sentences is true?
   a. The LAPD has a total of 18 aircraft.
   b. The LAPD has 17 fixed-wing aircraft.
   c. The LAPD shares its aircraft.
   d. The LAPD is the second largest unit tracked by ALEA.

59. As of 2006, ALEA was tracking how many airborne units?
   a. 185
   b. 18,000
   c. 17
   d. 18

60. According to the passage, when a city contracts with another city for helicopter services, how are the helicopter services shared?
   a. by number of aircraft
   b. by flight time
   c. by calls for service
   d. by miles flown

Section Three: Judgment and Problem Solving

These questions ask you to use good judgment and common sense, along with the information provided, to answer each of the questions. Some passages may be followed by more than one question pertaining to the same set of facts.

Read the following information, then answer questions 61 and 62.

Officer Smith has recently received an updated department policy regarding police vehicle pursuits. Her department has changed the circumstances in which a police officer may initiate a vehicle pursuit to state: "Officers of this Department may only initiate a vehicle pursuit when the driver of the pursued vehicle is known to have committed a serious felony or high-grade misdemeanor and/or failure to pursue them is likely to endanger the public more than pursuit itself."

61. Under which of the following conditions would Officer Smith initiate a vehicle pursuit?
   a. The driver runs a stop sign.
   b. The driver fails to signal for a left turn in a school zone.
   c. The driver is traveling over 100 mph on a residential street.
   d. The driver runs a stop sign in a school zone.

62. Under which of the following would Officer Smith NOT initiate a vehicle pursuit?
   a. The driver is wanted for murder.
   b. The driver is suspected of shoplifting.
   c. The driver is wanted for shooting at police officers.
   d. The driver is wanted for child molestation.

Read the following information, then answer questions 63 through 65.

Officer Jones receives a radio call for a robbery in progress. The dispatcher gives him the following information: "Robbery in progress, 211 North Main Street. Suspect described as a male white, wearing a black jacket, white T-shirt, blue jeans, and red tennis shoes. Suspect has a large-caliber handgun."

63. On the way to the robbery call, Officer Jones sees the following individuals two blocks from the call; which should he detain?
- **a.** a male black wearing a white T-shirt, blue jeans, and black shoes
- **b.** a female white wearing a black jacket, black slacks, and white shoes
- **c.** a male white wearing a white T-shirt, blue jeans, and red shoes
- **d.** a female white wearing a brown jacket, blue jeans, and red shoes

64. Upon arrival at the call, what is the proper order in which Officer Jones should accomplish tasks?
- **a.** Ascertain whether a crime was committed, verify that the suspect is gone, complete a report, search for the suspect.
- **b.** Complete a report, interview the victim, ascertain whether a crime was committed, complete a report.
- **c.** Interview the victim, complete a report, search for the suspect, have the report approved by a supervisor.
- **d.** Verify that the suspect is gone, ascertain whether a crime was committed, interview the victim, complete a report.

65. On his arrival at 211 North Main Street, Officer Jones discovers that the address does not exist; what should he do next?
- **a.** Radio dispatch, tell them no crime occurred, and tell them he is available for another call.
- **b.** Radio dispatch and tell them the address does not exist, request additional information, and then check 211 South Main Street.
- **c.** Radio dispatch, tell them the address does not exist, and request additional information.
- **d.** Park where the address should be and wait to be approached by the victim.

While on patrol at 3:00 A.M., Officer Smith sees smoke coming out of the front windows of a house. As she stops at the curb, she sees a man run off the front porch of the house carrying a gas can.

66. Which of the following is the best order of actions she should take?
- **a.** Radio for the fire department, alert the people in the house, assist with evacuation, radio the suspect's description.
- **b.** Alert the people in the house, assist with evacuation, radio for the fire department, radio the suspect's description.
- **c.** Radio the suspect's description, assist with evacuation, alert the people in the house, radio for the fire department.
- **d.** Alert the people in the house, radio the suspect's description, assist with evacuation, radio for the fire department.

Officer Jones has been told that no overtime will be authorized. It is five minutes before the end of his shift and he is driving back to the police station. He observes a three-car accident and one of the vehicles has overturned. There are no emergency services at the scene.

67. What is his best course of action?
  a. Drive to the station and inform his supervisor of the accident.
  b. Drive by and tell the parties he is calling another patrol car for them.
  c. Drive by and use the radio to call for another patrol car.
  d. Stop and assist the parties.

Officer Smith receives a radio call about a six-year-old child who is missing. She goes to the location and, after interviewing the parents and assisting them with a second, more thorough search of the house, the child is located asleep in her brother's room. During the initial interview, Smith took the following notes:

> Child's Name: Antonia Isabella Garcia
> Parents' Names: Maria and Raymundo Garcia
> Location: 18853 E. Galleano Street
> Date/Time: 11/01/10, 1500 hours
> Disposition: Child found asleep in bedroom

68. Which is the best summary paragraph of the incident?
  a. On November 1, 2010, at 1500 hours, I responded to a call of a missing child at 18853 E. Galleano Street. I met with the parents of the missing child, Maria and Raymundo Garcia. They stated their six-year-old daughter, Antonia Isabella Garcia, was missing. After obtaining basic information I assisted the parents in searching their residence for the child. The missing child was located asleep in her brother's bedroom.
  b. I helped the parents find their missing child at 18853 E. Galleano Street. The child was named Antonia Isabella Garica and the parents were Maria and Raymundo with the same last name. We looked around their house and found the kid in her brother's room, asleep.
  c. On November 1, 2010, at 1600 hours, I responded to a call of a missing child at 13358 E. Galleano Street. I met with the parents of the missing child, Maria and Raymundo Garcia. They stated their six-year-old daughter, Antonia Isabella Garcia, was missing. After obtaining basic information I assisted the parents in searching their residence for the child. The missing child was located asleep in her brother's bedroom.
  d. I helped the parents find their missing child at 13358 E. Galleano Street. The child was named Antonia Isabella Garica and the parent were Maria and Raymundo with the same last name. We looked around their house and found the kid in her brother's room, asleep.

69. Which of the following assumptions can the officer make?
  a. The child is a habitual runaway.
  b. The parents speak Spanish.
  c. There are at least two children in the family.
  d. The parents did not look for the child.

Read the following paragraph, then answer questions 70 through 72.

On November 1, 2010, at 1600 hours, Officers Smith and Jones were on patrol in a black and white police vehicle when they received a radio call about a burglary investigation at 145 N. Old Road. When they arrived, the officers observed that the location was a single-family residence on the east side of the street, with a detached garage. The detached garage was down a driveway on the south side of the house. The officers met with the person who called the police, Michael Bentway. Bentway told the officers that he lived at the address. He went to work at 9:00 A.M. that morning and returned at 3:30 P.M. to find that someone had broken into his home. Bentway emphasized to the officers that his house was fine before he left for work at 9:00 A.M. The officers conducted an investigation and found that an unidentified suspect had used a pry tool, possibly a large screwdriver, to force open the back sliding glass door of the residence. The officers observed that the suspect(s) had ransacked Bentway's home. With Bentway's assistance, the officer cataloged the missing items and determined that among the items taken was Bentway's 72-inch rear-projection television. In addition to the investigation inside the residence, the officers spoke to the neighbors. They found that the neighbor just south of Bentway's house, Sally Forth, heard a vehicle in Bentway's driveway during the early afternoon. She looked out the window on the north of her house and saw a white pickup truck parked in the driveway. Later, she heard male voices, and looked out the same window, but only saw a large television in the bed of the pickup.

70. When did the burglary occur?
  a. 11-1-10 at 1600 hours
  b. on November 1, 2010, between 9:00 A.M. and 3:30 P.M.
  c. on November 1, 2010, between 3:30 A.M. and 9:00 P.M.
  d. There is insufficient evidence to determine when.

71. Which of the following is an assumption the officers could make?
  a. There was only one suspect.
  b. There were two suspects.
  c. There were at least two suspects.
  d. There was a gang of suspects.

72. The officers decided to put out a crime broadcast about the burglary. Which is the most complete and most accurate?
  a. A burglary occurred at 145 N. Old Road, suspects used a white pickup truck and took miscellaneous property, including a 72-inch rear-projection television
  b. A burglary occurred at 145 N. Old Road, suspects used a white pickup truck and took a 72-inch rear-projection television
  c. A burglary occurred on Old Road, suspects used a white pickup truck
  d. A burglary occurred on Old Road, suspects used a pickup truck and took a 72-inch television

Answer questions 73 and 74 based on the following information.

A person committing assault with a deadly weapon is defined as "any person who commits an assault upon the person of another with a deadly weapon or instrument other than a firearm or by any means of force likely to produce great bodily injury; any person who commits an assault upon the person of another with a firearm; any person who commits an assault with a firearm upon the person of a peace officer or firefighter, and who knows or reasonably should know that the victim is a peace officer or firefighter engaged in the performance of his or her duties, when the peace officer or firefighter is engaged in the performance of his or her duties."

73. According to the definition, which of the following would qualify as an assault with a deadly weapon?
- **a.** a little league umpire hits a parent with a baseball glove
- **b.** a store clerk hits a customer on the head with a beer bottle
- **c.** a firefighter hits a doctor with his open palm
- **d.** a police officer hits a suspect with his open palm

74. Which of the following is not an assault with a deadly weapon?
- **a.** In a drive-by shooting, four gang members are wounded.
- **b.** An on-duty firefighter is shot and wounded by gang members.
- **c.** During a traffic stop, a violator attempts to run over a police officer with his car.
- **d.** An on-duty firefighter is bitten on the arm by a drunk.

75. Officer Jones is in pursuit of a vehicle being driven by a man wanted for murdering a police officer. The suspect's vehicle collides with a smaller vehicle, causing significant damage and likely injuring the occupants. The suspect's vehicle continues away from the scene at a high rate of speed. What is Officer Jones's best course of action?
- **a.** Stop and render aid to the victims of the crash, look for the suspect later.
- **b.** Stop and render aid to the victims of the crash, radio the last known direction of the suspect.
- **c.** Radio the location of the accident and request paramedics and another police unit to handle it, continue with the pursuit.
- **d.** Ignore the crash and continue with the pursuit.

76. The promotion list for sergeant has been released. Officer Smith finds out he is number 10 on the list. Officer Jones is 12 positions on the list behind Smith. Officer Smart is 18 positions ahead of Jones. What number is Smart on the list?
- **a.** 3
- **b.** 4
- **c.** 30
- **d.** 33

77. Officer Smith has been a police officer for 8 years. Officer Jones has been a police officer for 5 years less than Officer Smart. Officer Smart has been a police officer for 10 years longer than Officer Smith. How long has Jones been a police officer?
- **a.** 10
- **b.** 11
- **c.** 12
- **d.** 13

Answer questions 78 and 79 based on the following definition.

> According to the vehicle code, "A person who drives a vehicle upon a highway or in an off-street parking facility in willful or wanton disregard for the safety of persons or property is guilty of reckless driving."

78. Which of the following is most likely reckless driving?
  a. driving 70 miles an hour in the store parking lot at 2:00 P.M.
  b. running a traffic light at 2:00 A.M.
  c. running a traffic light at 2:00 P.M.
  d. driving 5 miles over the speed limit in a school zone

79. Which of the following is LEAST likely to be considered reckless driving?
  a. at 1:00 P.M., on a Wednesday, driving 25 miles an hour over the speed limit in a school zone
  b. at 1:00 P.M., on a Wednesday, driving 25 miles an hour over the speed limit in a residential zone
  c. at 2:00 P.M., on a Thursday, driving 25 miles an hour over the speed limit, on the highway
  d. at 2:00 P.M., on a Thursday, driving 25 miles an hour over the speed limit, in a downtown area

80. Officer Smith is manually fingerprinting a suspect in the jail. Smith knows that excessive perspiration can interfere with obtaining useful fingerprints. The suspect being fingerprinted is perspiring profusely and it is clear to Smith that she may not be able to take fingerprints. What is her best course of action?
  a. Provide the suspect with a towel to wipe his fingers and continue with fingerprinting.
  b. Give the suspect medication to control the perspiration, wait until it takes effect, and then fingerprint.
  c. Write "unable to fingerprint" on the fingerprint card and return the suspect to a cell.
  d. Call for a supervisor; after an inspection by the supervisor, write "unable to fingerprint" on the fingerprint card and return the suspect to a cell.

Answer questions 81 and 82 based on the following information.

> Police officers are trained to handle radio calls and observation activities based on the following formula:

1. make sure the scene is safe
2. request fire rescue if medical attention is necessary
3. obtain a brief synopsis of the incident and a description of suspect(s) and vehicle(s)
4. relay information to dispatch to notify other police units
5. take a detailed report from the victim
6. question witnesses
7. collect physical evidence
8. give the victim a report number for the incident
9. attempt to conclude the investigation with action most applicable to the situation

81. Officer Jones is the first officer to respond to a call about a shooting in a parking lot. He sees the victim on the ground, bleeding and moaning. The victim is lying next to a large panel van, with the side doors open. What should Jones do first?
   a. use his radio to call for an ambulance
   b. give first aid to the victim
   c. make sure the suspect isn't in the van or the immediate surrounding area
   d. ask the victim what happened

82. At the scene of the same shooting, what is Officer Jones's most likely LAST course of action?
   a. collect the expended shell casing from the suspect's gun
   b. use his police radio to inform nearby police units of the suspect's description
   c. interview witnesses at the scene of the shooting
   d. go to the suspect's house based on a license plate number provided by the victim

83. According to Officer Smith's department policy, she should take a traffic collision report if "the crash resulted in bodily injury to or death of any person; or, damage to any vehicle or other property in an apparent amount of at least $500." Based on that policy, which of the following is NOT a situation wherein Smith would take a traffic collision report?
   a. a car strikes a pedestrian, causing the pedestrian to scrape his knee on the pavement
   b. a shopping cart bumps the rear bumper of a 1995 Chevrolet
   c. a car traveling at 50 miles an hour hits a telephone pole
   d. a truck backs into the side of a 2010 Mercedes

84. Sergeant Dale supervises bicycle patrol officers. Her department policy states, "Bike officers are expected to ride their bikes in varying weather conditions. Officers and supervisors should take a common-sense approach toward riding in extreme conditions, which would pose an obvious threat to their physical health." Under which of the following conditions should Sergeant Dale order his bicycle officers to ride in patrol cars?
   a. Intermittent drizzle is expected in the morning, clearing in the afternoon.
   b. The high temperature of the day is expected to be 85 degrees.
   c. There is a thunderstorm warning in effect for the city.
   d. The low temperature is predicted to be 55 degrees.

85. Officer Smith's department policy states, "Arresting officers who suspect a prisoner of putting in their mouth, swallowing, or attempting to swallow any substance or item suspected as capable of causing physical harm, injury, or death will immediately request a supervisor and a Fire Department response to the scene." Which of the following is an incident wherein Smith should request a supervisor and the fire department?
   a. On the way to jail, a suspect in custody for drug possession swallows a balloon filled with heroin.
   b. A traffic violator eats and swallows the citation Smith issued.
   c. At a radio call, a mother reports that her three-year-old daughter has swallowed drain cleaner.
   d. While eating in a restaurant, Smith observes a man choking on a piece of steak.

Read the following passage, then answer questions 86 and 87.

According to Officer Smith's department policy, "Any responsible and competent adult whose whereabouts are unknown by his choice will not be reported as missing. Investigating officers are required to determine, based on the individual circumstances of each case, the age of the missing person and whether or not foul play and suspicious circumstances exist. Any further action will be determined based upon that investigation."

86. Under which circumstances should Smith immediately take a missing persons report?
   a. a 22-year-old female college student misses a college final exam
   b. an Alzheimer's patient wanders away from a semisecure facility
   c. a 32-year-old male is three hours late coming home from work
   d. a 42-year-old truck driver is six hours overdue from making a delivery

87. Under which of the following circumstances should Smith NOT immediately take a missing persons report?
   a. a 29-year-old male is despondent and left a suicide note
   b. a 41-year-old female's abandoned car was found with her purse inside and blood on the seat
   c. a 56-year-old male cancer patient has spoken of suicide with family members and has not returned home in 24 hours
   d. a 28-year-old female is three hours late for work

Read the following paragraph, then answer questions 88 and 89.

Officer Smith's department policy says, "because of the circumstances involved in a 911 silent/disconnect call and panic/duress alarms, every effort should be made to determine the cause of the call. When unable, further investigation is necessary." Moreover, Smith knows that the United States Supreme Court has held that police officers "may make warrantless, and presumably, forcible entry into a home where they reasonably believe a person within is in need of immediate aid."

88. Under which of the following circumstances should Officer Smith force entry into a home without a warrant?
   a. Responding to a 911 hang-up call, Smith talks to a woman through a small window in her front door. She says everything is okay, but refuses the officer entrance because she says her house is dirty.
   b. Arriving at the scene of a panic alarm, Smith observes a broken side window, but no one will answer the door.
   c. Arriving at a 911 hang-up call, Smith is met by two teenage boys who are inside the house. They tell Smith, by talking through the closed door, that they accidentally dialed 911, but will not allow Smith inside.
   d. Upon arrival on a 911 hang-up call, the door is answered by a 28-year-old female. She opens the door partway and tells Smith that her 8-year-old boy accidentally called 911. Smith can hear the boy crying inside. The woman tells Smith that the boy is standing in the corner, being punished for the 911 call.

89. Under which of the following circumstances should Smith NOT make an immediate warrantless forced entry into a home?

a. At a duress alarm call, Smith is met by the family in residence, who say they have handled their mother's medical emergency.

b. At a 911 hang-up call, when he looks through a window, Smith sees a body on the floor of the living room.

c. At a duress alarm call, no one answers the door, but the alarm repeatedly goes off.

d. At a 911 hang-up call, no one answers the door, but Smith hears the sounds of a fight inside the location.

90. Officer Jones works in a small town of less than 4,000 people. On a Friday night, he is driving on the town's main street. He stops a car for exceeding the speed limit by 30 mph. As he approaches the driver, he recognizes her to be the town mayor. What is his best course of action?

a. issue the mayor a citation

b. issue the mayor a warning

c. call for a supervisor, issue the mayor a citation

d. call the senior city council member, issue the mayor a citation

91. A criminal gang is defined as an ongoing formal or informal organization, association, or group of three or more persons to which all the following apply:

- It has as one of its primary activities the commission of one or more of the following offenses: Any Felony; Any Offense of Violence; Unlawful Sexual Conduct with a Minor; Criminal Damaging; Aggravated Trespassing; Failure to Disperse; Interference with Custody; Contributing to Unruliness/Delinquency of a Child; Intimidation of Attorney, Victim, or Witness in a Criminal Case; Improper Handling of a Firearm in a Motor Vehicle; Trafficking in Marijuana; or, Ethnic Intimidation.
- It has a common name or one or more common, identifying signs, symbols, or colors.

Based on the definition, which of the following is NOT a Criminal Gang?

a. six teenagers who wear the same color clothing and call themselves the 3rd Street Boys, who commit a drive-by shooting at three members of a known gang

b. six members of a motorcycle club, riding similar motorcycles and wearing similar leather gear, who conspire to sell cocaine

c. three members of a white-only motorcycle club, who ride similar motorcycles and wear similar leather gear, who threaten to lynch an African American male

d. three teenagers who wear the same color clothing and call themselves the 3rd Street Boys, who hang around an after-school recreation center

92. Officer Jones receives a radio call about a vicious dog. Which of the following would be the LEAST recommended tactic for dealing with the dog?
a. using meat to bait the dog into a neighbor's fenced-in front yard and calling animal control
b. spraying the dog with chemical irritant to dissuade it from biting the officer
c. shooting the dog in the body if it were biting the officer's leg
d. wrapping his police jacket around his arm, allowing the dog to bite it and then pulling the dog into an enclosed area

93. Police officers respond to a life-threatening emergency. Sometimes, they use the emergency lights and siren on their vehicles to make their way through traffic. Which of the following is NOT an example of a situation wherein the use of the emergency lights and siren is justified?
a. women screaming for help
b. a shoplifting suspect being detained by store security
c. a bank robbery in progress
d. a shooting in progress

Police officers are often given multiple calls for service at the same time. The individual police officer decides, based on the nature of the call and the information given, which call should be handled first. Additionally, police officers often see things happen on their way to calls for service. A police officer must use his or her judgment on what to do first. For the next three questions, use your judgment on which call or observation to handle first, or which has the highest priority.

94. Which has the highest priority?
a. a domestic dispute
b. a burglary investigation
c. a missing three-year-old
d. a robbery investigation

95. Which has the highest priority?
a. a traffic collision with injuries
b. a trespass suspect at a scene
c. a theft investigation
d. an abandoned vehicle

96. Which has the highest priority?
a. a man disturbing the peace
b. a robbery investigation
c. a traffic collision without injuries
d. a man with a knife

97. Penal Code Section 470b states, "Every person who displays or causes or permits to be displayed or has in his possession any driver's license or identification card of the type with the intent that such driver's license or identification card be used to facilitate the commission of any forgery, is punishable by imprisonment in the state prison, or by imprisonment in the county jail for not more than one year." A forgery is, in essence, the presentation of a false document for gain. Which of the following would NOT be a crime pursuant to this section?
a. an 18-year-old with a false ID attempts to buy beer with cash
b. an 18-year-old in possession of an altered driver's license
c. an 18-year-old uses an altered driver's license to cash a check from a fictitious account
d. an 18-year-old presents an altered driver's license to a police officer during a traffic stop

98. Officer Smith responds to a traffic collision. At the scene he is met by the three drivers, none of whom are injured. Where is it safest for Smith to interview the drivers?
   a. in the street, behind the crashed vehicles
   b. on the sidewalk
   c. in the street, behind the flare pattern
   d. in the street, in front of the crashed vehicles

99. Officer Smith observes four vehicles speeding on the freeway. The speed limit is 55 mph. The red car is going 20 mph faster than the white car. The white car is going 5 mph over the speed limit. The blue car is going 10 mph slower than the red car. The yellow car is going 15 mph faster than the blue car. Which car should Smith stop?
   a. red
   b. white
   c. blue
   d. yellow

100. Officer Jones knows his department policy is that "in a hostage, barricade, threatened suicide, or other applicable situation, a crisis negotiations team will respond and attempt to resolve the situation by utilizing the skills of trained police negotiators." Which of the following situations is one in which Jones should call for a crisis negotiations team?
   a. a domestic violence radio call
   b. a foot pursuit of carjacking suspect
   c. a petty theft suspect resisting arrest
   d. a man threatening to jump off a bridge

Answers

Section One: Memorization and Visualization

1. b. Henry Jacob Foster and Brian James Mesina are considered armed and dangerous.

2. a. One of the wanted persons is female—Cynthia Josephine Dean.

3. d. Henry Jacob Foster is the tallest and has a tattoo of a sword on his neck.

4. b. Brian James Mesina and Robert Percy Smith have facial hair.

5. a. Henry Jacob Foster and Brian James Mesina are wanted by the Chicago Police Department.

6. c. Brian James Mesina was wearing eyeglasses in the drawing.

7. b. Cynthia Josephine Dean has the most visible piercings.

8. d. Raymond Eugene Miller has curly hair.

9. a. Cynthia Josephine Dean is wanted only for Unlawful Flight to Avoid Prosecution.

10. c. Only Henry Jacob Foster frequents motorcycle clubs and strip bars.

11. a. Cynthia Josephine Dean is most likely to be apprehended while shoplifting.

12. d. Raymond Eugene Miller is the shortest male suspect.

13. b. Robert Percy Smith uses the alias David R. McIntyre.

14. a. Cynthia Josephine Dean is missing her lower two front teeth.

15. c. Brian James Mesina's hair can best be described as a flattop.

16. c. The first sentence of the passage reads, "Good police management requires clear rules, regulations, procedures, and policies," not values.

17. b. The passages reads, "In order to craft the proper response, a police manager must consider *the nature of police misconduct*, the employee's history, the legal ramifications of the response, and the organizational values."

18. a. While the others are likely to be written down, *organizational values* is the only response that is among the four factors.

19. d. The passages reads, "the three primary categories of police misconduct are: *occupational deviance*, noble cause misconduct, and brutality."

20. b. The passage reads, "Noble cause misconduct is sometimes referred to as the Dirty Harry syndrome."

21. a. The passage indicates that *misuse of the law* is part of brutality, not noble cause.

22. c. The passages reads, "Before a police manager can appropriately weigh these four factors, he or she must *have a complete understanding of them*."

23. a. The passage reads, "The important distinction is that *job-related misconduct* almost always involves a violation of the public trust whereas non-job-related misconduct does not."

24. c. The other three are clearly identified as examples of occupational deviance. Brutality is a separate category under job-related misconduct.

25. b. The passage describes misuse of the law as, "a police officer will have a personal zero tolerance policy for minor violations of the law that is directed at one particular group in society."

26. a. Statements from offenders is not one of the stated ways a police manager can determine factors about a police officer's personal work history.

27. c. The passage reads, "What is generally misunderstood or cloudy in law enforcement is the *nature of police misconduct*."

28. d. The end justifies the means best describes the attitude of police officers when they commit *noble cause misconduct*. The passage states that this is a key component of this type of misconduct.

29. a. The passage reads, "Occupational deviance is like job-related misconduct."

30. d. The passage reads, "noble cause generally targets an offender because the police officer believes he or she is a criminal."

Section Two: Reading Skills

31. c. The donut shop is located in the northwest corner of the map.

32. b. Proceed eastbound on Main Street, turn left on Orozco Avenue, and then left on Broadway.

33. c. The are four two-way streets: Durango, Washington, Mason, and Orozco.

34. a. Grand Avenue goes north only.

35. d. Officer Jones will be on Broadway and must travel west.

36. b. Her best route of travel is westbound on Mason Street to northbound on Grand Avenue. A car parked legally on the north side of Mason would be facing west.

37. c. The fire department is on the northeast corner of the map.

38. c. Officer Smith's best route is east on Main Street, then north on Orozco.

39. a. Gas stations are found on the northeast and southwest corners of the map.

40. b. Officer Smith's best route of travel is north on Hellena Avenue, east on Angelus Street, south on Anthony Avenue, then west on Bluebird.

41. d. Marianus Avenue is west of the school.

42. d. Officer Smith's best route is south on Anthony Avenue, right turn onto Bluebird Street, then north on Marianus Avenue.

43. c. Jameson Lane gives access to Zachariah Lane.

44. c. Officer Smith's best route to the the alley behind the gas station is south on Marianus, left turn into the alley, then drive across Anthony Avenue.

45. a. The school is located on the northwest corner of Anthony Avenue and Bluebird Street.

46. c. The passages states that the tax was imposed to finance night watchmen.

47. a. The passages reads, "modern police officers in large cities work out of precincts or stations and patrol specific geographic areas."

48. d. The passage reads, "a police agency is headed by a *chief* who is assisted by captains, lieutenants, and sergeants."

49. b. The passage reads, "*Vigiles urbani* (literally, watchmen of the city) were founded primarily as a fire-prevention force."

50. a. The passage states that the Roman cohorts patrolled one of 14 administrative districts.

51. a. The passage reads, "The Judiciary Act of 1789 created the office of attorney general and the first law enforcement agency, the U.S. Marshal Service (USMS)."

52. b. Organized crime investigation is not one of the U.S. Marshals professional services. They run the witness protection program but do not conduct the investigations.

53. d. The U.S. Marshals Service is the oldest federal law enforcement agency.

54. b. The passage reads, "7,500 witnesses and over 9,500 family members have entered the program and have been protected, relocated, and given new identities by the Marshals Service."

55. b. The passage reads, "The Witness Security Program was authorized by the Organized Crime Control Act of 1970."

56. c. All the choices except contracting from the military are mentioned in the passage.

57. a. The passage states the opposite: "A number of research studies have observed that rapid response to calls for service is not correlated with an increase in solving a crime or capturing an offender."

58. a. The passages reads "LAPD has 17 helicopters and one fixed-wing aircraft." This is 18 total.

59. a. According to the passage, as of 2006, ALEA was tracking 185 airborne units.

60. b. The passage reads, "a nearby small city will contract for flight time with a larger city that has an airborne unit."

Section Three: Judgment and Problem Solving

61. c. Of the potential answers, choice **c** is the only one that attains the level of a misdemeanor, and a vehicle traveling four times the speed limit is likely to endanger the public more than a police pursuit.

62. b. Suspicion of shoplifting is a nonviolent misdemeanor and would not qualify per the policy statement.

63. c. Of the descriptions given, "Male white wearing a black jacket, white T-shirt, blue jeans, and red shoes," *a male white wearing a white T-shirt, blue jeans, and red shoes* is the closest, and the jacket is the easiest item of apparel to take off and discard.

64. d. Of the choices, this is best because the officer should make sure a potential suspect with a gun is not at the location first. This is the safest course of action. Then, the officer must establish that a crime did occur, after which he would conduct an in-depth interview and then complete a police report.

65. b. This is the best answer because in addition to asking dispatch for additional information, the officer will take the initiative and check the south address while waiting.

66. a. This is the best order of action because the immediate safety of the people inside the residence is much more important than the capture of the potential suspect. However, the first step in rescuing people is ensuring that the fire department has been notified.

67. d. There may not be any overtime, but public safety requires the officer stop and render assistance.

68. a. Both choices **a** and **c** are very similar. However, choice **c** has the time wrong and the address of the radio call is incorrect.

69. c. There is no information to indicate the child is a habitual runaway. While the parents and children have Hispanic surnames, there is no information to indicate they speak Spanish. The officer assisted with a second search, suggesting that the parents had already conducted one.

70. b. The burglary occured on November 1, 2010, between 9:00 A.M. and 3:30 P.M.

71. c. The officers can assume that there were at least two suspects. It would more than likely take at least two people to move a 72-inch rear-projection television.

72. a. This is the best choice. Although choices **a** and **b** are similar, **a** informs officers that other property was taken in addition to the television.

73. b. Of all the choices, a store clerk hitting a customer on the head with a beer bottle is the one most likely to cause great bodily injury.

74. d. Choices **a** and **b** involve the use of a firearm and therefore automatically qualify. A vehicle is capable of causing great bodily injury. A bite to the arm is very unlikely to be considered an assault with a deadly weapon.

75. c. Officer Jones's best course of action is to radio the location of the accident and request another unit to handle it, and continue with the pursuit. A suspect wanted for murdering a police officer is a substantial threat to the community. Generally, at the scene of accidents, police officers request paramedics and conduct traffic control and the collision investigation. Therefore, when weighing the benefit of stopping at the accident against continuing to pursue the suspect, the officer's best course of action is **c**.

76. b. Smart is fourth on the list. Always begin with known information. The equation is $10 + 12 = 22$. $22 - 18 = 4$.

77. d. Always begin with known information. The equation is 8 (Smith) + 10 (Smart) − 5 (Jones) = 13

78. a. While all four are traffic violations, driving 70 mph in the store parking lot is the only one that displays a clear wanton and reckless disregard for the safety of others.

79. c. Driving 25 miles an hour over the speed limit on the highway is fast and still worthy of a citation, but it is the LEAST likely to be considered reckless driving. For the other answers, 25 miles an hour over the speed limit is usually more than twice the posted speed. As an example, most school zone limits are 25 mph; 25 mph over that limit is 50 mph. On the highway, however, the posted speed could be anywhere between 55 mph and 75 mph.

80. a. Provide the suspect with a towel to wipe his fingers and continue with fingerprinting. Sometimes the simplest answer is the best answer.

81. c. Based on the information, the first task is to make sure the scene is safe—make sure the suspect isn't in the van or the immediate surrounding area.

82. d. Going to the suspect's house based on a license plate number provided by the victim falls under the category of attempting to conclude the investigation by identifying and arresting the suspect.

83. b. A shopping cart bumping the rear bumper of a 1995 Chevrolet is the least likely to have caused an injury or damage in excess of $500.

84. c. The lightning accompanying thunderstorms is dangerous, and thunderstorms are often accompanied by intense downpours of rain.

85. a. A suspect in custody for drug possession swallowing a balloon filled with heroin on the way to jail is cause for Officer Smith to request a supervisor and the fire department. For choice **b**, an officer might strongly consider calling a supervisor because of the bizarre behavior, but the citation, when ingested, is not life threatening. In choices **c** and **d**, the officer would certainly call for emergency medical services, but in these cases neither is a person in custody—therefore, there is no need to call a supervisor.

86. b. An Alzheimer's patient who wanders away from a semisecure facility is the most likely not "responsible or competent."

87. d. In this choice, there are no indications of foul play or suspicious circumstances.

88. b. In all the choices, Smith would likely continue with his investigation, but for choices **a**, **c**, and **d**, the circumstances aren't such that he would make a forced warrantless entry. In choice **b**, he is most likely to use the forced entry option.

89. a. Of these situations, only Smith being met by the family, who say they have handled their mother's medical emergency, provides the officer with enough information to avoid a forced entry.

90. c. The person's status as the mayor should have little bearing on the decision to issue a citation; however, it will likely have ramifications in the community. Therefore, calling a supervisor to the scene and then issuing a citation affords the officer and the department the best alternative.

91. d. The definition requires the group to have two or more common signs and a common name, and the commission of a defined set of crimes. In choice **d**, there is no crime.

92. d. Tricking or baiting the dog into an enclosed area and waiting for animal control is probably the best solution. If the dog is trying to bite the officer, spraying it with chemical irritant is appropriate. If the dog is biting the officer, shooting it is justified. The least recommended tactic would be purposely using your jacket-covered arm as a means to control the dog.

93. b. A shoplifting suspect being detained by store security is the only clearly non-emergency call.

94. c. The word "investigation" denotes the crime has occurred. A domestic dispute can be a high-priority call, but a missing three-year-old is unable to care for or defend herself from danger.

95. a. A traffic collision with injuries is the only call with a clear public safety issue.

96. d. A man with a knife is the clearest public safety issue.

97. b. For a forgery to be present, the person must have a driver's license and use it to facilitate a forgery.

98. b. The sidewalk is a better choice than any location in the street.

99. d. The speed limit is 55. The white car is going $55 + 5 = 60$. The red car is going 60 (white car speed) $+ 20 = 80$. The blue car is going 80 (red car speed) $- 10 = 70$. The yellow car is going 70 (blue car speed) $+ 15 = 85$. The officer should stop the fastest car, yellow.

100. d. While the other calls may have an element of danger, a man threatening to jump off a bridge is a threatened suicide and clearly meets the criterion given.

Scoring

Use this practice exam to analyze where you have improved since Practice Exam 2 and where you continue to have weaknesses. As you did with the earlier exams, break down your score by section by writing down the number of correct answers for each section. When you add up the sections, remember that each correct answer is worth one point. You should be aiming for a score of at least 70. The better you do on the practice exams, the better your chance of not only passing the real exam, but scoring high enough to be among the first applicants called in for the later steps in the hiring process. If your score is 70 or lower, it is particularly important for you to review the individual section scores to see where you need to concentrate your additional study efforts.

POLICE OFFICER PRACTICE EXAM 5

CHAPTER SUMMARY

Practice Exam 5 tests your basic reading and writing skills. Compare your performance with earlier practice exams. If you have reviewed the earlier exams carefully, you should have a better idea of how to analyze the questions to arrive at the best answers.

Like Practice Exam 1 (Chapter 2), this practice exam is an example of a basic reading and writing skills exam like those used by many agencies around the country. This exam also contains 100 questions and is divided into two parts, although Part Two is somewhat different from the earlier practice exams.

Part One: 60 clarity of expression (grammar), vocabulary, spelling, and reading comprehension questions.

Part Two: 40 questions that require you to fill in the missing words in a two-paragraph passage. This portion of the exam is different from fill-in exams you may be familiar with. Read the instructions carefully before filling in any blank spaces.

The directions for each type of question are included in the test. Since you are now experienced at taking the practice exams, decide before you begin whether you will take your time and analyze along the way how you are doing or whether you will create conditions similar to the actual test and time yourself closely. Since the amount of time you will be given for the actual test may be different for different departments, rather than setting a hard time limit, see how long it takes you to complete the test and then try to find out what the time limits are for the departments you plan to test for.

When you turn the page, you will find the answer sheet for Part One, followed by the answer sheet for Part Two, the test itself, the answers and explanations, and, finally, instructions for scoring this practice exam.

Police Officer Practice Exam 5: Part One

1.	ⓐ	ⓑ	ⓒ	ⓓ
2.	ⓐ	ⓑ	ⓒ	ⓓ
3.	ⓐ	ⓑ	ⓒ	ⓓ
4.	ⓐ	ⓑ	ⓒ	ⓓ
5.	ⓐ	ⓑ	ⓒ	ⓓ
6.	ⓐ	ⓑ	ⓒ	ⓓ
7.	ⓐ	ⓑ	ⓒ	ⓓ
8.	ⓐ	ⓑ	ⓒ	ⓓ
9.	ⓐ	ⓑ	ⓒ	ⓓ
10.	ⓐ	ⓑ	ⓒ	ⓓ
11.	ⓐ	ⓑ	ⓒ	ⓓ
12.	ⓐ	ⓑ	ⓒ	ⓓ
13.	ⓐ	ⓑ	ⓒ	ⓓ
14.	ⓐ	ⓑ	ⓒ	ⓓ
15.	ⓐ	ⓑ	ⓒ	ⓓ
16.	ⓐ	ⓑ	ⓒ	ⓓ
17.	ⓐ	ⓑ	ⓒ	ⓓ
18.	ⓐ	ⓑ	ⓒ	ⓓ
19.	ⓐ	ⓑ	ⓒ	ⓓ
20.	ⓐ	ⓑ	ⓒ	ⓓ

21.	ⓐ	ⓑ	ⓒ	ⓓ
22.	ⓐ	ⓑ	ⓒ	ⓓ
23.	ⓐ	ⓑ	ⓒ	ⓓ
24.	ⓐ	ⓑ	ⓒ	ⓓ
25.	ⓐ	ⓑ	ⓒ	ⓓ
26.	ⓐ	ⓑ	ⓒ	ⓓ
27.	ⓐ	ⓑ	ⓒ	ⓓ
28.	ⓐ	ⓑ	ⓒ	ⓓ
29.	ⓐ	ⓑ	ⓒ	ⓓ
30.	ⓐ	ⓑ	ⓒ	ⓓ
31.	ⓐ	ⓑ	ⓒ	ⓓ
32.	ⓐ	ⓑ	ⓒ	ⓓ
33.	ⓐ	ⓑ	ⓒ	ⓓ
34.	ⓐ	ⓑ	ⓒ	ⓓ
35.	ⓐ	ⓑ	ⓒ	ⓓ
36.	ⓐ	ⓑ	ⓒ	ⓓ
37.	ⓐ	ⓑ	ⓒ	ⓓ
38.	ⓐ	ⓑ	ⓒ	ⓓ
39.	ⓐ	ⓑ	ⓒ	ⓓ
40.	ⓐ	ⓑ	ⓒ	ⓓ

41.	ⓐ	ⓑ	ⓒ	ⓓ
42.	ⓐ	ⓑ	ⓒ	ⓓ
43.	ⓐ	ⓑ	ⓒ	ⓓ
44.	ⓐ	ⓑ	ⓒ	ⓓ
45.	ⓐ	ⓑ	ⓒ	ⓓ
46.	ⓐ	ⓑ	ⓒ	ⓓ
47.	ⓐ	ⓑ	ⓒ	ⓓ
48.	ⓐ	ⓑ	ⓒ	ⓓ
49.	ⓐ	ⓑ	ⓒ	ⓓ
50.	ⓐ	ⓑ	ⓒ	ⓓ
51.	ⓐ	ⓑ	ⓒ	ⓓ
52.	ⓐ	ⓑ	ⓒ	ⓓ
53.	ⓐ	ⓑ	ⓒ	ⓓ
54.	ⓐ	ⓑ	ⓒ	ⓓ
55.	ⓐ	ⓑ	ⓒ	ⓓ
56.	ⓐ	ⓑ	ⓒ	ⓓ
57.	ⓐ	ⓑ	ⓒ	ⓓ
58.	ⓐ	ⓑ	ⓒ	ⓓ
59.	ⓐ	ⓑ	ⓒ	ⓓ
60.	ⓐ	ⓑ	ⓒ	ⓓ

Police Officer Practice Exam 5: Part Two

WRITE 1ST LETTER OF WORD HERE

CODE LETTERS HERE

1	2	3	4	5	6	7	8	9	10

A B C D E F G H I J K L M N O P Q R S T U V W X Y Z (columns 1–10)

11	12	13	14	15	16	17	18	19	20

A B C D E F G H I J K L M N O P Q R S T U V W X Y Z (columns 11–20)

21	22	23	24	25	26	27	28	29	30

A B C D E F G H I J K L M N O P Q R S T U V W X Y Z (columns 21–30)

31	32	33	34	35	36	37	38	39	40

A B C D E F G H I J K L M N O P Q R S T U V W X Y Z (columns 31–40)

Practice Exam 5: Part One

Section One: Clarity

In each of the following sets of sentences, select the one that is most clearly written.

1. a. During his shift, the officer issued 14 traffic citations.
   b. During his shift the officer, issued 14 traffic citations.
   c. During his shift, the officer issue 14 traffic citations.
   d. During his shift, the officer issued 14 traffic citation.

2. a. The altercation lasted 20 second.
   b. The altercation lasted 20 seconds.
   c. The altercation lasts 20 seconds.
   d. The altercation was for twenty seconds.

3. a. The suspect were unarmed at the time of his apprehension.
   b. As he was apprehended, the suspect was unarmed.
   c. The suspects was unarmed at the time of apprehension.
   d. The suspect was unarmed at the time of his apprehension.

4. a. The seatbelt was being worn by the passenger in the vehicle.
   b. The passenger had been wearing her seatbelt.
   c. While seated in the vehicle, the passenger had been wearing the seatbelt.
   d. While seated in the vehicle the passenger, had been wearing the seatbelt.

5. a. The police officer testified, after taking the oath.
   b. The police officer's testifying was after the oath.
   c. After taking the oath, the police officer testified.
   d. After taking the oaths, the police officer testified.

6. a. The emergency lights were activated during the traffic stop.
   b. The emergency lights was activated during the traffic stop.
   c. At the time of the traffic stop, the emergency lights were activated.
   d. At the time of the traffic stop, the emergency lights was activated.

7. a. The verdict was "not guilty."
   b. The court found the defendant not guilty.
   c. The defendant was, not guilty.
   d. The trial resulted in the defendant being found not guilty.

8. a. The suspect's was advised of his Miranda rights before the detective questioned him.
   b. Before questioning the defendant was told about his Miranda rights by the detective.
   c. Questioning of the suspect took place after he was advise of his Miranda rights by the detective.
   d. Before questioning, the suspect was advised of his Miranda rights by the detective.

9. a. The field of sociology includes the subject of Criminal Justice.
   b. Criminal Justice is a subject within the field of sociology.
   c. Criminal Justice was a subject within the field of sociology.
   d. Included within the field of sociology, is the study of the subject of Criminal Justice.

10. a. Officer Smith's arrived before Sergeant Jones arrived.
   b. Sergeant Jones's arrival was after Officer Smith's.
   c. Officer Smith arrived before Sergeant Jones.
   d. Officer Smith arrived before Sergeant Jones arrived.

11. a. On January 1, 2011, at 1500 hours, the police officers left the roll call room.
   b. On January 1 2011 at 1500 hours, the police officers left the roll call room.
   c. On January 1, 2011, at 1500 hours the police officers left the roll call room.
   d. On January 1 2010 at 1500 hours the police officers left the roll call room.

12. a. There were forty feet of skid marks from where the vehicle began to brake and it finally collided with the lamppost.
   b. The vehicle left 40 feet of skid marks preceding the impact into the lamppost.
   c. 40 feet of skid marks preceded the vehicle's impact with the lampost.
   d. The vehicle left 40 feet of skid marks on the pavement preceding the impact into the lamppost.

13. a. Officer Jones' appear in court after working his shift.
   b. Officer Jones appeared in court, after working his shift.
   c. After his shift, Officer Jones went to court.
   d. After his shift Officer Jones went to court.

14. a. Yesterday after leaving a burglary call, the officers saw, a stolen car.
   b. Yesterday, the officers' saw a stolen car after they had left a burglary call.
   c. Yesterday after they had left a burglary call the officers saw a stolen car.
   d. Yesterday, after leaving a burglary call, the officers saw a stolen car.

15. a. The sergeant corrected the officer's report with a red pen.
   b. Using a red pen, the officer's report was corrected by the sergeant.
   c. A red pen was used by the sergeant to correct the officer's report.
   d. The officer's report was corrected by the sergeant who used a red pen.

Section Two: Vocabulary

In each of the following sentences, select the word or phrase that most nearly means the same as the underlined word.

16. The field training officer <u>provided</u> the rookie with instruction.
   a. furnished
   b. encouraged
   c. overwhelmed
   d. assisted

17. The detective was unable to <u>substantiate</u> the suspect's alibi.
   a. discern
   b. verify
   c. accept
   d. eliminate

18. The penal code provided a <u>variety</u> of additional charges.
  a. amount
  b. uniformity
  c. type
  d. assortment

19. The changes to the police officers' union contract were <u>significant</u>.
  a. important
  b. meaningless
  c. apparent
  d. definitive

20. The undercover officer learned the <u>vernacular</u> of the streets.
  a. distance
  b. direction
  c. sense
  d. jargon

21. The police officer's training made her reactions <u>spontaneous</u>.
  a. deliberate
  b. perfect
  c. automatic
  d. rehearsed

22. The narcotics officers seized an <u>immense</u> amount of cocaine.
  a. illegal
  b. large
  c. minute
  d. indefinable

23. The fraud victim was <u>gullible</u>.
  a. injured
  b. overweight
  c. unsuspicious
  d. intoxicated

24. The evidence was <u>essential</u> in prosecuting the case.
  a. necessary
  b. incidental
  c. elementary
  d. secondary

25. The police officer <u>informed</u> the sergeant of his mistake.
  a. hid
  b. assured
  c. disclosed
  d. secreted

26. The witnesses <u>disagreed</u> in their testimonies.
  a. fought
  b. contravened
  c. contradicted
  d. supplanted

27. The prosecutor had a <u>casual</u> conversation with the police officers.
  a. dressed
  b. idiotic
  c. recorded
  d. informal

28. The driver of the vehicle could not <u>prevent</u> the accident.
  a. leave
  b. avoid
  c. determine
  d. access

29. The public placed the <u>blame</u> for the accident on the police department.
  a. fault
  b. pity
  c. appease
  d. offense

30. The police officers found the apartment to be a <u>mess</u> before the search warrant was served.
 a. methodical
 b. disordered
 c. closed
 d. arranged

Section Three: Spelling
In each of the following sentences, select the correct spelling of the missing word.

31. The witness was an _____ of the suspect.
 a. acquaintance
 b. acquainence
 c. acquaenence
 d. acquaineince

32. The robbery suspect was _____.
 a. disperate
 b. disperete
 c. desperate
 d. despirate

33. The new police vehicles were _____ with rotating emergency lights.
 a. equepped
 b. equipped
 c. equiped
 d. equeped

30. The light from the neon sign gave the crime scene a _____ glow.
 a. mysterious
 b. misterious
 c. mystereos
 d. mystereous

35. The defendant had _____ as well as motive to commit the crime.
 a. opportunety
 b. opportunity
 c. oportunity
 d. oportunety

36. The domestic violence incident occurred after the couple's _____.
 a. seperation
 b. siperetion
 c. seperration
 d. separation

37. The police officer's uniform shirt was soaked with _____ after the foot chase.
 a. prespiration
 b. perspiration
 c. persperation
 d. pirspiration

38. The chief of police made the _____ decision after consultation with the mayor.
 a. controversial
 b. contraverisal
 c. contraveresal
 d. contraversial

39. The parents _____ searched for their missing child.
 a. franticaly
 b. franttically
 c. frantically
 d. frantickaly

40. The _____ budget projections resulted in a shortfall of funds.
 a. optomistic
 b. optimestic
 c. optimistec
 d. optimistic

41. Sometimes the _____ of the graveyard shift made the police officers congregate at the coffee shop.
   a. lonelyness
   b. lonliness
   c. loneliness
   d. lonlyness

42. The police officer fired the bullets in rapid
   _____.
   a. sucession
   b. succession
   c. succesion
   d. successeon

43. The lineup was for _____ as well as identification.
   a. elemination
   b. elimenation
   c. elimination
   d. ellimination

44. The sergeant's _____ justified her actions.
   a. explanetion
   b. explanation
   c. explannation
   d. expliniteon

45. In good or bad _____, police officers patrol their beats.
   a. whether
   b. wheather
   c. weathier
   d. weather

Section Four: Reading Comprehension

For each of the reading passages, answer the questions based on what is stated or implied in the passage.

Read the following passage, then answer questions 46 through 50.

Generally, there are two broad classifications of police employees: sworn police officers and civilian police employees. Indeed, work traditionally performed by uniformed officers has increasingly been given to civilian employees. Usually, these are jobs that don't require enforcement of the law, such as repairing motor vehicles, programming computers, analyzing forensic evidence, and operating radio dispatch systems. Indeed, of all police employees, 27% in the United States are now civilians; 35% in Great Britain; 20% in Canada and Australia; and 12% in Japan.

Police officers are commonly referred to as sworn employees because they have taken an oath of office. As such, a police officer can make an arrest for a felony if he or she has sufficient probable cause to believe a felony was committed, whereas a civilian can only make an arrest for a felony if a felony has actually been committed.

As we examine policing, it is necessary to explore the roles of both sworn and nonsworn employees because civilian employees are taking an increasingly large and important role in law enforcement. Moreover, according to the Bureau of Justice Statistics (BJS) 2000 Census of State and Local Law Enforcement Agencies, of the 1,019,496 state and local law enforcement employees who are employed by 17,784 organizations nationwide, 311,474, or just over 27%, are nonsworn employees.

46. According to the passage, which of the following is true?
   a. Civilian employees are doing more law enforcement work.
   b. Civilian employees are doing more work that used to be performed by police officers.
   c. Law enforcement officials are doing more civilian work.
   d. Law enforcement officials are working less.

47. An examination of law enforcement must take into account civilian employees because
   a. they can arrest people.
   b. it is illegal to do otherwise.
   c. they are increasing in number and responsibility.
   d. they do so in other countries.

48. Police officers are commonly referred to as
   a. law enforcement officials.
   b. sworn employees.
   c. non-civilians.
   d. police employees.

49. Civilian police employees can
   a. make arrests for probable cause.
   b. not make any arrests.
   c. make arrests under the supervision of a police officer.
   d. make arrests only for felony crimes that have been committed.

50. Which has the highest percentage of civilian employees?
   a. the United States
   b. Great Britain
   c. Japan
   d. Canada and Australia, combined

Read the following passage, then answer questions 51 through 55.

The FBI has over 30,000 employees, including over 12,500 agents. The FBI term for a sworn law enforcement officer is *agent*. Generally, federal, state, and local law enforcement agencies use the terms *agent*, *detective*, and *investigator* to mean a sworn law enforcement employee whose primary job is conducting investigations. Conversely, federal, state, and local law enforcement agencies use the terms *police officer*, *peace officer*, *officer*, and *trooper* to describe a sworn law enforcement official whose primary duties are performed in uniform. These titles can get a little confusing, especially at the state and local levels.

While the FBI has over 12,500 agents, it has nearly 18,000 civilian employees. As in most other federal, state, and local agencies, civilian employees at the FBI provide critical support functions. The FBI also has civilian intelligence analysts, language specialists, scientists, and information technology specialists. While the FBI is headquartered in Washington, DC, the Bureau has 56 field offices in the United States and a presence in more than 50 countries. The FBI agent who is in charge of a field office is called the special agent in charge (SAC, pronounced SACK), and those who are attached to American embassies are called legal attaches.

51. The FBI uses which term to describe sworn law enforcement officials?
   a. detective
   b. investigator
   c. agent
   d. SAC

52. Which of the following is NOT one of the functions outlined in the passage for civilian employees?
   a. legal attache
   b. information technology specialist
   c. language specialist
   d. intelligence analyst

53. The FBI has how many agents?
   a. 500
   b. over 30,000
   c. over 12,500
   d. 50

54. According to the passage, which is true?
   a. A peace officer could be the title of a state or local law enforcement official.
   b. An FBI agent is a peace officer.
   c. A peace officer is a law enforcement official whose primary function is conducting investigations.
   d. A civilian employee is considered a peace officer.

55. How many special agents in charge (SAC) are there?
   a. at least 56
   b. no more than 50
   c. nearly 12,500
   d. The passage doesn't state.

Read the following passage, then answer questions 56 through 60.

In the 1960s, the United States began to experience a nationwide increase in crime. One of the ideas to combat the crime problem was the establishment of a nationwide database of wanted persons, stolen vehicles, stolen license plates, stolen handguns, and other stolen property that could be identified by a serial number. In 1965, in order to accomplish the task of establishing a nationwide database, the FBI created a working group that consisted of state and local law enforcement personnel from around the country. The working group established the first nationwide standards for a database that could be added to or queried by any law enforcement agency in the United States. In January of 1967, 15 computer terminals in several states and metropolitan areas went online with the NCIC database.

When NCIC first started, there were 95,000 records in the database. By 1971, all 50 states and the District of Columbia had access to NCIC. In addition to being available to agencies nationwide, one of the things that makes NCIC unique is that each participating agency is responsible for entering, updating, and deleting its own records. This is a means of ensuring accuracy and timeliness. The premise is that the agency that makes the entry into NCIC has the most up-to-date information. If the authority to enter, update, or delete information were centralized, the NCIC staff would need to increase in size and probably be the slowest bureaucracy imaginable.

56. Which of the following is NOT mentioned as an item to be included in the original nationwide database?
   a. stolen handguns
   b. stolen license plates
   c. wanted persons
   d. missing persons

57. By what year did all 50 states have access to NCIC?
   a. 1960
   b. 1971
   c. 1967
   d. 1965

58. Who is responsible for entering data into NCIC?
 a. the FBI working group
 b. NCIC staff
 c. the participating agencies
 d. the District of Columbia

59. Today, how many records are in NCIC?
 a. over 95,000
 b. under 95,000
 c. exactly 95,000
 d. The passage doesn't state.

60. Who, according to the passage, is presumed to have the most up-to-date information on records?
 a. the NCIC staff
 b. the participating agencies
 c. the FBI working group
 d. the 15 computer terminals

Practice Exam 5: Part Two

This is a test of your reading ability. In the following passages, words have been omitted. Each numbered set of dashed blank lines indicates where a word is left out; each dash represents one letter of the missing word. The correct word should not only make sense in the sentence but also have the number of letters indicated by the dashes.

Read through the whole passage, and then begin filling in the missing words. Fill in as many missing words as possible. If you aren't sure of the answer, take a guess.

Then mark your answers on the answer sheet on page 140 as follows: Write the first letter of the word you have chosen in the square under the number of the word. Then blacken the circle of that letter of the alphabet under the square.

Only the blackened alphabet circles will be scored. The words you write on this page and the letters you write at the top of the column on the answer sheet will not be scored. Make sure that you blacken the appropriate circle in each column.

Passage 1

A procedure is a step-by-step set of instructions on **1** _ _ perform a task. Perhaps, at your school there is a specific **2** _ _ _ _ _ _ _ _ _ for adding or dropping courses. You must do all the steps in a certain **3** _ _ _ _ _ so that you can add or drop. For instance, you must use an add card signed by the instructor to **4** _ _ _ a course that has **5** _ _ _ _ closed. You must get the card before the instructor can **6** _ _ _ _ it, you must approach the instructor before you get **7** _ _ _ or her signature, and you must obtain the signature before it can be added. In a procedure, it doesn't work if you do it **8** _ _ _ of order or **9** _ _ _ _ a step. For example, you can't get the signature without the **10** _ _ _ _ .

In policing, there are many procedures. After an arrest and transportation to the station, the offender must be officially recorded as being **11** _ _ _ _ _ _ _ _ by the police. The procedure of officially documenting the **12** _ _ _ _ _ _ is called "booking." During the **13** _ _ _ _ _ _ _ procedure, police **14** _ _ _ _ _ _ _ _ obtain an offender's personal information, fingerprints, and photograph, and record the arrest charge. During booking, **15** _ _ _ _ _ _ _ _ _ are thoroughly searched, screened for medical conditions and special considerations such as gang **16** _ _ _ _ _ _ _ _ _ _ , and generally processed before entering the jail.

Booking is a specific police procedure with steps that must be completed in a certain order. For example, the **17** _ _ _ _ _ _ officer completing the booking must thoroughly search the offender prior to obtaining fingerprints. Imagine the police officer who doesn't thoroughly search the offender first and begins to take the offender's fingerprints. During the **18** _ _ _ _ _ _ _ _ _ _ _ _ _ _, the police officer, who has placed his or her firearm in a special locker, suddenly finds that the offender had a knife **19** _ _ _ _ _ _ on his or her person. By not following what seems like a simple procedure, a police officer can find himself or herself in a dangerous, often **20** _ _ _ _-threatening situation.

Passage 2

In almost all local police departments you start out in **21** _ _ _ _ _ _. That's right! If you want to be a homicide **22** _ _ _ _ _ _ _ _ _ , in most police agencies you have to learn to be a good patrol officer first. Police officers working patrol **23** _ _ _ considered generalists. Whether it's a dispute at the local gas **24** _ _ _ _ _ _ _ , a terrorist attack, or a homicide, a uniformed police officer is likely the first one on scene. As such, he or she has to have a general working knowledge of all types of police procedure, incident management, and **25** _ _ _ _ _ scene investigation.

While some police officers spend their entire **26** _ _ _ _ _ _ in uniform and on patrol, most do **27** _ _ _. As a police officer works through his or her career, he or she tends to develop specializations. Specialization is developed within an organization for two chief reasons. First, the nature of bureaucracy demands specialization. The foundation of the modern **28** _ _ _ _ _ _ _ _ _ _ _ is the

development of bureaus of specialization. Some police officers **29** _ _ _ _ _ _ administrators, some become detectives, and some people are hired as **30** _ _ _ _ _ _ _ _ _ to fill needed positions. As organizations become larger, their **31** _ _ _ _ _ _ _ _ _ _ _ _ _ becomes more complex; someone patrols, someone investigates, someone handles payroll and benefits, and so on.

The second **32** _ _ _ _ _ _ for specialization has to do with human nature. We all have different talents and learn different skills. We have different interests that drive us to pursue a **33** _ _ _ _ _ _ _ degree of specialization. Some want to work narcotics and will be drawn to **34** _ _ _ _ _ _ _ _ about drugs and undercover work, while others want to be **35** _ _ _ _ _ _ _ _ detectives and will pursue a different body of policing knowledge. The combination of organizational need and **36** _ _ _ _ _ nature has created a strong sense of specialization in policing. Within the professional model of **37** _ _ _ _ _ _ _ _, specialization strengthens both the organizational and individual responses to problems; however, it is **38** _ _ _ without its downside. Specialization can lead to problems such as not **39** _ _ _ _ _ _ _ critical information. Or, it might lead to units within the same **40** _ _ _ _ _ _ _ _ _ _ _ working at cross purposes.

Answers: Part One

Section One: Clarity

1. **a.** In sentence **b**, the comma is incorrectly placed; in sentence **c**, the word *issue* is the wrong tense; and in sentence **d**, the word *citations* is singular.

2. **b.** In sentence **a**, the word *second* is not pluralized; in sentence **c**, the word *lasts* is the wrong tense; and in sentence **d**, the word *was* is not the best choice for communicating clearly. When numbers are written, one through ten are represented by words and 11 or more, generally, by the numerical.

3. **d.** Three of the four sentences indicate there was a single, male suspect. Sentence **c** lacks clarity in that number and gender are not indicated, and it lacks subject-verb agreement in tense. Likewise, sentence **a** also lacks subject-verb tense agreement. Sentence **b** is two poorly joined phrases.

4. **b.** This is the shortest, most clearly written sentence, containing the most information. It is the only sentence that tells us all the information, including the gender of the passenger.

5. **c.** In sentence **a**, the acts are written out of order. In sentence **b**, the acts are recorded out of order (*testifying* is mentioned before the oath, but the oath actually took place first) and testifying is a verb, an action, whereas testimony would be a noun. In sentence **d**, *oath* is incorrectly pluralized.

6. **a.** Sentence **b** has an incorrect form of the verb "to be." The focus of the thought is the activation of the emergency lights. In both sentences **c** and **d**, the focus shifted to the traffic stop (thus the sentences are less clear) and in **d** the form of the verb "to be" (was) is improperly conjugated.

7. **a.** All the sentences are correct. However, sentence **a** is the simplest way to state what happened.

8. **d.** In sentence **a**, the word *suspect* has an unnecessary apostrophe. Sentence **c** is too complex. In sentence **b**, a comma is missing after *questioning*.

9. **b.** Sentence **d** is too complex. Sentence **c** states that criminal justice "was" a field in sociology. In sentence **a**, criminal justice, subject of the sentence, would be most correctly stated first.

10. **c.** Sentence **a** has an unnecessary apostrophe attached to Smith. Sentence **b** converts the action word *arrived* to a noun, making the sentence ungrammatical. The word *arrived* at the end of sentence **d** is redundant.

11. **a.** The commas in sentence **a** are all correctly placed.

12. **b.** Sentence **a** is unnecessarily complex and uses "forty" where the numerical should be used. On the other hand, sentence **c** should use the word "forty" and not the numerical representation. Simply put, anytime a sentence begins with a number, that number should be represented by the word. Sentence **d** unnecessarily tells us the skid marks were left on the pavement.

13. **c.** Sentence **a** uses the wrong tense of *appear*. Sentence **b** places an unnecessary apostrophe on *Jones*. Sentence **d** lacks a comma between *shift* and *Officer*.

14. **d.** This sentence has the commas correctly placed. Additionally, sentence **b** has an unnecessary apostrophe attached to *officers*.

15. **a.** In this sentence the subject is the sergeant. What the sergeant did was correct a report. What he used was a red pen. In this instance, sentence **a** is the most correctly ordered.

Section Two: Vocabulary

16. a. To *provide* means to make available, or to *furnish*.

17. b. To *substantiate* means to establish by proof, or to *verify*.

18. d. A *variety* is a number of different types, or an *assortment* of things.

19. a. Something *significant* is of consequence; it is *important*.

20. d. *Vernacular* is the *jargon*, or the language specific to a place.

21. c. *Spontaneous* is an adjective that means resulting from a natural or *automatic* impulse.

22. b. Something *immense* could be described as extremely *large*.

23. c. A victim who is *gullible* is unsuspicious of those committing the fraud.

24. a. Something *essential* is totally *necessary*, or indispensible.

25. c. To *inform* is to impart or *disclose* information.

26. c. To *contradict* is to *disagree* with someone on a subject or matter.

27. d. A *casual* conversation would be an *informal*, unimportant one.

28. b. To *prevent* something means to *avoid* it.

29. a. To place the *blame* is the act of attributing *fault* for something.

30. b. A *mess* describes a dirty or *disordered* condition.

Section Three: Spelling

31. a. This is the proper spelling of *acquaintance*.
32. c. This is the proper spelling of *desperate*.
33. b. This is the proper spelling of *equipped*.
34. a. This is the proper spelling of *mysterious*.
35. b. This is the proper spelling of *opportunity*.
36. d. This is the proper spelling of *separation*.
37. b. This is the proper spelling of *perspiration*.

38. a. This is the proper spelling of *controversial*.
39. c. This is the proper spelling of *frantically*.
40. d. This is the proper spelling of *optimistic*.
41. c. This is the proper spelling of *loneliness*.
42. b. This is the proper spelling of *succession*.
43. c. This is the proper spelling of *elimination*.
44. b. This is the proper spelling of *explanation*.
45. d. This is the proper spelling of *weather*.

Section Four: Reading Comprehension

46. b. The passage states "work traditionally performed by uniformed officers has increasingly been given to civilian employees."

47. c. While all the choices may contain an element of truth, the main idea of the passage is that the number and responsibilities of civilian employees is growing.

48. b. The passage states "Police officers are commonly referred to as sworn employees."

49. d. The passage states "a civilian can only make an arrest for a felony if a felony has actually been committed."

50. b. Great Britain has the largest percentage of civilian employees—35%.

51. c. The FBI uses the term *agent* to describe sworn law enforcement officials.

52. a. *Legal attache* is not one of the functions outlined in the passage for civilian employees.

53. c. The passage states that the FBI has over 12,500 agents.

54. a. The passage states "federal, state, and local law enforcement agencies use the terms *police officer*, *peace officer*, *officer*, and *trooper* to describe a sworn law enforcement official whose primary duties are performed in uniform." Therefore the title of a state or local law enforcement agent *could be* peace officer.

55. a. The passage states there are "56 field offices in the United States and a presence in more than 50 countries. The FBI agent who is in charge of a field office is called the special agent in charge." There must be, therefore, at least 56 SACs.

56. d. *Missing persons* is not mentioned as an item to be included in the original nationwide database.

57. b. The passage states "By 1971, all 50 states and the District of Columbia had access to NCIC."

58. c. The passage states "each participating agency is responsible for entering, updating, and deleting its own records."

59. d. While the passage tells us how many records there were when the database began, no information is provided on the current number of records.

60. b. The passage states "the premise is that the agency that makes the entry into NCIC has the most up-to-date information." The premise is also a presumption.

Answers: Part Two

1. to
2. procedure
3. order
4. add
5. been
6. sign
7. his
8. out
9. skip
10. card
11. arrested
12. arrest
13. booking
14. officers
15. offenders
16. membership
17. police
18. fingerprinting
19. hidden
20. life
21. patrol
22. detective
23. are
24. station
25. crime
26. career
27. not
28. organization
29. become
30. civilians
31. specialization
32. reason
33. greater
34. learning
35. homicide
36. human
37. policing
38. not
39. sharing
40. organization

Scoring

Scoring this exam is identical to Practice Exam 1. Since each correct answer was worth one point, your total number of correct answers gives you your percentage. Since most police departments require a score of at least 70%, you will need to answer at least 70 questions correctly in a 100-question exam. If you did not improve your score from the earlier practice exams, try to analyze where your errors are occurring. Closely review the areas where you are having the most difficulty. Once you have completed your review, consider retaking a practice exam you have already completed before going on to a new one. Taking the same exam more than once, particularly if you separate your test taking by a few days or even a week, may provide you with a deeper understanding of where your difficulties are arising.

In addition to studying, give some thought to whether your nerves are preventing you from doing well on the practice exams. If that is the case, try to give yourself positive motivation so that you do not undermine the benefits of study by allowing yourself to become too jittery or tense before taking the practice exams. To boost your own confidence, remind yourself that the power practice exams will help you prepare for your actual test—and give you a strong advantage over those who come into the test site unprepared.

7 ▶ POLICE OFFICER PRACTICE EXAM 6

CHAPTER SUMMARY

Practice Exam 6 tests map reading, memory, judgment, common sense, reading, and math. It is similar in structure to Practice Exams 2 and 4. Compare your performance specifically with Practice Exam 2, but also with the other practice exams you have completed.

This practice exam is an example of a test that focuses on job-related skills. Even if the exam you take does not look exactly like this one, many police exams test for the same skills, so taking the exam will provide you with important practice and with an opportunity to analyze your test-taking abilities.

In addition to the pencils you will need to fill in the answer sheet, try to take this exam using an alarm clock or stopwatch. Set the timer for 15 minutes to study the memory materials that come directly after the answer sheet.

Then reset your timer for $2\frac{1}{2}$ hours, which is about the amount of time you can expect on an actual test to answer 100 questions. To do this properly, you should set aside at least $3\frac{1}{2}$ hours, including the 15-minute study time, the time for the test, and time after the test to review your answers and see where you need to continue studying.

As in the other practice tests, the study material, answer sheet, and test questions are followed by an explanation of the correct answers and information on how to score your exam.

Police Officer Practice Exam 6

1.	(a)	(b)	(c)	(d)
2.	(a)	(b)	(c)	(d)
3.	(a)	(b)	(c)	(d)
4.	(a)	(b)	(c)	(d)
5.	(a)	(b)	(c)	(d)
6.	(a)	(b)	(c)	(d)
7.	(a)	(b)	(c)	(d)
8.	(a)	(b)	(c)	(d)
9.	(a)	(b)	(c)	(d)
10.	(a)	(b)	(c)	(d)
11.	(a)	(b)	(c)	(d)
12.	(a)	(b)	(c)	(d)
13.	(a)	(b)	(c)	(d)
14.	(a)	(b)	(c)	(d)
15.	(a)	(b)	(c)	(d)
16.	(a)	(b)	(c)	(d)
17.	(a)	(b)	(c)	(d)
18.	(a)	(b)	(c)	(d)
19.	(a)	(b)	(c)	(d)
20.	(a)	(b)	(c)	(d)
21.	(a)	(b)	(c)	(d)
22.	(a)	(b)	(c)	(d)
23.	(a)	(b)	(c)	(d)
24.	(a)	(b)	(c)	(d)
25.	(a)	(b)	(c)	(d)
26.	(a)	(b)	(c)	(d)
27.	(a)	(b)	(c)	(d)
28.	(a)	(b)	(c)	(d)
29.	(a)	(b)	(c)	(d)
30.	(a)	(b)	(c)	(d)
31.	(a)	(b)	(c)	(d)
32.	(a)	(b)	(c)	(d)
33.	(a)	(b)	(c)	(d)
34.	(a)	(b)	(c)	(d)
35.	(a)	(b)	(c)	(d)

36.	(a)	(b)	(c)	(d)
37.	(a)	(b)	(c)	(d)
38.	(a)	(b)	(c)	(d)
39.	(a)	(b)	(c)	(d)
40.	(a)	(b)	(c)	(d)
41.	(a)	(b)	(c)	(d)
42.	(a)	(b)	(c)	(d)
43.	(a)	(b)	(c)	(d)
44.	(a)	(b)	(c)	(d)
45.	(a)	(b)	(c)	(d)
46.	(a)	(b)	(c)	(d)
47.	(a)	(b)	(c)	(d)
48.	(a)	(b)	(c)	(d)
49.	(a)	(b)	(c)	(d)
50.	(a)	(b)	(c)	(d)
51.	(a)	(b)	(c)	(d)
52.	(a)	(b)	(c)	(d)
53.	(a)	(b)	(c)	(d)
54.	(a)	(b)	(c)	(d)
55.	(a)	(b)	(c)	(d)
56.	(a)	(b)	(c)	(d)
57.	(a)	(b)	(c)	(d)
58.	(a)	(b)	(c)	(d)
59.	(a)	(b)	(c)	(d)
60.	(a)	(b)	(c)	(d)
61.	(a)	(b)	(c)	(d)
62.	(a)	(b)	(c)	(d)
63.	(a)	(b)	(c)	(d)
64.	(a)	(b)	(c)	(d)
65.	(a)	(b)	(c)	(d)
66.	(a)	(b)	(c)	(d)
67.	(a)	(b)	(c)	(d)
68.	(a)	(b)	(c)	(d)
69.	(a)	(b)	(c)	(d)
70.	(a)	(b)	(c)	(d)

71.	(a)	(b)	(c)	(d)
72.	(a)	(b)	(c)	(d)
73.	(a)	(b)	(c)	(d)
74.	(a)	(b)	(c)	(d)
75.	(a)	(b)	(c)	(d)
76.	(a)	(b)	(c)	(d)
77.	(a)	(b)	(c)	(d)
78.	(a)	(b)	(c)	(d)
79.	(a)	(b)	(c)	(d)
80.	(a)	(b)	(c)	(d)
81.	(a)	(b)	(c)	(d)
82.	(a)	(b)	(c)	(d)
83.	(a)	(b)	(c)	(d)
84.	(a)	(b)	(c)	(d)
85.	(a)	(b)	(c)	(d)
86.	(a)	(b)	(c)	(d)
87.	(a)	(b)	(c)	(d)
88.	(a)	(b)	(c)	(d)
89.	(a)	(b)	(c)	(d)
90.	(a)	(b)	(c)	(d)
91.	(a)	(b)	(c)	(d)
92.	(a)	(b)	(c)	(d)
93.	(a)	(b)	(c)	(d)
94.	(a)	(b)	(c)	(d)
95.	(a)	(b)	(c)	(d)
96.	(a)	(b)	(c)	(d)
97.	(a)	(b)	(c)	(d)
98.	(a)	(b)	(c)	(d)
99.	(a)	(b)	(c)	(d)
100.	(a)	(b)	(c)	(d)

Practice Exam 6

Section One: Memorization and Visualization

You have 15 minutes to study the memory material at the beginning of the exam before starting the practice test, which begins with questions about what you have memorized.

The memory questions are divided into two distinct forms of memorization. The first part contains wanted posters and the second part is an article on law enforcement concerns about the dangers of text messaging while driving. After reviewing the posters and reading the article for a total of 15 minutes for both sections, turn the page and answer the test questions about the material. To create the same conditions as the actual test, **do not refer back to the study booklet to answer the questions**.

You have two options when you complete Part One. If you want to continue to create actual test conditions, go directly on to the rest of the test. If you are curious about how well you answered these questions, review the answers for this portion before continuing with the rest of the exam.

WANTED

Peter Thomas Anderson

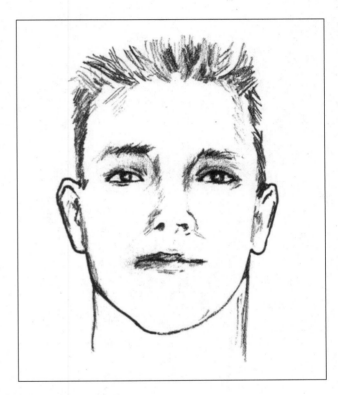

ALIASES: Pete, Tom
WANTED BY: Nassau County, NY Sheriff's Department
CHARGES: Attempted murder
DESCRIPTION:
Age: 19
Race: White
Height: 6′1″
Weight: 155 lbs.
Hair: Blond
Eyes: Blue

IDENTIFYING SCARS OR MARKS: Tattoo of a naked woman on left forearm.
REMARKS: Fired at coworker after an argument. Tall and thin. Walks with a limp.

WANTED

James Michael Thompson

ALIASES: Jim Michelson
WANTED BY: Philadelphia, PA Police Department
CHARGES: Assault with a deadly weapon

DESCRIPTION:
Age: 32
Race: Black
Height: 5'10"
Weight: 180 lbs.
Hair: Brown
Eyes: Brown

IDENTIFYING SCARS OR MARKS: Tattoo of a sun on left forearm and scar above left eye.
REMARKS: Stabbed a fellow resident of a homeless shelter after an argument over who would shower first.
CAUTION: Known to carry a knife and has a history of mental illness.

WANTED

Aaron Jay Johnson

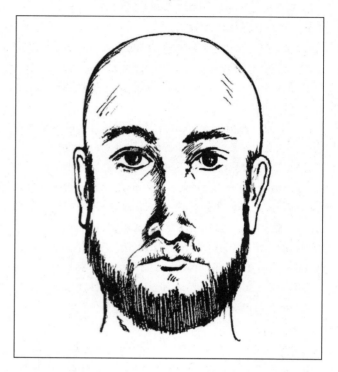

ALIASES: Ray, Joe-Joe
WANTED BY: Newark, NJ Police Department
CHARGES: Rape, attempted rape

DESCRIPTION:
Age: 27
Race: White
Height: 6'0"
Weight: 175 lbs.
Hair: Bald
Eyes: Green

IDENTIFYING SCARS OR MARKS: Scar on right side of neck. Wears a beard and is bald.
REMARKS: Raped three college students walking to their cars between 8 and 10 P.M. Attempted a fourth rape at 11 P.M., but was interrupted by campus security officer.

WANTED

Jose Juan Suarez

ALIASES: Juan Suarez
WANTED BY: Los Angeles County, CA Police Department
CHARGES: Robbery, assault

DESCRIPTION:
Age: 40
Race: Hispanic
Height: 5′6″
Weight: 215 lbs.
Hair: Brown
Eyes: Brown

IDENTIFYING SCARS OR MARKS: Tattoo of an eagle on right bicep.
REMARKS: Wanted for robbing two women working alone on the overnight shifts at convenience stores in rural areas.
CAUTION: Known to carry a .57 caliber gun.

WANTED

William Kirk Ericson

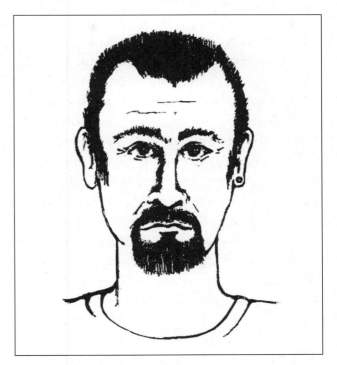

ALIASES: Bill, Captain Kirk
WANTED BY: El Dorado, TX Police Department
CHARGES: Burglary

DESCRIPTION:
Age: 32
Race: White
Height: 6′3″
Weight: 195 lbs.
Hair: Black
Eyes: Brown

IDENTIFYING SCARS OR MARKS: Tattoo of a spaceship on right bicep. Wears an earring in left ear.
REMARKS: Breaks into homes in the suburbs during the day when no one is home. Breaks the glass of a back door.
CAUTION: Known to carry a .38 caliber gun.

Reading Passage

Speeding is a social issue that affects anyone who is a driver or passenger in any type of motor vehicle—whether personal or public. Speeding is one of the most commonly violated laws in the United States. When a driver is late for school or work, or simply wants to arrive at a destination faster, he or she will speed. In some places it can feel as though a person is expected to speed. In many states it is almost guaranteed that if you are driving at the posted speed limit on a major roadway you will be honked at or tailgated or drivers will give you any number of rude gestures as they go around you and speed past. Approximately 13,000 people die each year from car crashes related to speeding. Speeders include drivers who travel above the posted speed limit as well as drivers who travel at inappropriate speeds for the road conditions. There are numerous situations in which driving slower than the posted speed limit is appropriate, such as where there are many pedestrians present, where the road is damaged, or in adverse weather conditions when visibility may be poor or the road surface is slippery or wet. But justifications for speeding are few.

Research has shown that a number of factors can predict who is most likely to speed and when speeding is most likely to occur. Income has been found to be related to patterns of speeding. Individuals who make less money or are paid an hourly wage are less likely to speed. It is hypothesized that people with lower incomes speed less often than their wealthier counterparts because they cannot afford the consequences of speeding—both the monetary punishment and the lost time sitting on the side of the road as the officer writes a ticket. In order to further deterrence goals, some have recommended that fines should be proportional to a person's income. Hence, a wealthier person would pay substantially more for the same speeding violation than would a person with a lower income.

Another factor related to speeding is an individual's type and color of car. People who drive sportier cars are more likely to speed than are those who drive sedans. For example, a person who drives a Saturn station wagon is less likely to speed than is someone driving a Porsche. This is not to say that the Saturn driver will never speed, just that the car type is weakly correlated with speeding when compared to a sports car. Another factor that has been found to have a minor relationship is the color of a person's car. Not surprisingly, people with cars that are brightly colored, such as red or yellow, are more likely to speed, followed by people with black cars; people driving white or beige cars have been found to be least likely to speed.

Age and gender also have been found to influence a person's likelihood of speeding. Drivers 25 years old and younger receive more tickets than older people. It is hypothesized that younger drivers are more likely to be fearless and want to express their sense of freedom. Since younger drivers are not as skilled as experienced drivers, they are more likely to cause accidents, especially when they speed. Increased numbers of accidents are also associated with people over the age of 65. In terms of gender, males comprise the vast majority of people caught speeding. Approximately 80% of drivers who receive tickets for speeding are male. Interestingly, the number of females caught speeding increases every year.

Several related social issues also contribute to the problem of speeding. The capability of cars to go faster and faster increases with each new model year. In addition, as the cost of public transportation increases while services are cut and quality decreases, more Americans are using their personal vehicles to get around. With a greater number of cars on roads that have not been improved at a pace to accommodate these vehicles, the potential for danger and even death increases. In an effort to increase safety, some people have suggested implementing laws that require people to take driving tests periodically. Others want to see mandatory revocation of licenses when a person turns a certain age or cannot reasonably pass a vision test. As the United States population ages, these proposals may get more attention. However, suggesting policies to revoke a person's driver's license is not a politically popular idea. And as is commonly known, older people are more likely to vote than are younger people.

One of the largest problems with speeding is developing successful means to stop it. According to one research group, there are four points that are most influential on speeding.

1. Appropriate speed limits, based on the nature of the road, will decrease speeding. A straight road that goes through a rural area should have a reasonably higher speed limit than a curved road on a major city highway.
2. The design of the road also influences the likelihood that a person will speed. For example, drivers are more likely to speed on a straight and wide flat road than on a narrower road surrounded by trees. The trees create a sense of being in a tight space, which has been found to decrease speeding. However, an issue with narrower roads lined with trees is that when an accident does occur there is more likely to be injury to a driver.
3. The third factor is to increase the number of signs that indicate the speed limit on a road. It is not helpful for a driver to go miles without seeing a speed limit sign.
4. Finally, it is believed that if more people were caught speeding, fewer would do it. However, with so many drivers on the road, there are simply not enough law enforcement personnel to catch even half of all speeders. Using technology, such as cameras, can supplement the presence of human efforts, but the technology is flawed. The accuracy of these cameras is still being debated.

Section One: Memorization and Visualization

Answer questions 1 through 15 based on the wanted posters you have just studied. Do not refer back to the study material to answer these questions.

1. How many individuals were described as having tattoos?
   a. one
   b. two
   c. three
   d. four

2. Which individual walks with a limp?
   a. James Thompson
   b. Aaron Johnson
   c. Peter Anderson
   d. Jose Suarez

3. How many individuals were described as known to be armed?
   a. one
   b. two
   c. three
   d. four

4. How many people were described as being Hispanic?
   a. one
   b. two
   c. three
   d. four

5. Which individual was pictured wearing an earring?
   a. James Thompson
   b. Aaron Johnson
   c. Jose Suarez
   d. William Ericson

6. How many individuals were described as being shorter than six feet tall?
   a. one
   b. two
   c. three
   d. four

7. Who was described as being bald?
   a. Aaron Johnson
   b. Peter Anderson
   c. William Ericson
   d. James Thompson

8. How many individuals were described as having a scar?
   a. two
   b. three
   c. four
   d. five

9. Who fired a gun at a coworker?
   a. James Thomson
   b. Juan Suarez
   c. Peter Anderson
   d. William Ericson

10. How many individuals were described as in their 30s?
   a. one
   b. two
   c. three
   d. four

11. Who is being sought for rape and attempted rape?
   a. Aaron Johnson
   b. James Thompson
   c. William Ericson
   d. Jose Suarez

12. Which individual is known to carry a knife?
   a. William Ericson
   b. Jose Suarez
   c. James Thompson
   d. Aaron Johnson

13. How many individuals are pictured with facial hair?
   a. two
   b. three
   c. four
   d. five

14. Who is wanted for burglary?
   a. James Thompson
   b. Peter Anderson
   c. William Ericson
   d. Jose Suarez

15. How many individuals were described as being wanted for an offense against females?
   a. one
   b. two
   c. three
   d. four

Answer questions 16 through 30 based on the reading passage. Do not refer back to the study material to answer these questions.

16. Which of the following is the best title for the reading passage?
   a. *Issues Surrounding Texting and Driving*
   b. *New York and New Jersey Speeders*
   c. *Issues Surrounding Speeding*
   d. *Federal Laws Regulate Speeding*

17. Approximately how many people die each year as a result of car crashes?
   a. 3,000
   b. 13,000
   c. 31,000
   d. 33,000

18. According to the passage, what are two groups of people more likely to speed?
   a. younger people and older people
   b. people who wear glasses and people who wear contact lenses
   c. females and younger people
   d. people in their car alone and people late for work

19. What is one consistently successful response to speeding?
   a. building wider roads
   b. installing technology inside cars to limit maximum speed
   c. building roads lined with metal barriers
   d. the use of cameras on roads

20. How many states currently require people to retake their driver's license test when they turn 65 years of age?
   a. 0
   b. 10
   c. 12
   d. 15

21. According to the passage, what is one of the most commonly broken laws related to driving?
   a. using the phone while driving
   b. driving in unsafe weather conditions
   c. speeding
   d. texting while driving

22. According to the passage, people who drive cars of two specific colors are more likely to speed. What are those colors?
   a. white and beige
   b. gray and silver
   c. black and white
   d. red and yellow

23. According to the passage, approximately what percentage of people caught speeding are male?
   a. 20%
   b. 30%
   c. 50%
   d. 80%

24. According to the passage, what is one reason to drive slower than the posted speed limit?
   a. the presence of large vehicles on the road
   b. the presence of many pedestrians
   c. the presence of cameras
   d. the presence of law enforcement personnel

25. According to the passage, what is one suggestion to reduce speeding?
   a. paying a fine proportional to one's income
   b. sentencing people to community service rather than paying a fine
   c. installing speed-limiting technology in speeders' vehicles
   d. building more roads

26. Which of the following was not mentioned in the passage as a factor that contributes to speeding?
   a. age
   b. income
   c. level of education
   d. gender

27. According to the passage, what is the group that each year is increasingly getting more tickets?
  a. younger people
  b. females
  c. older people
  d. wealthy people

28. According to the passage, what is one of the effects of lining roads with trees?
  a. an increased number of cars on those roads
  b. an increased rate of speeding on those roads
  c. an increased rate of injury when accidents occur
  d. an increased rate of drivers hitting wildlife

29. According to the passage, law enforcement is able to catch how many speeders?
  a. fewer than half of speeders
  b. greater than half of speeders
  c. the majority of speeders
  d. most speeders

30. According to the passage, what is a factor that prevents the mandatory revocation of a driver's license when a person turns a certain age?
  a. a federal ban
  b. the decisions of courts
  c. funding
  d. politics

Section Two: Reading Skills

Map 1

Answer questions 31 through 38 based on Map 1. Review the directional arrows and the map key. You are not permitted to go the wrong way on a one-way street.

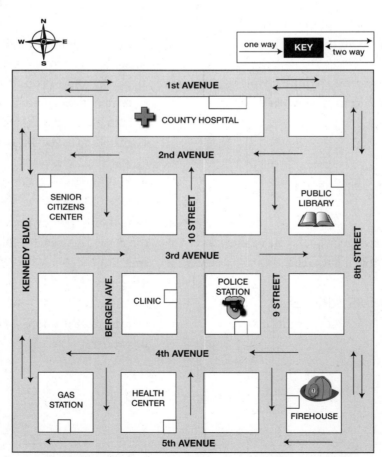

31. You are transporting an arrestee from the police station, exiting onto 4th Avenue, to the county hospital. Taking the most direct legal route, which building will you NOT pass?
a. clinic
b. senior citizens center
c. firehouse
d. gas station

32. A library patron decides to get gas before returning home. She exits the library garage directly onto 8th Street. The most direct legal route to the gas station is
a. south on 8th Street, then west on 5th Avenue.
b. north on 8th Street, then west on 5th Avenue.
c. south on 8th Street, then west on 4th Avenue.
d. north on 8th Street, then west on 2nd Avenue.

33. Dr. Ranjan works at the county hospital and needs to see a patient at the health center. She wants to avoid the traffic on the two-way streets of 8th Street and Kennedy Boulevard. She exits the hospital directly onto 1st Avenue. The most direct legal route to the health center is
a. south on 9th Street, then west on 4th Avenue.
b. south on 9th Street, then east on 3rd Avenue.
c. east on 1st Avenue, south on 9th Street, then west on 5th Avenue.
d. south on Bergen Avenue then east on 5th Avenue.

34. A member of the senior citizens center needs to be rushed to the county hospital. Exiting directly onto 2nd Avenue, the most direct legal route is
a. south on Kennedy Boulevard, then east on 1st Avenue.
b. north on Kennedy Boulevard, then east on 1st Avenue.
c. north on Kennedy Boulevard, then west on 1st Avenue.
d. south on Kennedy Boulevard, then east on 1st Avenue.

35. You and your partner are dispatched to a shooting at the gas station. Exiting directly onto 4th Avenue, the most direct legal route is
a. north on Bergen Avenue, then south on Kennedy Boulevard.
b. south on Bergen Avenue, then east on 5th Avenue.
c. north on 10th Street, then west on 4th Avenue.
d. south on Bergen Avenue, then west on 5th Avenue.

36. A fire is reported at the public library. The fire engines exit the firehouse directly onto 9th Street. The most direct legal route to the library is
a. west on 5th Avenue, north on 10th Street, east on 3rd Avenue, then north on 8th Street.
b. west on 5th Avenue, north on 10th Street, west on 9th Street, then south on 8th Street.
c. east on 5th Avenue, south on 8th Street, east on 9th Street, then north on 8th Street.
d. west on 5th Avenue, north on 10th Street, east on 2nd Avenue, then west on 1st Avenue.

37. You and your partner are posted at the corner of 8th Street and 1st Avenue. A man approaches you and asks you the most direct route to walk to the health center. You should tell him to walk

a. south on 8th Street, then east on 5th Avenue.

b. south on 8th Street, then west on 5th Avenue.

c. north on 8th Street, then west on 5th Avenue.

d. north on 8th Street, then east on 5th Avenue.

38. How many roadways on the map are designated one-way (streets, avenues, boulevards, or lanes)?

a. 3

b. 4

c. 5

d. 6

Map 2

Answer questions 39 through 45 based on Map 2. Review the directional arrows and the map key. You are not permitted to go the wrong way on a one-way street.

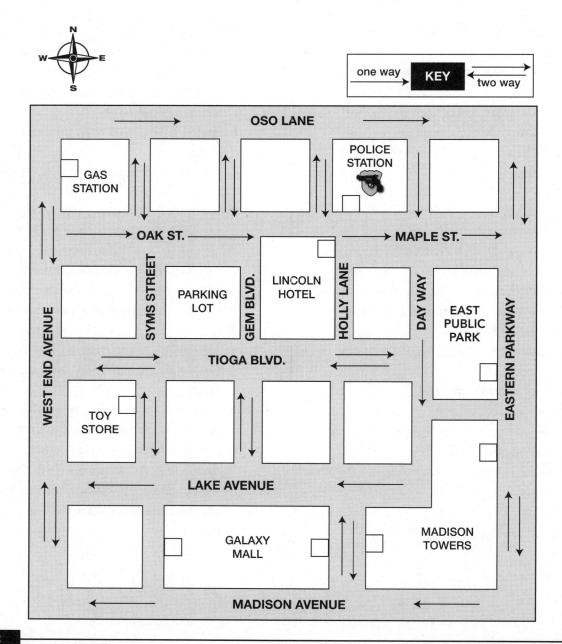

39. Officers Andrews and Pedro are patrolling East Public Park when they are dispatched to the Galaxy Mall to respond to a report of shots fired. They exit the park onto Eastern Parkway. The most direct legal route to the mall is
   a. east on Madison Avenue, then south on Holly Lane.
   b. south on Eastern Parkway, west on Madison Avenue, then north on Holly Lane.
   c. south on Day Way, then east on Lake Avenue.
   d. south on Day Way, then west on Lake Avenue.

40. How many roadways are designated on the map as two-way (streets, avenues, boulevards, or lanes)?
   a. 3
   b. 4
   c. 5
   d. 6

41. How many avenues are designated on the map as one-way?
   a. 1
   b. 2
   c. 3
   d. 4

42. You are on foot patrol in front of the Lincoln Hotel on Holly Lane when a tourist approaches you and asks you the most direct way to walk to the toy store. You tell him to go
   a. south on Holly Lane, west on Lake Avenue, then north on Syms Street.
   b. west on Maple Street, south on Gem Boulevard, then east on Tioga Boulevard.
   c. south on Holly Lane, east on Lake Avenue, then north on Syms Street.
   d. east on Oak Street, south on Gem Boulevard, then west on Lake Avenue.

43. Two paramedics are sitting in their ambulance in front of the east entrance of Madison Towers when they get a call about an injured child in the parking lot. The most direct legal route is
   a. north on Eastern Parkway, west on Oso Lane, then south on Syms Street.
   b. south on Eastern parkway, west on Tioga Boulevard, then north on Syms Street.
   c. south on Eastern Parkway, west on Madison Avenue, then north on Syms Street.
   d. north on Eastern Parkway, east on Oso Lane, then south on Gem Boulevard.

44. You just filled your patrol car with gas at the gas station and have been called to a disturbance at the Lincoln Hotel. You exit the gas station directly onto West End Avenue. The most direct legal route is
   a. north on West End Avenue, west on Tioga Boulevard, then south on Day Way.
   b. north on West End Avenue, east on Oso Lane, then south on Holly Lane.
   c. south on West End Avenue, west on Oak Street, then south on Gem Boulevard.
   d. south on West End Avenue, east on Tioga Boulevard, then north on Holly Lane.

45. You and your partner are dispatched from the police station to a call of domestic violence at the Madison Towers. You were instructed to use the west entrance. You exit onto Maple Street. The most direct legal route is
   a. south on Eastern Parkway, east on Madison Avenue, then west on Lake Avenue.
   b. north on Eastern Parkway, west on Tioga Boulevard, then south on Holly Lane.
   c. north on Eastern Parkway, west on Lake Avenue, then south on Holly Lane.
   d. south on Eastern parkway, west on Madison Avenue, then north on Holly Lane.

Reading Passage 1

Read the following passage, then answer questions 46 through 52.

People rely on law enforcement officers to protect them against crime. At the same time, though, the public is exposed to stories of police misconduct. Officers have been accused of being racist, sexist, and corrupt. If citizens do not believe law enforcement can provide equal protection for all, then tension will arise. Members of the public may not trust law enforcement and may not report crimes or help law enforcement solve crimes or pursue offenders.

Research has explored the influence of demographic and situational variables on types of police suspicion of members of the general public. Researchers have examined whether a minority suspect is more likely to be viewed suspiciously by the police for non-behavioral reasons, such as style of dress. They also examined whether minority status plays a significant role in the decision to stop and question suspicious persons. Researchers observed police officers to examine how they formed suspicions and the reasons underlying their decisions to stop citizens. The researchers found that minority status does influence an officer's decision to form non-behavioral suspicion, but they also found that minority status does not influence decisions to stop and question citizens. The results showed that with the exception of race, other demographic variables did not play an important role in forming non-behavioral suspicion.

46. Which of the following would be the best title for this passage?
   a. *Citizen Perception and Law Enforcement Reality*
   b. *A Ride-Along with Law Enforcement*
   c. *Stories of Police Misconduct*
   d. *The Correlation of Style of Dress and Police Suspicion*

47. According to the passage, law enforcement officers have been accused of being
   a. overweight.
   b. lazy.
   c. racist.
   d. slow to respond.

48. Which of the following is mentioned in the article as a non-behavioral reason that researchers have examined that may cause a law enforcement officer to develop suspicion?
   a. the color of a person's shoes
   b. the way a person walks
   c. a person's hairstyle
   d. the way a person is dressed

49. The researchers found that
   a. minority status does not influence an officer's decision to form non-behavioral suspicion.
   b. minority status does influence an officer's decision to form non-behavioral suspicion.
   c. minority status does not influence an officer's decision to arrest a person.
   d. minority status does influence an officer's decision to arrest a person.

50. Researchers also found that
  a. minority status does influence decisions to stop and question citizens.
  b. gender influences decisions to frisk a person for weapons.
  c. minority status does not influence decisions to stop and question citizens.
  d. minority status does not influence decisions to arrive late to a call for assistance.

51. What is one result of citizens not trusting law enforcement?
  a. Citizens may not report crimes or help law enforcement solve crimes and pursue offenders.
  b. Citizens may protest against law enforcement.
  c. Citizens may disrespect law enforcement.
  d. Citizens may commit more crimes to insult the abilities of law enforcement officers.

52. Research has explored the influence of
  a. gender of the officer on the development of suspect suspicion.
  b. age of the suspect on the development of suspect suspicion.
  c. gender of the suspect on the development of suspicion.
  d. demographic and situational variables on the development of police suspicion.

Reading Passage 2

Read the following passage, then answer questions 53 through 60.

Law enforcement officers are assumed to have one of the most dangerous and stressful occupations. Anecdotal as well as research findings seem to support this idea. But the stress law enforcement officers face is multifaceted and, as a result, the coping mechanisms used differ from problem to problem and officer to officer. It is assumed that law enforcement officers rely on alcohol and tobacco to cope with stress. They are also known for having higher rates of domestic violence and rates of divorce.

Prior to discussing law enforcement officer stress, it is necessary to define stress. Most commonly, stress is regarded as a response of the body to any demand placed on it. Each person responds differently to internal and external demands of life, but each person does experience what can be regarded as stress. And while officers undergo extensive training for the proper procedures for negotiation, self-defense, and problem solving, learning these skills does not generally prepare officers for career-related stress. Today law enforcement officers have more support for dealing with stress than officers on the job in the past. Today programs exist that provide avenues for officers to express their emotions and vent their stress. Often, these programs consist of call-in hotlines that are operated by former law enforcement officers who have experienced similar anxiety, depression, or even post-traumatic stress disorder (PTSD). These types of hotlines offer officers a way to reach out to someone who has had similar experiences.

Arguably, the worst outcome of police stress is officer suicide. Statistics show that twice as many officers die at their own hand than in the line of duty. Officers who have been interviewed about suicide attempts have mentioned the horrible things they are forced to see each day coupled with the strong image they are expected to present. They often feel as if they are expected to be supermen.

53. What would be the best title for this passage?
  a. *Higher Divorce Rates among Law Enforcement Officers*
  b. *Law Enforcement Officer Stress and Coping Methods*
  c. *Post-Traumatic Stress Disorder and Law Enforcement Officers*
  d. *Suicide and Policing*

54. According to the passage, law enforcement officer stress is
  a. different from officer to officer.
  b. generally similar between officers.
  c. on the decline.
  d. rising each year.

55. According to the passage, law enforcement officers receive training in
  a. self-defense.
  b. negotiation.
  c. problem solving.
  d. all of the above.

56. Based on the passage, which of the following statements can be concluded as true?
  a. The suicide rate among police offficers is higher now than it was 30 years ago.
  b. In the past, there were fewer programs to help police officers cope with on-the-job stress.
  c. Police officers are less likely to remarry after a divorce.
  d. Movie portrayals of police officers are often highly inaccurate.

57. According to the passage, a common model of programs that are designed to assist law enforcement officers in coping with their stress is
  a. individual psychotherapy.
  b. group therapy.
  c. call-in phone hotlines.
  d. There are no programs designed to assist officers with their stress.

58. One of the reasons current programs aimed at combating officer stress are successful is that
  a. the services are free.
  b. the services are offered by males only.
  c. officers receive pay for utilizing the services.
  d. the services are offered by former law enforcement officers.

59. Statistics show law enforcement stress has created a situation that has
  a. led to more officers committing suicide than dying in the line of duty.
  b. led to more officers quitting the job.
  c. led to fewer people applying to become law enforcement officers.
  d. led to increased tension with the public.

60. According to the passage, factors that contribute to officer suicide include
  a. low pay.
  b. lack of family support.
  c. exposure to horrific scenes.
  d. access to firearms.

Section Three: Judgment and Problem Solving

These questions ask you to use good judgment and common sense, along with the information provided, to answer each of the questions. Some passages may be followed by more than one question pertaining to the same set of facts.

Read the following information, then answer questions 61 and 62.

Officer Jeremy is stationed in her patrol car three blocks away from the local supermarket when she receives a radio dispatch call concerning a shooting. Based on the information she receives, she responds to the scene and calls for an ambulance while beginning to identify and question witnesses to the shooting. Her scratch sheet on this case reads as follows:

Date of occurrence:	March 27, 2011
Time of occurrence:	Approximately 10: 00 P.M.
Place of occurrence:	Europa Market
Reporting person:	Elizabeth James
Victim:	Oliver Valez
Disposition:	Mr. Valez found shot on the floor of the market, and taken to Palisade General Hospital by ambulance. There was one shopper at the time and no employees of the store; the shopper was questioned as a witness.

61. Of the following assumptions you might make based on the fact pattern, which is most likely to be accurate based on the material provided?
   a. Locating witnesses will be difficult.
   b. Mr. Valez was shot for debts he owed to a grocery supplier.
   c. An employee of the store shot Mr. Valez out of revenge.
   d. Elizabeth Jones was shopping in the store at the time of the shooting.

62. Of the following assumptions you might make based on the fact pattern, which is most likely to be accurate based on the material provided?
   a. Mr. Valez's store was being robbed.
   b. Elizabeth James was an accomplice to the offender.
   c. Mr. Valez shot back at the offender.
   d. Elizabeth James will never shop at the Europa market again.

Read the following information, then answer questions 63 and 64.

Last month, Officer Cameron had more arrests than Officers Ament and Scalzo. Officer Ament had more arrests than Officer Gurick but fewer than Officer Scalzo.

63. Given the information provided, which officer most likely had the fewest arrests?
   a. Officer Cameron
   b. Officer Ament
   c. Officer Gurick
   d. Officer Scalzo

64. Given the information provided, which officer had the most arrests?
   a. Officer Cameron
   b. Officer Ament
   c. Officer Gurick
   d. Officer Scalzo

Read the following information, then answer questions 65 through 67.

Police Officers Cho and Matthews were dispatched to investigate a report of attempted rape. They obtained the following information:

Date: July 11, 2011
Victim: Diana Sampson
Suspect: Joseph Edwards, the victim's landlord
Disposition: Suspect arrested

65. Officer Matthews is writing up the crime report. Which of the following expresses the information most clearly and accurately?
  a. During an argument about the end of their romantic relationship, the suspect, Joseph Edwards, attempted to rape the victim, Diana Sampson.
  b. During an argument about the payment of rent, the suspect, Joseph Edwards, attempted to rape the victim, Diana Sampson.
  c. Joseph Edwards, the suspect, was stalking his tenant, Diana Sampson, and attempted to rape her on July 11, 2011.
  d. On July 11, 2011 Joseph Edwards, the landlord of the victim, Diana Sampson, was arrested on charges of attempting to rape her.

66. Which of the following is an *incorrect* assumption based on the material provided?
  a. Joseph Edwards is the landlord of Diana Sampson.
  b. Diana Sampson is married to Joseph Edwards.
  c. Joseph Edwards attempted to rape Diana Sampson on July 11, 2011.
  d. none of the above is incorrect

67. Which of the following is a correct assumption based on the material provided?
  a. Diana Sampson is divorced from Joseph Edwards.
  b. Joseph Edwards was hired by another person to rape Diana Sampson.
  c. Diana Sampson rented a home from Joseph Edwards.
  d. Joseph Edwards has raped his tenants before.

Read the following information, then answer questions 68 and 69.

In the K-9 Division, Officer Rodriguez is partnered with Tioga, Officer Mattice is partnered with Roscoe, Officer Dobson is partnered with Emma, Officer Vedder is partnered with Sparky, and Officer Jenson is partnered with Sasha.

68. If Officer Rodriguez switches partners with Officer Mattice and Officer Mattice switches with Officer Vedder, who is Officer Mattice's new partner?
  a. Sasha
  b. Tioga
  c. Sparky
  d. Emma

69. If Officer Vedder switches partners with Officer Dobson and Officer Dobson switches with Officer Jenson, who is Officer Dobson's new partner?
  a. Sasha
  b. Tioga
  c. Emma
  d. Roscoe

Read the following information, then answer questions 70 and 71.

Burglary happens when a person unlawfully breaks into and enters a domicile with the intent to commit a felony within.

70. Which situation is the best example of burglary?
   a. John, a homeless person, enters an empty summer home through an open window in order to find shelter for the night.
   b. Eric is a representative from the electric company. He convinces the homeowner he needs to check something in the house. He asks her for a glass of water and when she leaves the room he notices a $100 bill on the dresser, which he takes.
   c. Jane uses a hammer to smash the window of a house's back door, enters the home, and takes as much jewelry and cash as she can find.
   d. Pete enters an empty home through an open window. He makes himself a sandwich and watches cable TV. He showers before he leaves.

71. Based on the definition, two required elements of burglary are:
   a. knowledge and behavior
   b. conduct and intent
   c. conduct and ignorance
   d. none of the above

Read the following information, then answer questions 72 through 74.

Professor Latzer provides his criminal law class with the following information: Assault is a less serious crime than rape. Rape is a more serious crime than extortion, but less serious than homicide, and extortion is more serious than assault. Assault is more serious than petty theft. Petty theft is less serious than burglary.

72. Which crime is the most serious according to the above?
   a. homicide
   b. assault
   c. extortion
   d. burglary

73. Which crime is the least serious according to the above?
   a. rape
   b. assault
   c. petty theft
   d. burglary

74. Which crime is the second most serious according to the above?
   a. rape
   b. assault
   c. extortion
   d. burglary

Read the following passage, then answer questions 75 through 83.

At approximately 9:30 A.M. on a rainy morning, Irving Greenberg of 127 Madison Avenue called his local police department to report a vehicle accident on Madison Avenue near Gorge Road. He said he had just arrived home when he heard a collision while he stood in the kitchen washing dishes. When Officer Fischer arrived on the scene at 9:40 A.M., she observed two vehicles that appeared to have been involved in the collision. She also observed that the passenger in a red sedan that appeared to have been involved in the collision appeared to be unconscious. She checked the injured passenger of the other vehicle, a gray pickup truck, who was bleeding from the head, and covered him with a blanket that was provided by Mr. Greenberg. She then notified the dispatcher to send two ambulances and additional backup officers to the scene. Susana Isly of 555 Gorge Road, the driver of the red sedan, identified the passenger as Raymond Holland, her neighbor, who resided at 557 Gorge Road.

The ambulance arrived at 9:52 A.M. One minute later, three additional officers arrived, including Lieutenant Waynes, who became the senior officer at the scene. She assigned officers Fischer and Lane to block off both streets and control local traffic and Officer Gasper to examine the skid marks on Gorge Road. Isly told Waynes that she had stopped at the corner of Gorge Road and then turned right onto Madison Avenue. Isly further explained that the rear of the vehicle in which she was driving was struck by the pickup truck, which was skidding down Madison. The impact caused Isly's vehicle to spin and hit a tree on the lawn of 129 Madison Avenue. The driver of the gray pickup truck, Mike Jakes, stated that he lost control of the vehicle when he attempted to stop at the intersection, but he was not speeding. After checking with Waynes and Gasper, Fischer issued Jakes citations for speeding, failing to obey a stop sign, and driving with an expired license.

75. Which vehicle had been traveling on Madison Avenue prior to the accident?
   a. the red sedan
   b. the gray pickup truck
   c. the ambulance
   d. the sedan and the pickup truck

76. Who examined the evidence relating to Mike Jakes's claim that he lost control of the vehicle?
   a. Lieutenant Waynes
   b. Officer Fischer
   c. Officer Gasper
   d. Officer Lane

77. What can be concluded about the Madison Avenue–Gorge Road intersection?
   a. There is a stop sign at the intersection.
   b. Madison Avenue is a one-way street.
   c. Gorge Road is a one-way street.
   d. none of the above

78. Based on Isly's report that the rear of her car was hit after she made a right onto Madison, we can assume the pickup truck was traveling in what direction?
   a. east
   b. north
   c. west
   d. It is not possible to be sure in what direction the pickup truck was driving.

79. Who would have been taken away or checked by the paramedics?
   a. the passenger in the red sedan and the passenger in the gray pickup truck
   b. the driver of the red sedan and the passenger in the gray pickup truck
   c. the passenger in the red sedan and the driver of the gray pickup truck
   d. the drivers of both vehicles

80. Which of the following is the most likely factor that led to the accident?
- **a.** The driver of the red sedan was drunk.
- **b.** The passenger in the red sedan distracted the driver.
- **c.** The gray pickup truck was being driven on a slippery road.
- **d.** The driver of the gray pickup truck was driving with an expired license.

81. What additional citation could the driver of the gray pickup truck have been issued?
- **a.** having a cracked windshield
- **b.** giving false information in a traffic investigation
- **c.** verbally assaulting the driver of the red sedan
- **d.** attempted murder of the passenger of his car

82. Which vehicle had been traveling on Gorge Road prior to the accident?
- **a.** the red sedan
- **b.** the gray pickup truck
- **c.** the ambulance
- **d.** the sedan and the pickup truck

83. Which scenario best describes the order in which the accident occurred?
- **a.** The red sedan hit the gray pickup truck, which hit the tree.
- **b.** The gray pickup truck hit the red sedan, which then hit the tree.
- **c.** The red sedan hit the gray pickup truck and the red sedan hit the tree.
- **d.** The gray pickup truck hit the tree and spun out of control and hit the red sedan.

Read the following information, then answer questions 84 through 86.

After arresting a person, officers should conduct a search for weapons and contraband by performing the following:

1. Make sure the prisoner's hands are handcuffed securely behind his or her back.
2. Check the waistband area within reach of the prisoner's handcuffed hands.
3. Check the prisoner's cap or hat.
4. Check the neck area and both arms.
5. Check the prisoner's front pockets.
6. Check the inseam of the pants and crotch area.
7. Check the legs and ankles.
8. Check the prisoner's shoes.

84. Officer Thomas arrests a woman for stealing a shopping cart. She is wearing jeans, red sneakers, and a black sweater. The officer cuffed the suspect and began checking the suspect's pockets. What should Officer Thomas have done instead, after cuffing the suspect?
- **a.** Check the inseam of the pants and crotch area.
- **b.** Check her legs and ankles.
- **c.** Check the waistband area within reach of the suspect's handcuffed hands.
- **d.** Check the suspect's neck area and both arms.

85. Officer Markus arrests a man for loitering outside a school. He is wearing a gray sweatshirt, khaki slacks, blue cap, and black sneakers. The officer cuffs the suspect, makes sure his hands are secured, and then checks his waistband. What should Officer Markus do next?
- **a.** Check his front pockets.
- **b.** Check under his hat.
- **c.** Check his shoes.
- **d.** Check his legs and ankles.

86. Officer Pilgrim arrests a man for public intoxication and vandalism. He is wearing a green shirt and jeans and is barefoot. The officer cuffs the suspect and makes sure his hands are securely behind his back. What is the last thing Officer Pilgrim should do?
   a. Check the waistband of the suspect's pants.
   b. Check under his hat.
   c. Check his shoes.
   d. Check his legs and ankles.

Read the following information, then answer questions 87 through 90.

Officer Nelson has been a police officer for 10 years, which is 4 years fewer than Officer Wilson but 6 more than Officer Osh. Officer Anderson has been a police officer for 7 years more than Officer Osh.

87. How many years has Officer Osh been a police officer?
   a. 14
   b. 10
   c. 7
   d. 4

88. Which officer has been a police officer for the most years?
   a. Officer Wilson
   b. Officer Anderson
   c. Officer Osh
   d. Officer Nelson

89. Which officer has been a police officer for the fewest years?
   a. Officer Wilson
   b. Officer Anderson
   c. Officer Osh
   d. Officer Nelson

90. Which officer has served for 11 years?
   a. Officer Wilson
   b. Officer Anderson
   c. Officer Osh
   d. Officer Nelson

91. Officer Manson is on a motorcycle pursuing a speeding vehicle. As the suspect and Officer Manson reach 68th Street, the suspect makes a sharp right turn. Officer Manson makes the turn too fast and the motorcycle slides out from under him. He runs over to the bike. What should he do next?
   a. Turn off the ignition.
   b. Stand the bike up and continue the pursuit.
   c. Call for backup.
   d. Call in a description of the car.

92. The police file information on crimes by date committed. Barnard burglarized a house after Woods raped a woman but before Cho assaulted his wife. Williams stole a car before Woods committed his crime. Who was the first to commit a crime?
   a. Barnard
   b. Cho
   c. Williams
   d. Woods

Read the following information, then answer questions 93 through 95.

Police officers are required to give out physical descriptions of suspects over police radios so that other officers can assist in locating the person. A description should be given out in the following order:

   1. race and sex
   2. weapons the suspect may be carrying
   3. approximate height and weight
   4. color and length of hair

5. baseball hat or other headgear
6. coat, jacket, or shirt
7. long or short pants
8. footwear

93. Officer Kidde was on patrol when he saw a woman gesturing for him to come over to her. She reported having just been robbed by a Hispanic man carrying a shiny object she believed was a gun. The victim described the suspect as 18 or 19 years old, wearing black work boots, a black jacket, blue jeans, and a red baseball cap. The victim could not give an approximation of the suspect's height or weight. What is the first thing Officer Kidde should put out on the radio when he begins describing the suspect?
    a. an estimate of the suspect's age
    b. a warning that the suspect may be armed with a deadly weapon
    c. a description of the suspect's clothing
    d. a description of the suspect's race and sex

94. Officer Cadre is on the scene investigating the possible burglary of a home. Suddenly, he hears a man and woman talking and is hit from behind with a blunt object. When he opens his eyes, he sees a white male wearing blue jeans and white sneakers and a black female wearing black pants and black sneakers. They run from the house, and Officer Kidde hears what sounds like a loud sports car take off. What is the first thing Officer Cadre should put on the radio when he begins describing the suspects?
    a. that he was responding to a possible burglary
    b. that there were two suspects: a white male and a black female
    c. that he may need backup
    d. that the suspects may be speeding around in a sports car

95. Officer Mitchel is on foot chasing a suspect in a possible assault. Officer Mitchel can only tell that the person is wearing a gray hooded sweatshirt and black sweatpants with white sneakers. What is the first thing Officer Mitchel should put on the radio when he begins describing the suspect?
    a. a description of the suspect's hooded sweatshirt
    b. a description of the suspect's hair color
    c. a description of the suspect's sneakers
    d. With so little to go on, the officer should first provide his location.

96. The police are staking out a drug house. Officer Johnson is positioned south of officers Betts and Childe. Officer Alpert is stationed north of Officer Johnson. Given the facts, which is the only statement that can be true?
    a. Officer Betts is positioned farthest south of all the officers.
    b. Officer Johnson is positioned farthest south of all the officers.
    c. Officer Betts is positioned farthest north of all the officers.
    d. none of the above

Read the following information, then answer questions 97 through 99.

When called on to work a collision scene, a police officer should follow the steps below:

1. Have all drivers move all vehicles not in need of a tow truck off the street.
2. Position the patrol car behind the disabled vehicles to prevent other vehicles from becoming involved.
3. Turn on the patrol car's emergency lights to warn other motorists of the problem.
4. Call tow trucks if needed.

5. Put on a reflective traffic vest if traffic direction becomes necessary.

6. Have the drivers, passengers, and witnesses move off the road.

7. Collect information from drivers, passengers, and witnesses.

97. Officer Carlson is dispatched to a three-car collision at mile marker 34 on Route 98. When she arrives, all three cars are in the same lane of traffic and appear to have run into each other. The front car is driving to the side of the road. A group of five people is standing on the side of the road. What is the first thing she should do?

a. Position her patrol car to prevent other vehicles from becoming involved.

b. Direct the drivers of the other two vehicles to move off the road if possible.

c. Direct the group of people to remain on the side of the road.

d. Call an ambulance.

98. The second car involved is not able to move off to the side of the road. What should Officer Carlson do next?

a. Call a tow truck for the second vehicle.

b. Direct the group of people to remain on the side of the road.

c. Position her patrol vehicle so no other cars become involved.

d. none of the above

99. Upon reaching her patrol vehicle, Officer Carlson is told that backup is going to take 15 minutes to reach her due to the traffic buildup. What should Officer Carlson do next?

a. get the group of people to remain on the side of the road

b. call a tow truck

c. begin directing traffic herself

d. none of the above

100. Officer Spring arrives at the scene of a three-car accident. She discovers that there was a fourth car that drove off. Four witnesses provide the first three number/letter combinations listed below. Which is most likely to be true?

a. VB6

b. V97

c. VC1

d. GB3

Answers

Section One: Memorization and Visualization

1. **d.** Four individuals were described as having tattoos—Jose Suarez, William Ericson, Peter Anderson, and James Thompson.
2. **c.** Peter Anderson walks with a limp.
3. **c.** Three individuals were described as known to be armed—Jose Suarez, William Ericson, and James Thompson.
4. **a.** One person was described as being Hispanic—Jose Suarez.
5. **d.** William Ericson was pictured wearing an earring.
6. **b.** Two individuals were described as being shorter than six feet tall—Jose Suarez and James Thompson.
7. **a.** Aaron Johnson was described as being bald.
8. **a.** Two individuals were described as having a scar—James Thompson and Aaron Johnson.
9. **c.** Peter Anderson fired a gun at a coworker.
10. **b.** Two individuals were described as in their 30s—William Ericson (32) and James Thompson (32).
11. **a.** Aaron Johnson is being sought for rape and attempted rape.
12. **c.** James Thompson is known to carry a knife.
13. **b.** Three are pictured with facial hair—William Ericson, James Thompson, and Aaron Johnson.
14. **c.** William Ericson is wanted for burglary.
15. **b.** Two individuals were described as being wanted for an offense against females—Jose Suarez and Aaron Johnson.
16. **c.** The entire passage discusses the different issues surrounding speeding.
17. **b.** The first paragraph of the passage states that approximately "13,000 people die each year from car crashes related to speeding."
18. **a.** The passage's fourth paragraph states that younger people and older people are more likely to speed.
19. **d.** The final paragraph of the passage states "it is believed that if more people were caught speeding, fewer would do it," but "with so many drivers on the road, there are simply not enough law enforcement personnel to catch even half of all speeders. Using technology, such as cameras, can supplement the presence of human efforts."
20. **a.** Although the passage mentions that some people "want to see mandatory revocation of licenses when a person turns a certain age or cannot reasonably pass a vision test," it goes on to state that "suggesting policies to revoke a person's driver's license is not a politically popular idea." Currently, no states require a driver to retest.
21. **c.** The second sentence of the passage states: "Speeding is one of the most commonly violated laws in the United States."
22. **d.** The passage states that drivers of red and yellow cars are more likely to be issued speeding tickets.
23. **d.** The passage's fourth paragraph states that "Approximately 80% of people who receive tickets for speeding are male."
20. **b.** The first paragraph of the passage states that one of the situations where driving slower than the posted speed limit is appropriate is "when there are many pedestrians present."
25. **a.** The passage's second paragraph suggests that paying a fine proportional to one's income may reduce speeding.
26. **c.** Education level was not mentioned in the passage as a factor that contributes to speeding.

27. b. Although men are overwhelmingly issued more speeding tickets than women, the passage notes that "interestingly, the number of females caught speeding increases every year."

28. c. The passage states lining roads with trees has been found to decrease speeding, but an unfortunate side effect of this road design is that "there is more likely to be injury to a driver" when an accident occurs.

29. a. The final paragraph states that "there are simply not enough law enforcement personnel to catch even half of all speeders."

30. d. The passage states that "suggesting policies to revoke a person's driver's license is not a politically popular idea. And as is commonly known, older people are more likely to vote than are younger people."

Section Two: Reading Skills

31. c. If you take the most direct legal route from the police station to the county hospital, you will not pass the firehouse.

32. a. The most direct legal route from the library garage on 8th Street to the gas station is south on 8th Street, then west on 5th Avenue.

33. c. The most direct legal route from the hospital on 1st Avenue to the health center is east on 1st Avenue, south on 9th Street, then west on 5th Avenue.

34. b. The most direct legal route from the senior citizens center on 2nd Avenue to the county hospital is north on Kennedy Boulevard, then east on 1st Avenue.

35. d. The most direct legal route from 4th Street to the gas station is south on Bergen Avenue, then west on 5th Avenue.

36. a. The most direct legal route from the firehouse on 9th Street to the library is west on 5th Avenue, north on 10th Street, east on 3rd Avenue, then north on 8th Street.

37. b. You should tell the man to walk south on 8th Street then west on 5th Avenue.

38. d. There are six roadways designated as one-way on the map.

39. b. The most direct legal route to the mall from East Public Park is south on Eastern Parkway, west on Madison Avenue, then north on Holly Lane.

40. d. Six roadways on the map are designated as two-way.

41. b. Two avenues on the map are designated as one-way.

42. a. You would tell the tourist to go south on Holly Lane, west on Lake Avenue, then north on Syms Street.

43. c. The most direct legal route for the paramedics is south on Eastern Parkway, west on Madison Avenue, then north on Syms Street.

44. b. The most direct legal route to the Lincoln Hotel is north on West End Avenue, east on Oso Lane, then south on Holly Lane.

45. d. The most direct legal route from the police station to the west entrance of the Madison Towers is south on Eastern Parkway, west on Madison Avenue, then north on Holly Lane.

46. a. A title generally provides a summary of the topic; choices **c** and **d** are mentioned in the reading but are not its main themes; choice **b** does not at all capture what the reading is about.

47. c. The second sentence of the passage states that "Officers have been accused of being *racist*, sexist, and corrupt." There is no mention of accusations of being overweight (choice **a**), lazy (choice **b**), or slow to respond (choice **d**).

48. d. The passage states: "Researchers have examined whether a minority suspect is more likely to be viewed suspiciously by the police for non-behavioral reasons, such as style of dress." Shoe color (choice **a**), gait (choice **b**), and hairstyle (choice **c**) are not mentioned.

49. b. The passage states that "The researchers found that minority status does influence an officer's decision to form non-behavioral suspicion."

50. c. The passage states that researchers "also found that minority status does not influence decisions to stop and question citizens."

51. a. As the passage states: "If citizens do not believe law enforcement can provide equal protection for all, then tension will arise. Members of the public may not trust law enforcement and may not report crimes or help law enforcement solve crimes or pursue offenders."

52. d. The passage states that "Research has explored the influence of demographic and situational variables on types of police suspicion of members of the general public." Gender of the officer or the suspect (choices **a** and **c**) and age of the suspect (choice **b**) are not specifically mentioned in the passage.

53. b. A title generally provides a summary of the topic; choices **a**, **c**, and **d** are all discussed in the reading but are not its main themes.

54. a. The second sentence of the passages states that "Each person responds differently to internal and external demands of life, but each person does experience what can be regarded as stress."

55. d. According to the passage, law enforcement officers receive training in self-defense (choice **a**), negotiation techniques (choice **b**), and problem solving (choice **c**).

56. b. The passage states "Today law enforcement officers have more support for dealing with stress than officers on the job in the past." Thus, it can be concluded that in the past there were fewer programs to help officers cope with stress. From that information, you can conclude that suicide rates among police officers have probably dropped, so choice **a** is incorrect. Although a higher divorce rate among police officers is mentioned, nothing suggests that they are more or less likely to remarry than any other group (choice **c**). And while choice **d** may often be true, it not discussed anywhere in the passage.

57. c. The last two sentences of the second paragraph discuss call-in phone hotlines for law enforcement officers.

58. d. The passage states that many of the phone hotlines are manned by "former law enforcement officers who have experienced similar anxiety, depression, or even post-traumatic stress disorder (PTSD). These types of hotlines offer officers a way to reach out to someone who has had similar experiences."

59. a. The passage states that statistics "show that twice as many officers die at their own hand than in the line of duty." There are no statistics in the passage related to officer resignation and hiring rates (choices **b** and **c**) or increased tension with the public (choice **d**).

60. c. The passage states that officers "who have been interviewed about suicide attempts have mentioned the horrible things they are forced to see each day coupled with the strong image they are expected to present." Although easy access to firearms (choice **d**) may indeed be a factor, it is not mentioned or implied in the passage. Salary and family concerns (choices **a** and **b**) are not discussed.

Section Three: Judgment and Problem Solving

61. d. The person most likely to report the shooting would be someone who was present at the time—either an employee or a shopper. Only a shopper was given as a choice.

62. a. Given the time of the occurrence, 10 P.M., it is likely that the offender believed the store would have the fewest number of shoppers and employees.

63. c. Cameron had the highest number of arrests, followed by Scalzo, Ament, and then Gurick, who had the fewest.

64. a. Cameron had the highest number of arrests, followed by Scalzo, Ament, and then Gurick, who had the fewest.

65. d. Of the choices, **d** presents the given information most clearly and accurately. There is no mention of a romantic involvement (choice **a**), an argument over the rent (choice **b**), or stalking (choice **d**).

66. b. If Sampson and Edwards were married, this would have been mentioned in the material.

67. c. As the material states, Joseph Edwards is Diana Sampson's landlord.

68. c. After the switches were made, Officer Rodriguez's partner was Roscoe, Officer Mattice's partner was Sparky, Officer Dobson's partner was Emma, Officer Vedder's partner was Tioga, and Officer Jenson's partner was Sasha.

69. a. After all the switches were made, Officer Rodriguez's partner was Tioga. Officer Mattice's partner was Roscoe, Officer Dobson's partner was Sasha, Officer Vedder's partner was Emma, and Officer Jenson's partner was Sparky.

70. c. Only Jane broke into the home with a premeditated plan to steal all the jewelry and cash she could find. John (choice **a**) did not break and enter and had no intent to steal. As a representative, Eric (choice **b**) was invited into the home and during the course of his work noticed the money lying on the dresser—he did not enter with the intent to steal. Pete (choice **d**) did not commit a felony.

71. b. Burglary requires unlawfully breaking and entering (conduct) in order to commit a felony (intent).

72. a. Based on the information provided in the passage, here are the crimes listed in order of decreasing seriousness: homicide, rape, extortion, assault, burglary, petty theft. Thus, homicide is the most serious crime of those listed.

73. c. Based on the information provided in the passage, here are the crimes listed in order of decreasing seriousness: homicide, rape, extortion, assault, burglary, petty theft. Thus, petty theft is the least serious crime of those listed.

74. a. Based on the information provided in the passage, here are the crimes listed in order of decreasing seriousness: homicide, rape, extortion, assault, burglary, petty theft. Thus, rape is the second-most serious crime of those listed.

75. b. The red sedan turned onto Madison Avenue and was hit by the pickup truck, which was already traveling on the road.

76. c. Officer Gasper inspected the skid marks on the street that indicated the pickup truck was braking.

77. a. Officer Fischer issued a ticket to Jakes for failing to obey a stop sign, thus it can be concluded that there is a stop sign at the intersection.

78. d. We do not know which street runs north-south and which runs east-west.

79. a. The passenger in the red sedan appeared to be unconscious and the passenger in the gray pickup truck was bleeding from the head.

80. c. The accident occurred on a rainy morning and it was the gray pickup truck that skidded.

81. b. There were skid marks on the road where the gray pickup truck was traveling, indicating the driver slammed on the breaks and had been traveling at a fast rate of speed. There is no indication that the driver of the gray pickup truck had intended for the passenger to be injured or killed.

82. a. The red sedan had been traveling on Gorge Road and then made a right turn onto Madison Avenue. It was hit by the pickup truck, which was already traveling on Madison.

83. b. The red sedan was hit by the gray pickup truck. The force of being hit caused the red sedan to spin out of control and hit a tree on the lawn of 129 Madison Avenue.

84. c. The next step after handcuffing a suspect should always be checking the waistband area within reach of the prisoner's handcuffed hands.

85. b. The next step after securing and checking a suspect's hands is to check under the suspect's hat, if he or she is wearing one.

86. b. The suspect is not wearing shoes, so the last step is checking his legs and ankles.

87. d. Officer Wilson has served for 14 years, Officer Anderson for 11 years, Officer Nelson for 10 years, and Officer Osh for 4 years.

88. a. Officer Wilson has served for 14 years, Officer Anderson for 11 years, Officer Nelson for 10 years, and Officer Osh for 4 years. Officer Wilson has served the most years.

89. c. Officer Wilson has served for 14 years, Officer Anderson for 11 years, Officer Nelson for 10 years, and Officer Osh for 4 years. Officer Osh has served the fewest years.

90. b. Officer Wilson has served for 14 years, Officer Anderson for 11 years, Officer Nelson for 10 years, and Officer Osh for 4 years.

91. a. The first step is to always turn the engine off. In the heat of the moment the officer may want to continue the pursuit, but the first step is to secure the motorcycle by turning off the engine.

92. c. Williams. The order in which the crimes were committed is: Williams, Woods, Barnard, and then Cho.

93. d. The first step is to give the suspect's race and sex.

94. b. The first step is to give the suspect's race and sex, even if there are two suspects. Each person's sex and race should be described before going on to describe their other characteristics.

95. a. Without knowing race, sex, or hair color, or being able to approximate height and weight, the officer must start with the sweatshirt, which includes a head cover—the hood. The question is about a description of the suspect—do not be distracted by choice **d**.

96. b. Given the facts, the only true statement is that Officer Johnson is positioned farthest south of all the officers.

97. b. The first step is for the officer to have the other drivers move their cars off the road if possible. Don't be distracted by the group of people on the side of the road.

98. c. Since there is still one car remaining on the road, it is necessary to prevent other vehicles from hitting it.

99. d. Once the patrol car is positioned to prevent other vehicles from becoming involved, she should turn on the patrol car's emergency lights to warn the other vehicles.

100. a. Three of the witnesses agree that the first letter is V. Two agree that B is next. Choice **a** is the best choice because it contains the letters that most of the witnesses agree they saw.

Scoring

Based on the amount of studying and practice you have done, you will hopefully have seen improvement over your score on Practice Exam 2. Regardless of how much your overall score improved, use this practice exam to analyze where you have improved and where you continue to have weaknesses. As you did with the earlier exams, break down your score by section by writing down the number of correct answers for each section. When you add up the sections, remember that each correct answer is worth one point. You should be aiming for a score of at least 70. The better you do on the practice exams, the better your chance of not only passing the real exam but scoring high enough to be among the first applicants called in for the later steps in the hiring process. If your score is 70% or lower, it is particularly important for you to review the individual section scores to see where you need to concentrate your additional study efforts.

GLOSSARY

Americans with Disabilities Act   this law, which came into effect in 1990, prohibits discrimination against those with disabilities in a number of areas, including employment. It has had a major impact on the order in which police departments administer portions of their entry requirements, particularly the medical exam and physical agility tests.

arraignment   a hearing before a court having jurisdiction in a criminal case at which the defendant is identified, informed of his or her rights, and required to enter a plea.

arrest   an arrest occurs when any sworn officer deprives a person of his/her liberty by taking that person into custody to answer for a criminal offense or a violation of a code or ordinance that the officer's jurisdiction is authorized to enforce. Most arrests are made by police officers, peace officers, troopers, or sheriff's deputies, but depending on the jurisdiction or circumstances, probation, parole, or court officers may be authorized to arrest all or certain categories of people.

auxiliary/reserve/part-time police officer   designations that refer to different types of officers in different areas of the United States; regardless of title, they are found in many police departments and sheriffs' offices but rarely in state police agencies. Depending on local usage, these officers may be volunteers or may be paid; they generally perform in uniform a certain number of hours per week or per month, supplementing regular officers during certain times of the year (such as in resort communities when populations increase substantially), or for certain events, including traffic control or work at fairs or civic or cultural events; in other jurisdictions, they have the same duties as fully sworn, full-time officers. Many officers employed in these positions are interested in employment as full-time law enforcement officers. In some jurisdictions, this type of employment is viewed as a stepping-stone to full-time employment, offered first to those who are Police Explorers or others involved in similar programs, or to those who are on the civil service eligibility list and are awaiting being called for full-time police employment.

background investigation a key element in the hiring process, it delves into a candidate's past life, including education, employment, military service, criminal history, credit and driving records, and past associations. A candidate must provide information that is verified by the hiring agency to help in determining whether the candidate is suitable for law enforcement employment. Deliberate falsehoods are automatic grounds for a candidate to be dropped from further consideration for employment.

beat the smallest geographical area that an officer is assigned to patrol. In large cities and in high-density jurisdictions (e.g., airports, large rail stations), an officer will likely be assigned to walk the beat; in rural areas or agencies that cover a large geographical area (state police, suburban agencies), an officer will likely be assigned to patrol the beat from a vehicle. Some departments rely on other motorized vehicles, such as scooters or three-wheeled carts, and some assign officers to patrol beats in parks and recreation areas on bicycles.

booking the process of fingerprinting, processing, and photographing a suspect who has been taken into custody by a police officer and placed under arrest.

bureaucracy any organization with a strictly defined hierarchy, a defined promotion policy generally based on written tests, a career path, reliance on rules and regulations, and a formal and impersonal style of management. Police agencies, regardless of size, are considered to be bureaucracies.

burnout a form of stress associated with policing and many other emergency service positions that involve constant interaction with members of the public. Burnout manifests in feelings of fatigue, frustration, and cynicism, all of which may ultimately end in depression and extremely negative attitudes toward the employing agency or the public. See also: police cynicism.

chain of command each person in the organization is supervised and reports to one person, generally one or two ranks above him or her. For example, a police officer reports to a sergeant in most agencies, sometimes to a lieutenant, but almost never to a captain. A lieutenant reports to a captain or higher rank, never to a sergeant or police officer, both of whom are lower in the chain of command than the lieutenant.

chain of custody the witnessed, unbroken, written chronological history of who had any piece of evidence at any time.

civil service system a system of hiring and promoting employees that is designed to eliminate political influence, nepotism, and bias, generally involving a written examination on factual material and sometimes combining interviews and other criteria as part of the process of hiring or promoting personnel. Most municipal, county, and state police departments and most federal law enforcement agencies are covered by civil service regulations; some sheriffs' and special-jurisdiction departments are not.

civilianization the trend of agencies hiring non-sworn employees (civilians) to fill positions that were once filled by police officers. Among these jobs have been answering non-emergency and emergency phones, dispatching beat officers, investigating traffic accidents and civil infractions, and media relations. In recent decades, civilians have been hired to provide computer services and web design; crime and crime scene analysis and technical services; and budget, legal, and financial expertise. Departments may also call on civilians who are multilingual for interpreting services.

collective bargaining an employer and its employees, represented by their union, negotiate a formal agreement over salaries, hours, benefits, and other conditions of employment.

community policing   a philosophy of policing that gained public attention beginning in the 1970s. Also called community-oriented policing or COP, it is based on police agencies developing close relationships with civilian populations and developing partnerships with the community to develop solutions to persistent crime problems.

conditional offer of employment   a job offer from a police agency to an applicant, extended with the understanding that there are still steps in the employment process that the applicant must complete, and that if these are completed successfully, the agency intends to hire the applicant.

confession   a formal, written document in which a person admits to having been involved in specific criminal activity.

consent decree   an agreement that requires an agency to take specific actions involving hiring and promoting minority group members and/or women. A law enforcement agency that is operating under a consent decree will often hire or promote individuals on a basis not limited to test scores.

crime (criminal offense)   legal definition of an act that the government (local, state, federal) has declared to be unlawful; a crime is defined by law (statute) and is prosecuted in a criminal proceeding.

crime prevention   activities undertaken by police officers and agencies to help the community reduce crime and support community safety. Crime prevention efforts by police might include such activities as patrol or community outreach efforts; efforts by companies or institutions might include developing access control policies, installing surveillance cameras or video systems, and using landscaping and building placements to minimize areas that are dark, unattended, or unobserved.

crime scene/crime scene investigators   the location where a crime has occurred; over the past decade, the emergence of television programs that feature crime scene investigators has led the public to focus on crime scenes and evidence obtained at them in greater detail than in the past. The expectation of jurors that there will always be physical evidence of a crime has led to what has become known as the *CSI effect*, which has resulted in juries failing to convict defendants without the types of evidence they have come to expect via television. In most large city police departments, crime scene investigators are sworn police officers selected for the job on a number of criteria. In this regard, they differ from detectives, who may or may not gather physical evidence but who are also responsible for interviewing victims, witnesses, and suspects and following up on various aspects of the crime. In some police and investigative agencies, those who collect and analyze certain types of evidence may be civilians hired specifically for these tasks. See also: detective.

crime-fighter style   a philosophy of policing, popular particularly from the 1930s to the 1970s, that focused almost solely on the police fighting crime and enforcing the law rather than also providing community services. This is the police role featured most frequently in fictional portrayals of the police and that many police candidates incorrectly believe will form the largest portion of their job responsibilities.

criminal justice system   the term used to encompass the police, the judicial system, and correctional facilities and to show their interrelatedness. The police are viewed as the gatekeepers to the system because they make the initial contact with lawbreakers and, through the arrest process, determine who will enter into the system. The judicial system is the middle phase, where guilt or innocence is determined, and correctional institutions are viewed as the final phase, where punishment is meted out. A broader description might also include probation and parole as alternatives to correctional institutions or post-correctional oversight of an offender.

custody   legal or physical control of a person or thing.

deadly physical force   physical force that, under the circumstances in which it is used, is readily capable of causing death or serious physical injury. Police officers are among the few government employees who are authorized to use deadly force under certain circumstances determined by department policies and court decisions.

decoy operations   a non-uniformed (plainclothes) assignment during which officers are assigned to play the role of potential victims with the goal of attracting and catching a criminal. Decoy operations can be very dangerous because the decoy is often unarmed and carries no police identification, which results in the decoy being totally dependent on the backup team (officers observing and positioned to assist) should the decoy be attacked or mistaken by other police or members of the public for an actual criminal.

detective   generally an experienced police officer who is assigned to investigate serious crimes by following up on initial information obtained at the crime scene by the patrol officers. In many police agencies, detectives are selected and appointed based on their active arrest records while police officers or having worked in plainclothes assignments; in some agencies, detective is a civil service rank for which police officers must take and pass a written test to be selected from a list. The position of detective is highly sought after because it means working out of uniform, provides more freedom than is provided to uniformed police officers, and carries prestige, particularly based on the media portrayal of what has come to be known as the *detective mystique*, a view that detective work is glamorous and dangerous and that only detectives ever have the opportunity to arrest criminals accused of serious crimes (felonies).

directed patrol   an assignment for officers to concentrate on areas where certain crimes have been known to occur and are a significant community problem.

discretion   freedom to act on one's own and make decisions from a wide range of choices. Although police officers are expected to act according to department rules and procedures, police work entails considerable discretion by officers because situations may develop or change in ways that cannot be predicted in advance. Policing is often singled out as a profession in which the most important discretionary decisions are made by the lowest ranking personnel; this view is based on the understanding that the officer who arrives on the scene of an event almost always makes decisions that more senior or higher-ranking personnel are not involved in until after the fact.

domestic (or family) violence   incidents of violence between spouses or partners or between family members; these calls are disliked by many police officers because they are often unpredictable and may turn violent when family members had intended for the police to simply defuse a situation, rather than possibly use force or make an arrest.

drug testing (or screening)   analysis of employees or applicants for use of illegal drugs or substances. Most agencies screen candidates at the time of hiring, and many also have policies for random testing of officers or for testing after a vehicle accident, shooting, or any situation in which impairment may have influenced the event. Drug screening is usually done via urinalysis, but some agencies also use hair analysis tests.

evidence   anything that tends to prove or disprove an alleged act (crime) or a fact or action pertaining to a crime. Direct evidence is generally defined as an eyewitness account, a confession, or a tangible link to the act; indirect evidence (or circumstantial evidence) is the deductive process of inferring an unknown fact from a known or proven fact; and physical evidence is anything tangible that links a person to the act under investigation.

field training (field training officer)   on-the-job training that generally occurs immediately after completion of the police academy when a new officer ("rookie") is assigned to work with an experienced officer (the field training officer). Depending on the agency, this period may be a few weeks and may be informal; in some agencies, field training may be a formalized program up to a year long, during which rookies are assigned sequentially to a number of training officers and the trainers file formal reports on the rookies' performance of particular tasks. In some agencies, failure of the rookie to be positively appraised by the training officer may result in termination during the probationary period.

foot patrol   the historical method of patrolling, particularly in large cities, that lost ground to patrolling in marked police cars in the 1930s but reemerged in the 1960s as a way to combat disorder. It gained additional attention in the 1970s and 1980s as a community policing technique to make officers more visible and accessible to members of the community. In many large cities, recent graduates of the police academy are often assigned to foot patrol as a way for them to gain experience interacting with the public.

hot spot   defines an area that is known for significant criminal activity, such as a storefront where drug sales or prostitution solicitations are common. A *hot time* is a period of day or the week when crime is a problem, such as a storefront on Saturday nights after 11 P.M.

incident report   the first recorded, official report prepared by an officer after responding to events. Some incident reports are not followed up, but others may be referred to detectives or investigators assigned to learn more about the event (generally referred to as a follow-up investigation).

informant   any civilian who brings information about a past or potential crime to the police. Informants may be individuals who are not involved in a crime but have knowledge of it and have no other involvement with the police, or they may be individuals who have been involved in criminal activity who assist the police in investigations, often for considerations of leniency in their cases. Although many types of enforcement (such as the purchase of narcotics or guns by police officers) depend on informants, police prefer not to rely on the testimony of informants in court and to verify information from informants through independent sources.

in-service training   general term used to describe training that occurs after a police officer graduates from the academy; it might occur on a regular basis or be scheduled occasionally to instruct officers in new techniques, policies, or laws. In some states, in-service training is mandated for officers to retain their commissions (legal status as officers empowered to make arrests).

job analysis   a scientific or quasi-scientific method to identify the tasks that police officers perform and the knowledge, skills, and abilities (often abbreviated as KSAs) required to perform those tasks. A job analysis is often performed by consultants who ride along with officers to observe their activities or who ask officers to list the KSAs they believe are needed to perform their jobs as a means of validating the requirements for employment. Agencies rely on these studies to create applicant tests that reflect the reality of police work.

jurisdiction   authority of a law enforcement agency to enforce particular laws in specific political and/or geographic boundaries. United States law enforcement is highly decentralized; no one law enforcement agency has total jurisdiction, which means that no one single agency has the authority to enforce all the laws in all places.

lateral transfer   the ability of an officer to transfer from one police agency to another while retaining rank or seniority gained in the original agency; these transfers are rare in the United States, where it is traditional that officers begin their careers at the lowest rank in one agency and remain there for their entire careers. The inability to transfer laterally is one reason that it is important for candidates to carefully consider the agencies to which they apply, since quitting one and joining another will often require the officer to begin as a rookie in the new agency.

mentor   a person who fulfills the role of teacher, model, motivator, or advisor; often a more senior member of the agency who takes an interest in the career of a new officer. The importance of mentors has been debated in leadership literature, but it is generally agreed that new officers benefit from having a senior person to whom they can turn for advice. Mentors can also come from outside the agency; they may be family members, teachers, or anyone who inspires or assists a person in setting and reaching goals.

misdemeanor   class of criminal activity below a felony. Although the exact definitions differ by state, this class of crime is generally punishable by a fine of $1,000 to $5,000, depending on jurisdiction, and a maximum of up to one year in a county or city correctional facility rather than a state prison.

moonlight   term used to describe the act of police officers working non-police jobs during their off-duty hours. In some parts of the country, it implies that the second job is in private security, but it may refer to any non-police work; regardless of the type of work, many agencies restrict the hours and types of jobs police officers may hold while off duty.

non-sworn (civilian) employees   members of a law enforcement agency who do not have traditional police powers and are generally assigned to a wide variety of non-enforcement tasks. See also: civilianization.

omnipresence   a concept associated with patrol that suggests that visibly patrolling on foot, in motorized vehicles, or on bicycles or horses will create the appearance that uniformed officers are always present. The officers' visibility will deter criminals from committing crimes and reassure citizens of their safety.

order maintenance   expands the police role beyond the crime fighter by emphasizing that officers are assigned to keep the peace and provide social services, not only to prevent crimes.

ordinance/infraction/violation   although not identical, these terms each refer to the least serious category of offense, generally punishable by a small fine and no more than a few days in jail, if any. They may not permit the right to trial because a conviction may not result in a permanent record.

physical agility test   portion of the entrance requirements for most police agencies that requires an applicant to complete strength and endurance activities required to perform police tasks; tests might include running a particular distance within a designated time or completing specific physical activities (such as sit-ups or push-ups) within a designated time.

police academy   the formal training that newly hired officers receive. When officers refer to the police academy, they may be speaking about their training or about an actual, physical place. Police academies differ among agencies; you may commute from home or live at the facility, or you may attend only with members of your agency or at a regional academy where new officers from many departments attend classes together.

police cadet   a position that differs in agencies around the country; in most agencies, it a non-sworn position for teenagers and young adults who are interested in a police career. Other agencies employ only cadets who are high school or college students who receive school credits or a financial stipend rather than a salary. In some agencies, if you are employed as a cadet and you pass the department's entry exam, you will be given certain preferences in the hiring process.

police cynicism   cynicism means seeing the worst in situations or in people and the belief that events or actions that appear positive will soon become negative. Police cynicism has been identified by sociologists as a belief that there is no hope for society and that people will always behave badly; it has been suggested that because police are often faced with negative situations, they are more cynical than other members of society. See also: burnout.

Police Explorers   a structured career and educational program that grew out of the Boy Scouts of America for young men but that now enrolls both men and women between the ages of 14 and 20 and allows them to explore policing through volunteer or work experiences in police agencies. Some Explorer programs provide accelerated entry into a department, making Explorers and similar internship, volunteer, and cadet programs popular with young people interested in police careers.

police officer   member of a police agency who is sworn to make arrests and in most departments carries handcuffs and various defensive weapons, including a firearm. The term *police officer* is most often used to denote the entry-level rank of sworn officers but is also used more broadly to define the status of anyone employed in a police department without an indication of rank. Thus, police officers are sworn members of the department, but not all sworn members are police officers since they may hold higher ranks. In state police and in some county police departments, the entry-level rank of police officer is called a trooper; in federal law enforcement, particularly if the individual does not work in uniform, the entry-level position is usually called a special agent or an investigator.

police subculture   a subculture is a combination of norms, values, goals, career patterns, lifestyles, and roles that define a group. Of the many professional subcultures that exist, sociologists have found the police subculture to be among the strongest; suggested reasons include the belief that people who are similar are attracted to police work; the structured style of training and operations; the reliance on other officers that the job tasks engenders; the potential danger the occupation presents; and the fear of being isolated from peers if officers do not adhere to the subculture's norms, which are viewed as secretive and as separating officers from civilians.

polygraph (or lie detector) test   test that relies on a polygraph machine to determine whether the person being tested is telling the truth; the machine measures physiological responses (such as perspiration and pulse) to psychological stimuli (the questions). Although many people question the validity of these tests, some police agencies use them in the hiring process to verify the truthfulness of an applicant's claims.

precinct/district/stationhouse   depending on local usage, these terms may refer to the collection of beats within a given geographic area or to the organizational substations of a law enforcement agency; generally, not all officers report to headquarters but to a building that is located within the area they patrol and that houses that area's equipment and supervisory personnel.

private security   the industry that provides uniformed or investigative functions by non-governmental agencies. Private security officers (sometimes called private police) are paid from private funds and may work directly for a company (termed proprietary officers) or for an outside provider (termed contract officers). The number of private security personnel far exceeds the number of police personnel in the United States; in 2011, the Department of Justice estimated that two million people were employed in private security, compared to approximately 600,000 police officers. Opinion differs as to whether working in private security provides experience helpful to a police career or whether the duties and legal responsibilities are too dissimilar to be helpful.

probationary period   the time from when an officer begins the academy until the officer becomes covered by civil service or other tenure regulations. During the probationary period (generally from six months to as long as two years depending on local law or union contract), an officer may be fired without a hearing or without the protections afforded by civil service law. Common reasons for termination during this period include conduct on- or off-duty that does not meet the department's standards or an issue in the candidate's background that was not uncovered prior to hiring or during academy training.

random patrol   tactic of having an officer walk or drive around a designated geographic area in what seems to the public to be a random manner but may be predetermined by patrol supervisors. The theory behind random patrol is that officers create a sense of omnipresence by appearing at unpredictable intervals; the tactic is based on the belief that the surprise presence of officers creates a fear of detection in criminals, and for that reason creates a sense of security in members of the public who feel safer knowing officers may be in the area.

reserve officer   usually a part-time employee who is a sworn police officer, often employed in communities with large population shifts during certain times of the year. In some parts of the country, reserve officers are not sworn and assist primarily with such non-enforcement duties as patrol at parades, fairs, and civic events or with traffic enforcement at major events. Not all reserve officers are interested in a full-time law enforcement career, but many consider this an excellent way to learn about the field and to establish positive relationships with their local police departments.

residency requirement   a requirement that officers must reside within the community they serve as a condition of employment; the community may be defined as within the city or town limits, within the county, or within jurisdiction(s) that are specified in the collective bargaining agreement.

squad   a group of officers who work together for a certain length of time under the supervision of the same sergeant or lieutenant. Police officers will often refer to themselves as part of a particular squad, identifying it by name or by tour of duty (such as "I work the 4 to 12 squad," which means the officer works the 4 P.M. to midnight shift, or "I work the burglary squad," which means the speaker is assigned to a group of officers who investigate past burglaries).

sting operation   an undercover operation where officers pose as someone they are not to surprise and arrest criminals. For instance, in some cases the police may pose as criminals by setting up a store to purchase stolen goods or to pretend to be looking for someone to commit a crime for them. Other types of stings have used a different element of surprise; for example, an officer may invite criminals with warrants for arrest to a party or event, which they attend with no expectation of being arrested.

SWAT   Special Weapons and Tactics (SWAT) teams began in the 1960s; the term is used to describe teams of officers who are specially trained and equipped to deal with situations that present a higher-than-usual level of danger, such as hostage taking, or situations in which it appears there are multiple aggressors. SWAT training varies across jurisdictions but generally ranges from hostage negotiation to special weapons training, including training as sharpshooters. In large agencies, SWAT members are permanently assigned to this team; in smaller agencies, they are likely to maintain their regular assignments but are called on when a situation occurs in which their skills are determined appropriate. There has been criticism of dedicated SWAT teams in smaller agencies because there are often few situations for which their skills are truly required, leading to their use at times when it is perceived as an overreaction to the event.

testimonial evidence   verbal testimony given by witnesses at trial, including police officers who testify about their observations or actions.

undercover operations or investigations   activity undertaken by police that is covert (hidden) and during which officers work in plainclothes (out of uniform and either in business attire or in clothing appropriate to the undercover situation). For instance, officers attempting to observe the purchase of guns or narcotics or pretending to be gun purchasers or drug dealers would dress differently than officers pretending to be businessmen attempting to purchase a restaurant to use as a front for money laundering. Undercover operations are seen as among the most dangerous in police work; officers must convince others that they are authentic in the roles they are portraying, must often work without their police identification and firearms, and in some undercover situations must position themselves to become crime victims while depending on a hidden, backup team of officers to come to their aid as the situation develops.

union   an organization that represents dues-paying officers for the purpose of negotiating a collective bargaining agreement (contract) with employers.

Using the codes below, you'll be able to log in and access additional online materials!

Your free online access codes are:

FVEDLL3GK5PKU86PKNHM

FVEFIS6EQMBM3D2D02C6

FVEXY038B76KBSDEG368

FVE7D636C7XF133S3XUJ

FVEDOTSXB04J1567TK3Q

Follow these simple steps to redeem your codes:

- Go to **www.learningexpresshub.com/affiliate** and have your access codes handy.

If you're a new user:

- Click the **New user? Register here** button and complete the registration form to create your account and access your products.
- Be sure to enter your unique access codes only once. If you have multiple acess codes, you can enter them all—just use a comma to separate each code.
- The next time you visit, simply click the **Returning user? Sign in** button and enter your username and password.
- Do not re-enter previously redeemed access codes. Any products you previously accessed are saved in the **My Account** section on the site. Entering a previously redeemed access code will result in an error message.

If you're a returning user:

- Click the **Returning user? Sign in** button, enter your username and password, and click **Sign In**.
- You will automatically be brought to the **My Account** page to access your products.
- Do not re-enter previously redeemed access codes. Any products you previously accessed are saved in the **My Account** section on the site. Entering a previously redeemed access code will result in an error message.

If you're a returning user with new access codes:

- Click the **Returning user? Sign in** button, enter your username, password, and new access codes, and click **Sign In**.
- If you have multiple access codes, you can enter them all—just use a comma to separate each code.
- Do not re-enter previously redeemed access codes. Any products you previously accessed are saved in the **My Account** section on the site. Entering a previously redeemed access code will result in an error message.

If you have any questions, please contact LearningExpress Customer Support at LXHub@Learning ExpressHub.com. All inquiries will be responded to within a 24-hour period during our normal business hours: 9:00 a.m.–5:00 p.m. Eastern Time. Thank you!

NOTES

NOTES

NOTES

NOTES

NOTES